THE FAR LEFT

for

JIMMY BAKER

20·11·52 – 30·10·64

THE FAR LEFT

An Exposé of the Extreme Left in Britain

BLAKE BAKER

Weidenfeld and Nicolson
London

The condition upon which God hath given
liberty to man is eternal vigilance.

John Philpot Curran

Copyright © 1981 by Blake Baker

First published in 1981 in Great Britain by
George Weidenfeld and Nicolson Ltd
91 Clapham High Street
London SW4

ISBN 0 297 78030 1 cased
ISBN 0 297 78033 6 paper

Printed in Great Britain by
Butler & Tanner Ltd
Frome and London

Contents

Foreword

For this book, I make no apologies. Writing it was not even my idea. It originated in a series of articles on the Trotskyists in the *Daily Telegraph* in spring 1981. Those, too, were not my idea, but sprang from personal concern voiced by a leading public figure.

Seldom, however, have I received so much correspondence and messages from the humble and great, expressing or indicating widespread concern at the growing influence in Britain of the Far Left. Its adherents probably total no more than 35,000: 20,000 Communists and 15,000 Trotskyists of various kinds. There are, of course, in addition many thousands more fellow-travellers and sympathizers.

It is customary to dismiss the Far Left or tolerate them in the assumption that they cannot seize control of, or scuttle, the great ship of British democracy. But most of the Far Left are dedicated activists who spend almost every waking hour and most of their energy in furthering their party interests. As the history of the Communist Party by George Matthews is entitled, 'All for the Cause'. They are, I imagine, similar to what the early Christians must have been, regarded by the Romans as dangerous ideological subversives, but who conquered in the end.

This book, again, is not intended to be polemical, but informative. I hope it draws attention to the activities of the Far Left for surprisingly little is known about them, even by most well-informed political observers. Although public concern has grown during the past year or so about the penetration of the Labour Party, the unions, local government, the public services and other areas by the Far Left, most of its activities are subterranean as far as the general public is concerned.

Doubtless, again, this book will provoke cries from the Far Left of 'reds under the bed' and witch-hunting. I myself have a long record of active opposition to the Far Left, which, as I am from time to time reminded, has neither been forgotten nor forgiven. My own anti-Communism, which has mellowed over the years so far as individuals are concerned, did not originate from political views. I have never been a member of a political organization in my life.

As I have explained to Russians, who can also prove likeable human beings, it stems from experiencing at first hand in 1947-8 the cruelties inflicted by Communists in Hungary and elsewhere on their opponents or, more often, merely their victims. I have seen a man weeping as he described how he was tortured until he denounced his aged mother and asking to be arrested for his own protection. I feel equally strongly about concentration camps of which I have far more personal knowledge and acquaintance than, for example, members of the so-called Anti-Nazi League. Few of them, I would guess, have ever met a real Nazi, and certainly not, like myself, reported the Auschwitz trial or stood in the Auschwitz gas-chamber or walked through the infamous gate, '*Arbeit Macht Frei*' or stood on the 'ramp' where the Jews were segregated for death or forced labour.

Inevitably, there will be some public denunciations. Not all are honest. On the day I was denounced in *News Line*, organ of the Workers Revolutionary Party, last April, its editor, Alex Mitchell, told me before colleagues that I had actually been quite fair and accurate about them. He also reminded me of a good turn I had done him about twelve years earlier when he was a Communist – defending him as a working journalist against criticism by an American – which I had forgotten.

Leading Communists, too, have expressed private appreciation to me, as a political opponent, for fair and objective treatment of the Party. Surprising though it may seem, I have nearly always, if not quite, got on well with Communists because they appreciate straightforwardness, even if they know you are against them. Trotskyists are less honest and open.

They are, indeed, characterized not only by unrelenting purpose, but by uncommon spleen and vindictiveness. They hate each other even more than society. They are like piranha fish, snapping at each other. During prolonged inquiries before writing this book, more thoughtful people have asked, as I have asked, what is their real motivation? It is difficult to answer. They profess opposition to every kind of injustice and discrimination and concern for democracy, but practise the opposite. The most apt parallel is perhaps Stavrogin and his fellow nihilists in *The Possessed* by Dostoievsky. The Far Left is dedicated to nihilism.

In this book, again, I make no apologies for citing other newspapers and colleagues' reports, not only from the *Daily Telegraph*, but also the *Daily Mail*, the *Daily Express*, *The Times*, the *Guardian*, the *Observer*, and others. The fact is that the activities of the Far Left are largely observed and reported by vigilant newspapers. I should also like to acknowledge the help of the following publications. Those who want a detailed but concise account of the Trotskyist movement in Britain, with much information on its constituent parties, will find it in a twenty-page publication of the Communist Party, *Trotskyist Organizations in Britain*, prepared by its Trotskyism study group. No doubt Trotskyists of all persuasions will protest at the citing of their ideological enemy. But who better than the Communist Party to keep a sharp eye on the Trotskyists? I am also indebted to Tom Forester's article on the Militant Tendency in *New Society* (10 January 1980); Peter Shipley's pamphlet 'Trotskyism: "Entryism" and Permanent Revolution', Conflict Studies no 81, published by the Institute for the Study of Conflict in 1977; and John Tomlinson's book *Left, Right: The March of Political Extremism in Britain* (1981). Those requiring a comprehensive account of Far Left activity in education should acquire 'Survey of Left Wing Plans for Transforming Education', Common Cause Publications, 1980, which gives 102 pages of detailed information.

One of the tribulations of researching this book was taking out subscriptions to a range of Trotskyist publications themselves. I still read them. It proved a revelation. With the Far Left, there is no need to use 'smear tactics'. One merely needs to quote them in what sometimes appears their astonishing frankness and naïvety. A prime requirement of revolutionary activity is a printing press. Finally, therefore, I would offer two apposite quotations. Bulwer Lytton noted, 'The pen is mightier than the sword.' For those Labour MPs threatened with re-selection and other moderates, used to calling each other 'Brother' or, as by Mr Wedgwood Benn, 'Comrade', some lines from Shakespeare's *Julius Caesar*, Act Four, scene one, when the triumvirate meet in Rome after the death of both Caesar and Pompey:

ANTHONY [*sic*]: These many shall die; their names are pricked.
OCTAVIUS: Your brother too must die. Consent you, Lepidus?
LEPIDUS: I do consent.
OCTAVIUS: Prick him down.

To those in the Labour Party, local government, the trade unions and the Establishment, who by now has been pricked down? If this book has any message, it is: Take note.

Introduction

The Far Left have often, and rightly, been likened to termites, gnawing away at the foundations of our society. Nor do they deny it.

In their numerous publications, they make no bones about their revolutionary aims and spell out with astonishing explicitness the methods by which they will be achieved. I will give many examples in this book from their own literature and internal bulletins. Yet most of these publications are never seen by the vast majority of the population. Nor, I would guess, are they seen regularly and comprehensively by many of those with a specialist interest in political and industrial affairs.

Until recently at least, there has been a widespread tendency to discount 'the Trots', with their high turnover of young adherents, as basically insignificant, the lunatic Left fringe. That is largely because the extent of their activities has been little appreciated or publicized. It was always the Communist Party which was regarded as the Red menace.

The Communist Party has been with us for a long time – it celebrated its sixtieth anniversary in 1980. Politically, it has never done well in its own right since post-war days although, as has often been said, it has not lacked fellow-travellers among Labour MPs, trade union officials, the Church, the Campaign for Nuclear Disarmament and other areas. There have also been Conservative MPs prepared, perhaps if only for financial gain, to make speeches in support of foreign Communist causes in parliament and, as in East Germany at the height of the Berlin crisis, to lend their presence against British political interests.

Industrially, however, the Communist Party has remained a formidable, disciplined force. It is suffering from association in the public mind with the Soviet Union, from which it has tried to dissociate itself, a lack of appeal to youth and shortage of finance. It has had setbacks in the unions, notably in the Engineering Union through determined opposition by moderates and the introduction of postal ballots, and in the Electricians Union, which it once controlled. But it is neither down nor out. The Communist Party, which remains well disciplined and highly organized, producing propaganda to high professional standards, may be likened to regular soldiers as against the guerrillas of the Trotskyist parties. It has opted for changing society through exploitation of 'democratic' methods and is still wooing the Labour Party for closer co-operation and possible affiliation.

But now the alarm bells have begun to ring, notably in the Labour Party, over the extent of Trotskyist penetration and agitation. This is partly because, despite their secretiveness and the undercover 'entryism' of some groups - 'moling away' inside the Labour Party, trade unions and other organizations - the Trotskyists have either by design or willy-nilly come more into the open.

The declared aim of all Trotskyist organizations in Britain - unlike the Communist Party which professes democratic reform - is to bring about the collapse of the established order, destroy democracy and substitute a revolutionary State, against which the Soviet Union would appear a capitalist country. For that reason, prime targets are the armed forces and the police, which would be disbanded and replaced by a 'workers' militia', and the judiciary. It goes without saying that the whole of industry would be nationalized and all land and property expropriated. Education would be Marxist, and free parliamentary elections a thing of the past.

Trotskyists have played an ugly part in racial demonstrations, such as at Southall in 1978, in industrial disputes, as at Grunwick, and in mass riots, where their main target has been the police. Their role in front organizations, such as the Campaign for Nuclear Disarmament, the Anti-Nazi League and the Right to Work Campaign, or the Workers Revolutionary Party's youth centres, has become obvious.

Far Left activists are everywhere. Including many middle-class academics, they are strong in education, particularly provincial universities, polytechnics and further education colleges, and some comprehensive schools. Action against their activities there has been taken by the National Union of Teachers and National Union of Students. Trotskyists are strong in the Civil Service, both in union activity and in departments, including, one Labour MP suggested to me, at policy advisory level in some key Ministries. There, as in organizations like the Campaign for Nuclear Disarmament, they fight a running battle or occasionally have uneasy alliances with the Communist Party. On the Far Left, expediency sometimes overcomes ideological differences. Trotskyists are well represented in acting and include many familiar faces on television; Equity, the actors' union, has long been a battleground between moderates and the Far Left.

Trotskyists are also strategically placed in journalism, in Fleet Street, both as journalists and among print workers in a number of national newspaper plants, in magazines and book publication, among London suburban journalists and parts of the provincial Press. There, too, there is war with the Communists. Trotskyists are also well represented on the executive of the National Union of Journalists, in Central London and other branches. They are active in television and broadcasting.

Extreme Left activists are also increasingly evident in local government, public, health and welfare services. And of course, they are extremely active in the unions, where all leading Far Left groups maintain their own caucuses, fractions and cells, and where they are constantly striving to increase their influence. They are active on the shopfloor at British Leyland and elsewhere. They organize and exploit factory occupations where plants are due to be closed down. All groups bombard workers with a stream of special pamphlets, leaflets and broadsheets. No major dispute occurs without Trotskyists and Communists getting on the picket line and producing special bulletins. There is a flood of such propaganda.

Similarly, no minority cause is overlooked for exploitation, not merely racial grievances among immigrant communities, black and Asian discontent, but homosexuals – 'gay rights' figure large in Far Left publications – women's liberation and the Irish. Unemployment, now a major public issue, is a prime target. The May 1981 Jobs March from Liverpool to London, nominally organized by the TUC, was the subject of exhaustive daily and weekly coverage in all Far Left publications, from the Communist *Morning Star* to the Trotskyist *News Line*, with all claiming major credit for supporting and publicizing it.

Even more so than Communism, Trotskyism is an international movement. Its funding is substantial, but not all sources clear. All larger groups have active international links with many countries. There are constant exchange visits, publication of mutual propaganda and joint conferences. In contrast, Communists maintain fraternal links, but do not give the impression of such conspiratorial international activity.

Trotskyist factions have several common characteristics. The larger groups, unlike the Communists who appear more democratic, are oligarchies, controlled by small groups of veteran revolutionaries without whose control, direction and ideological guidance they would disintegrate. They practise extreme secrecy, using code-names and initials in internal bulletins, and letting little emerge about their financial and other internal affairs.

The Far Left is prone to regular, ideological differences, its sects splitting and re-forming, only to split again, and express vituperative criticism and abuse of each other. Even the Communist Party has such internal disputes, as on whether it should concentrate on industry or seek affiliation to the Labour Party or re-form as a tightly knit organization of agitation.

While happy to exploit young people, the unemployed and others, the Far Left is extremely careful and selective on whom it recruits to its cadres, or admits to its inner circles. Once recruited, Far Left converts are subjected to iron discipline, exercised by the central caucus.

They are submitted to rigorous demands to attend incessant meetings, sell publications on the streets and at factory gates, become involved in industrial disputes, raise money and make their own regular and occasional financial contributions to the party, its special causes and appeals. Fund raising, through special events, workshop collections, and 'fighting funds' is relentless. They are ordered to attend various conferences of fringe organizations, told what motions to support or not support, whom to back and how to vote or for which candidates not to vote. Backsliding, particularly among Trotskyists, is subject to disciplinary action, sometimes by fines. Physical intimidation is not unknown. Ideological deviants are expelled.

As with the Communist Party and the *Morning Star*, larger Trotskyist groups have their own printing works, run on the cheap, publishing weekly or fortnightly papers, or, as with the Workers Revolutionary Party, a small but highly professional daily paper, *News Line*, with colour printing. They also have trade union wings, women's, coloured and youth sections, all with their own publications. They publish regular ideological or international reviews and journals, and produce special newspapers for unions where they are strong. They also do cheap commercial printing for many unions or union sections. Larger groups have their own bookshops.

Material resources are, despite the small membership, thus considerable, suggesting a sizeable full-time staff, in the case of the Militant Tendency at least sixty-three. All in all, the Far Left has a formidable field of activity, all co-ordinated from the centre, but, in the case of Trotskyists, with adherents usually and deliberately working from the wings or background, rather than adopting a central role. Communists actively seek union and other office and make no secret of their allegiance. In union branches, for example, Trotskyist activists are sometimes instructed to avoid being elected secretary, treasurer or social secretary because of the amount of work involved, but seek election to the organizing committee where they can exert political influence while reserving their time and energy for the cause.

Most of this widespread activity is unreported. Opinions vary on the significance and role of Trotskyist groups. But in my view and that of others who monitor their activities, they are a widespread and dangerous conspiracy with international links, which has made considerable advances in recent years.

Strongest evidence of this is provided by the divided and demoralized state of the Labour Party exacerbated by the entryism of the Militant Tendency over the past fifteen years or so. As a direct result of its persistent campaign, supported by other Far Left organizations, the Party voted at its special Wembley conference in January 1981 for election of the leader by a new electoral college based on a representation formula of 40 per cent for the unions, 30 per cent for constituency parties and only 30 per cent for the Parliamentary Party. Militant Tendency also secured mandatory re-selection of MPs. As a result of its systematic penetration of local parties, between seventy and one hundred of which it is believed to control, moderates, whether right or left wing, are increasingly threatened with being booted out.

One major result has been the formation of the Social Democratic Party. Let it not be thought that this was a setback for the Far Left. It was a prime policy aim to drive moderates out, declared in Militant Tendency's internal bulletins long before the issue became acute, in order to make easier full left-wing control. For the same reason, Mr Wedgwood Benn has full backing. Although he has tacitly accepted Militant support without committing himself explicitly, there can be little doubt that they regard him as a figurehead to be manipulated, or eventually replaced.

Growing alarm over the extent of Trotskyist penetration and influence is now felt even by orthodox left-wing Labour MPs. During my inquiries, I had private conversations with a number of MPs, only one of whom, Frank Field (Birkenhead), was prepared to be identified. Even Mr Field, who may be regarded as a well-meaning left-winger, felt himself under threat from the Militant Tendency. My impression was that demoralization, division and despair inside the Party were far deeper than might be supposed even from the daily ructions. Since then, divisions inside the Party have worsened. Despite the formation of the Labour Solidarity Campaign by alarmed moderates, it remains to be seen whether the Trotskyist bid for control can be checked.

Altogether, there are about fifteen Trotskyist organizations in Britain, although only one true Communist Party. Some are tiny, eccentric minnows, with perhaps as few as thirty or no more than a hundred members, with a confusing range of names which bear a similarity to each other, the Revolutionary this, Communist that, Party this, Tendency or Current that, hence the deep ideological differences. Some are virulently active, others almost invisible. They publish their bulletins, but give the impression that their main activity and obsession is revolutionary theory, a form of Trotskyist space-game, competing with each other through argument and abuse rather than active subversive action and agitation. The larger groups are a different matter. They mean business and go about it purposefully.

Two views might be taken of which is the most significant. The Militant Tendency, with an estimated 2,000 members (excluding the nearly 5,000-strong Labour Party Young Socialists, whom the Tendency controls – it claims up to 10,000 'supporters'), and led by Edward (Ted) Grant, has the greatest political influence through its penetration of the Labour Party. Its influence has increased most in recent years, and it poses the most direct political threat to parliamentary democracy. Others see the Socialist Workers Party, between 3,000 and 4,000 strong, and led by Tony Cliff, an anti-Zionist Israeli, as the most professional in its operations, the strongest in industry, where the Militant Tendency is trying to extend its own base and influence, and the most dangerous Trotskyist organization.

The third largest Trotskyist organization, and the most secretive and tightly disciplined, is the Workers Revolutionary Party with up to 2,000 members. Led by Gerry Healy, a veteran revolutionary and erstwhile Irish Communist, it has less overt influence. But with its daily paper, *News Line*, backed by its own printing firm and a fleet of heavy delivery lorries, not to mention its well-known Marxist training college in Derbyshire and its new chain of revolutionary youth centres, it represents a formidable, purely revolutionary force. It also claims up to 5,000 members of its own Young Socialists organization, the recruiting organization for the planned Workers' Militia.

The fourth group, the International Marxist Group, about 1,000 strong and led by Tariq Ali, the former student revolutionary leader, has less impact, and is constantly seeking alliances with the Socialist Workers Party and others. It is strong among students and academics, and still strives to extend its influence in industry.

Of the rest, the Workers Socialist League, led by Alan Thornett, the 'mole', and based in Oxford, is only around 200 or more strong, but active both on the shopfloor and internationally. A recent development is what appears to be a strong resurgence and advance of the International Communist League, estimated at only 100 hard-core members, but growing fast through the *Socialist Organiser* organization.

The history of Trotskyism in Britain and elsewhere has its effective beginning in 1938 when Trotsky, who had been expelled from Russia in 1929 for preaching world revolution, as well as more radical Bolshevism at home, launched the Fourth International at a founding Congress attended by thirty supporters from eleven countries. He urged concentration on international revolution in Western Europe with its highly industrialized society, and invented the concept of 'entryism', joining social democratic and other organizations secretly and working for their take-over from within. In 1935 he expressed the view that Britain was heading for a revolutionary explosion.

In its policy declaration, *The Death Agony of Capitalism and the Tasks of the Fourth International*, known as the *Transitional Programme*, the movement advocated revolution through the industrial working class, using its own independent organizations, trade unions, works committees and strike pickets with the aim of forming a 'workers' militia'. It advocated factory occupations. There should be a single world-wide organization under centralized leadership and discipline. The latter aim has fallen victim to repeated ideological differences, but otherwise, the basic aims of Trotskyism remain unchanged to this day.

Even before the founding of the Fourth International in 1938 (the Communist Party of Great Britain was formed in 1920), there were two Trotskyist organizations in Britain, the Workers International League, whose members included Gerry Healy, and the Militant Labour League. In 1937 a group of disillusioned Trotskyists, including Ted Grant, arrived in Britain from Johannesburg. They, too, joined the Workers International League.

In 1943-4, obeying a call for unity from the Fourth International's international secretariat, the two British organizations, the Workers International League and the Militant Labour League, merged to form a public organization, the Revolutionary Communist Party. Its members later included Tony Cliff, who also came to Britain via South Africa.

After the war, deep divisions developed in the Trotskyist movement, both internationally and in Britain, notably over the view of some radicals, including Tony Cliff, that the Soviet Union was really a form of state capitalism. Others, including Gerry Healy, favoured a new Bolshevik revolution in Russia to remove the Stalinist ruling class. Another group, led by Michael Pablo, a Greek, who became secretary-general of the Fourth International in 1951 with a new international secretariat, adhered to the view that the Soviet Union was a 'degenerated workers' state', but that with the possibility of a third world war, there should be co-operation in Stalinist-dominated countries, such as Italy and France, with the Communist Party, while in countries such as Britain, Trotskyists must infiltrate themselves into the social democratic movement.

These differences continued in all their complexity for the next twenty years and more, but resulted in the break-up of the Revolutionary Communist Party in 1949. The various factions went on their own ways over subsequent years until the position has been reached today where the three leading Trotskyist parties are each led, and were effectively founded, by men who were all once comrades in the Revolutionary Communist Party more than thirty years ago.

'Entryism', a classic Trotskyist term, means joining an organization with which one does not sympathize, concealing one's own true allegiance or membership of other rival or more radical organizations, but working within it to change its policies, constitution and ultimate aims and nature. It is an undermining from within, working like true 'moles', using and exploiting the rules, taking advantage of the procedure until others who are more moderate have been driven out, gone away or otherwise been excluded, whether by deliberate persecution or sheer exhaustion. Those practising it profess merely to be loyal and diligent activists, anxious to work for the good of the cause. In fact, their aim is a take-over, to win more recruits for their own subversive organization, increase influence by back-door methods and win power. Entryists are chameleons, adopting whatever colour is most opportunist and likely best to serve the ultimate aim.

Peter Shipley, in his invaluable paper on the Far Left, makes some astute judgements of entryism. 'Entryism is basically a solution to the problems created by the weakness of Trotskyism and its lack of direct appeal for the working class.' When the social and political climate is unfavourable for revolution, 'then the tiny Trotskyist cells have sought refuge in the Labour Party'. Entryism does not mean 'cautious co-operation'. Those involved must appear to be joining their new party as individuals, not as members of an existing political organization, which would make them ineligible for membership. 'It is a delicate systematic operation that must be carried out in secret. ... It masquerades as a Leftish ginger group that owes no allegiance except to the party it has infiltrated.'

Apposite here are the views of the Militant Tendency, now the main entryist organization in the Labour Party, where it has achieved considerable success and influence. The Tendency regards itself as an 'organic part of the labour movement' and sees the rival Trotskyist organizations as 'sects'. They in turn express contempt for the Tendency as not a truly Trotskyist organization.

In its October 1979 *British Perspectives*, the Tendency, in effect Ted Grant, its chief ideologist, said:

> The sects and sectlets which swarm in Britain – many of them claiming to be Marxist or Trotskyist – are incapable of maintaining a permanent base. The possible exception is in the student field, where their support shifts from one generation of students to another. But this is a quicksand, in the sense that students won to the sects, once they leave the universities and find work in the professions, in the great majority tend to drop out of these organizations.
>
> They invariably hold the workers responsible for the inadequacy of their ideas, methods and policies. Unless it is supplemented by a strong base amongst the industrial working class and white-collar workers – but especially among the industrial working class – such a basis can disappear quickly.... However, in the rarefied atmosphere of the universities ... the sects can find some echo. In this rarefied and exotic atmosphere the way-out and Ultra-Left ideas of the sects do not seem out of place....
>
> The sects vie with one another in swinging from Ultra-Leftism to opportunism and back in a frantic endeavour to build phantom 'revolutionary parties' outside the labour and trade union movement. They will be doomed to disappointment.... As the influence of the paper (*Militant*) and the editorial board is extended within the Labour Party, more and more of these workers will come into contact with the paper and supporters of the paper and under those conditions can be won to the ideas of Marxism....
>
> There are almost as many varieties of sects as there are of Heinz products; different varieties of middle-class radicalism. They expected that they would grow enormously as a consequence of the disillusionment in the Labour Government of 1974-9. On the contrary, we have seen a partial disintegration of the bigger of the sects and a split into innumerable sectlets. Like the poor are to the Christians, so the sects will always be with us.
>
> They will always attract a particular type of individual; those who are natural 'aginers', who are always against whatever ideas are in the majority in the labour and trade union movement. But the

sects, on the wave of radicalism that is developing, will succeed in picking up workers here and there.... They will inevitably repel the mass of workers. As an example, we have the Ultra Left's attitude of 'smashing' the 'Fascists' which involved them in attempting to substitute themselves for the organized working class....

In every field it is the same.... The sects will grow a little, then disintegrate and split, then unite, disintegrate and then split again. They have not the remotest chance of success. In the long run they will stagger into the Labour Party on an opportunistic basis.... We must brush aside the nuisance of the sects like so many noxious flies.... There is not one of the sects that does not reek with an organic contempt for the working class. They all wish to impose their 'leadership' on the workers whom they regard as an ignorant mass.

So much for the Militant Tendency, which regards its own entryism and broader appeal to the workers as a more promising road for true Trotskyism. Not all will agree with its dismissal of other Trotskyist groups as insignificant. But much of the observation is accurate.

To those who dismiss the constant activity of the Far Left as that of political eccentrics, I would draw the analogy of Adolf Hitler. He started with only six fellow members of the committee of the German Workers' Party in Munich in 1919. His movement initially was also at grass-roots level. His most important political principle was to go to the masses, in the first instance, the workers.

His movement, too, suffered from setbacks and splits. As with the Trotskyists, it believed in armed insurrection and physical violence, and formed what amounted to a 'workers' militia' in what became the SA. He, too, believed in demos and street action. In *Mein Kampf*, like the present Trotskyist gurus, Hitler spelled out exactly what his ideology and plans were, but was not taken seriously. Indeed, as with Trotskyist and Communist policy statements, not many people read him.

As with the Far Left, both through party membership and front organizations, Hitler gained the support of many well-meaning but not so ideologically dedicated people. As the social, economic and political climate worsened in Germany, just as is happening in Britain, Hitler gradually developed his at first obscure, minor, politically eccentric organization into a mass organization run, too, by a central caucus with strict discipline. He, too, purged those with ideological differences. It took him fourteen years from his beginning as a tiny 'sect' until he was elected Chancellor of Germany, able to carry out his policies in full, with what consequences the whole world knows.

That is not to say the Trotskyists and Communists will ever have the same mass appeal. What should be remembered is that with the steady disintegration of the Labour Party, and polarization of opinion between Far Left and radical Right, the state of Britain increasingly resembles the Weimar Republic. The Far Left will never succeed in its true colours. But it is bidding for power through entryism, with the inevitable right-wing backlash which that would bring. Some might think we are already well down that road.

1 The Workers Revolutionary Party

The Workers Revolutionary Party is best known for its two most prominent members, Vanessa Redgrave, the actress, and her actor brother, Corin, not to mention the considerable number of well-known entertainers and sportsmen who have lent their names to its causes, over the past few years.

The WRP, based in Clapham Old Town, is the most secretive, rigid and possibly the most disciplined, fanatical and sectarian of Trotskyist groups, despising entryism and the 'revisionist' ideologies of rival factions. The WRP regards itself, and is often so regarded by outside observers, as the British section of the Fourth International, which has itself been subject to divisions over the years. But a similar claim is made by the International Marxist Group. The WRP's membership is estimated at between 1,000 and 2,000, with up to 5,000 claimed for its Young Socialists. Like other major Trotskyist groups, it traces its origins back to the Revolutionary Communist Party, formed in 1944 and dissolved in 1949.

Leader and creator of the WRP is Gerry Healy, now in his late sixties, a grizzled Irish veteran revolutionary, once a Communist, who was active in the pre-war Trotskyist movement. After formation of the Revolutionary Communist Party, which achieved a membership of 400 at one stage but numbered only 100 at the end, Healy became leader of a RCP minority working in the Labour Party, work which was sanctioned by the Fourth International in 1947, and known as 'The Group'.

Following dissolution of the Revolutionary Communist Party, members were instructed to join the Labour Party under Healy's leadership. Later, Healy started the publication *Socialist Outlook*, but splits in the Fourth International between 1951 and 1953 disrupted its work, and although Healy finally won control, it ceased publication in 1954. Most of the support gained by entryism was lost.

Despite setbacks, The Group continued its work, publishing pamphlets under the New Park imprint. In 1956 came Mr Khrushchev's revelations on the evils of Stalinism at the Soviet Communist Party's twentieth Congress followed by the Hungarian uprising. Numerous prominent Communist Party members defected, some joining Healy whose Group had concentrated on exploiting the Communist Party's internal divisions. There followed in 1957 publication of the *Newsletter* and *Labour Review*.

Strengthened by Communist defections, Healy in 1959 founded the

Socialist Labour League, which continued to work inside the Labour Party with its main target the Party's Young Socialists, of which it soon gained control through the organization's national committee. But in 1964, under Harold Wilson, the Labour Party proscribed the Socialist Labour League and expelled its leading members, as well as the Young Socialists.

Following this setback, the League withdrew all its members from the Labour Party and its Young Socialists, and forsook entryism. Instead, it concentrated on building up its own membership and expanding its own organization. The Party set up the All Trades Union Alliance as its industrial wing devoted to rank-and-file agitation and its own Young Socialists organization. In September 1969 it transformed the *Newsletter* into the *Workers Press*, the first Trotskyist daily paper in the world. *Labour Review* was re-launched in June 1977 as the Party's monthly ideological journal. But despite following the precepts of the *Transitional Programme*, the founding document of the Fourth International in September 1938, which predicted the overthrow of capitalism if the working class was given the right revolutionary proletarian leadership, further difficulties followed.

In 1974 ideological splits led to the expulsion of about 200 members led by Alan Thornett, the Oxford activist who has been prominent in British Leyland labour disputes at its Cowley plant, as well as differences with the Transport and General Workers Union. Thornett subsequently formed the Workers Socialist League. Bitter mutual vituperation has characterized relations between the two cliques.

By early 1976, the Party's printing company, which printed *Workers Press* and *Keep Left*, was in acute financial trouble and was wound up later in the year. But simultaneously a new firm, Astmoor Litho, was set up at Runcorn, Cheshire. The Party's daily paper, which the firm printed with *Young Socialist*, was re-launched as the *News Line*, a sixteen-page tabloid which now has colour-printing facilities. Further financial difficulties have followed, with which I deal in Chapter 6. But the WRP is still going strong.

Where does the Workers Revolutionary Party stand today? Its 1981 Manifesto, adopted unanimously (of course) at its fifth Congress held from 31 January to 3 February, concentrates, as might be expected, on the fight against the Thatcher government and the Tories, who, it claims, are 'deliberately provoking a state of national emergency.... They are working towards violent class confrontation as a pretext to drive down living standards and do away with basic rights and liberties.

'Since coming to power in May 1979 the Thatcher Government has systematically prepared the army, the police, the judiciary and the capitalist state bureaucracy for a pre-emptive strike against the trade unions and the working class. Using the element of surprise, the Tories will bring out the army to terrorize the masses into dictatorship. That is why the Workers Revolutionary Party says – Watch out for this violent conspiracy by the Tories and the capitalist state machine. Prepare now!'

The paranoia of the WRP has strange manifestations. Thatcher government preparations for smashing the unions and enslaving the working class, the Manifesto says, include 'huge salary increases for the military and the police, the lavish recruitment campaigns for the armed forces, the unbridled use of telephone-tapping and mail-opening, the naked role of the Special Branch and the Special Patrol Group against the trade unions and the passing of Whitelaw's prison camp act which abolishes *habeas corpus.*...' Whitehall plans for a state of emergency includes recruitment of an 'army of blacklegs'. Restricted pickets will be provoked to enable unrestrained police violence and wholesale arrests. Labour Party and Trades Union Congress opposition are dismissed contemptuously. They both suffer from 'confusion and inertia' created by 'reformists', 'bureaucrats' foundering without policies. Even a Labour government of Foot and Healey 'would play the part of Allende's government in Chile. Its job would be to demoralize and divide the working class so that in a short time the military and the police would depose the Parliamentarians and install a junta.' It is difficult to imagine Mr Foot in this role.

Active Tory measures to stage the 'counter-revolution', the WRP warns, will include superseding parliament with 'a select group of non-elected Privy Councillors and generals representing big business, finance capital, the aristocracy, royalty and the armed forces'. The working and middle classes will be 'bullied into silence until they are ready to throw up their early morning street barricades and road blocks in the working-class estates and "dormitory areas".

'Then, armed with lists of names and addresses of leading trade unionists, Leftists and all known protesters, they will move into action with mass arrests in an atmosphere of terror, brutality and arrogance.' Preparations include 'special detention centres' in Britain. Particularly sinister, the WRP thinks, is the acquisition by Scotland Yard of two Bell 222 helicopters 'equipped with TV cameras, an illumination system, loudhailers, fixed binoculars, a winch and special infra-red sensory devices. This "spy in the sky" can be quickly converted into an aerial gunship with eight police snipers on board!'

But the prospect of police gunships strafing the citizenry is only part of the WRP's ghastly prediction of what awaits us:

Preparations have been made for the country to be divided into military sectors each ruled by martial law administration with its own pass system. They plan to isolate whole communities from each other and starve them into submission as the Bolivian miners were starved into submission.

Live military operations have been conducted in the art of sealing off the entrances to high-rise flats by the deployment of rubber-tracked light tanks and armoured cars. Since the beginning of this year night-time manoeuvres have been regularly taking place in the streets of London and other major cities. Detachments of troops, carefully selected for their racist views and brutality, are being selected for these monstrous tasks.

They are being modelled on the killers of the Special Air Service (SAS) and this explains why Thatcher was so eager to involve them in the Iranian embassy siege and then to glorify the cold-blooded executions they carried out. The Army Command has decided there will be no half-measures. Trade union activists, Labour Left Wingers, members of the Workers' Revolutionary Party, Communists etc will be interned without trial in the first hours of the Emergency.

Barmy though all this may sound, more relevant is what the Workers Revolutionary Party proposes to do, and is already doing, to prepare for revolution under the pretext of pre-empting a right-wing counter-revolution. It is setting systematically about what it preaches. It is also a blueprint for subversion, modelled on the Bolshevik Revolution in which Trotsky as well as Lenin played a leading part.

Following the 'cowardly acquiescence of the TUC leaders and Labour MPs' in sackings, closures and the rundown of social services, which 'must be ended by class action - the occupation of factories and workplaces' - the first step must be the formation of Occupation Committees. These would comprise representatives of the shopfloor, staff, technical and supervisory sections. Fighting to keep factories open, they would appoint groups of qualified technicians and workers to inspect company books, ending management financial secrecy and openly making out the case for nationalization and workers' control. 'The committees would constitute a preparatory step towards the conquest of political and industrial power and the nationwide administration of industry by a Workers' Revolutionary Government' – the ultimate WRP aim.

Parallel to this is the formation of Community Councils, Trotskyist front organizations acting under the cloak of defending local interests in towns and areas hard hit by industrial closures, redundancies and unemployment, such as the steel towns of Shotton, Corby, Consett and Port Talbot. Predicting 'spontaneous outbreaks of revolutionary struggle', the Manifesto says such councils must embrace all sections of the community involved in production, commerce and maintenance of local services. At their heart would be trade unions.

But they must also 'incorporate existing local community bodies which have sprung up almost overnight in some areas – for example, community groups against police violence, against racism, against hospital and school closures, against cutbacks in local facilities such as playgrounds and libraries, against the cuts in medical facilities and university education and also tenants' and ratepayers' organizations', opening the doors even to mistaken Tory voters.

Opposition to the government and denationalization would be led by Occupation Committees backed by Community Councils, leading to formation of a workers' militia on Bolshevik lines. 'The Community Councils', the Manifesto says, 'would take responsibility for uniting, organizing and mobilizing the masses in the area they cover against Tory class war attacks. They would be responsible for alerting and mobilizing the masses to the danger of a military coup. Their task would be to organize a round-the-clock vigilance to detect and compile information on the movement of troops, the police and blacklegs.

'They would create units of Workers' Defence Guards based on the trade unions, strikes, factory occupations and street committees, as well as the youth and immigrant organizations. They would take the initiative in mobilizing tens of thousands on to the streets the moment the Tories brought out the troops. To frustrate the terror and provocation of the capitalist state and its agents, the Workers' Defence Guards would create their own intelligence system.'

Prime target for penetration of building Community Councils would be Labour-controlled councils. On their own, the 1981 Manifesto states, they could not withstand the 'Tory onslaught on local government finances', but must put themselves 'at the head of the oppressed in the local communities. . . .' Such local councils must be supported in the fight against government economy measures. 'This is a necessary and correct tactical measure to defend all past gains and to create the conditions for nation-wide opposition to build up for the defeat of the government.'

Unions in the public service must give their full support. 'They must avoid at all costs fighting Labour councils on sectional issues.' Community Councils would be called on to deal with the 'mass of social problems caused by Thatcher's monetarist catastrophe'. They would not only have to prepare 'comprehensive building plans', but requisition 'all unoccupied property, large hotels and the homes of the aristocracy', as well as relieving exorbitant gas, water and electricity bills promptly. Rents and rates for the unemployed would be abolished immediately, and substituted by rates graduated according to income. 'In short, the Community Councils will form the local and regional basis for the Workers Revolutionary Government. . . .'

The Manifesto continues: 'Every step forward by the working class in resisting Tory conspiracies and building Community Councils, Occupation Committees, Workers' Defence Guards and Revolutionary Youth Committees poses directly the question: what kind of government will secure the basic democratic rights of workers, end unemployment and inflation and guarantee decent living standards? Unquestionably, only a Workers' Revolutionary Government which derives its power from the Community Councils will carry out such an historic task.' In other words, as the Party has acknowledged, Community Councils would be local Soviets.

The first Community Council was formed at Thetford, Norfolk in 1980. A prominent part was taken by the Thetford section of the All Trades Union Alliance, with chief speakers being Dave Hyland, an Engineering Union branch committee member, and Barry Lee, one of the union's local shop-stewards. The drive to build Community Councils, launched in August 1980, continues.

But most attention should be directed to the Workers Revolutionary Party's active campaign to mobilize young people. Whatever the protestations about wanting to relieve the evils of youth unemployment, the young are intended to form the recruits and foot-soldiers of the revolution.

'The youth', says Paragraph 16 of the 1981 Manifesto, 'who are among the hardest-hit by the Tories would be mobilized through Revolutionary Youth Committees to be active in the work of the Community Councils.'

With almost 300,000 young jobless (now more), 'the Revolutionary Youth Committees will organize unemployed youth, apprentices, student and immigrant youth. They will provide social and sporting activities as well as the opportunity to take part in the political struggles against Toryism. A central issue will be the demand for the trade unions to recruit unemployed youth as members.... The Revolutionary Youth Committees will take an active part in the Community Councils and form the backbone of the organization of the Workers' Defence Guards.' At the same time the WRP is currently engaged in founding and opening revolutionary youth centres through 'Youth Training'. Chairman is Vanessa Redgrave, a member of the Party's central committee, and secretary Claire Dixon, who is also secretary of the Young Socialists. Its declared purpose is to assist young people facing a lack of jobs and training. But at a meeting to celebrate eleven years of a daily Trotskyist newspaper, Miss Dixon stated: 'Our plan is to establish twenty-five of them as an initial step to develop their skills and their opposition to the capitalist system and all it stands for.' For her part, Miss Redgrave has denied any political purpose.

The first training centre was opened at Brixton by Helen Mirren, the distinguished actress, in January 1981. A large photograph of her doing so appeared with the text of the Manifesto as published in *News Line* on 7 February 1981. Following publicity, Miss Mirren denied any Trotskyist political commitment, expressing only concern for the young unemployed. Others present, apart from Miss Redgrave and Miss Dixon, included the actor Jeremy Kemp and Maurice Hope, then the world light middleweight boxing champion. Mr Hope was doubtlessly moved to do his best for the young black jobless in Brixton. But when questioned about his attendance, Terry Lawless, his manager, told the *News of the World* (8 March 1981), 'I'm shocked and so is Maurice. He went along to the youth centre in Brixton thinking he was helping the local kids. He wasn't aware this was the Workers' Revolutionary Party, and if they've used his name in connection with their party, then they're out of order. Maurice doesn't have any political views – he wants to help kids, he's a soft touch when it comes to that – and I wouldn't like to see him exploited.'

Involvement with unwitting, if politically naïve, well-wishers is, as will be further seen, a feature of the WRP and *News Line*. At Brixton an impressive list of courses available was stated to range from engineering to modern dancing. Developments there have included visits to local schools and signing up of young people outside Brixton Job Centre. Plans included visits to local factories, trade union branches and shops to seek materials and facilities for the centre. A drama course was conducted with the help of the playwright Michael Hastings and the actress Kika Markham. A film about the 'fight against Tory cuts in social services', called 'Lambeth', was shown. As might be expected in Lambeth, led by 'Red Ted' Knight, the Labour leader, himself a former active Trotskyist, 'Youth Training' was invited to see some of the council's workshops and taken 'in the Mayor's car' on a tour of borough training facilities by two Lambeth youth officers.

The second revolutionary youth centre was opened in early 1981 at Kensington, Liverpool where Trotskyists have traditionally been strong. According to the WRP, those attending the opening included Eddie Loyden, a Liverpool councillor and former Labour MP for Garston, Lancs; Bobby Owen, president of the Transport and General Workers Union's No. 6 Regional Committee; Alex Doswell, secretary of Liverpool Trades Council; Dave Martin, president of the Amalgamated Union of Engineering Workers' Liverpool District Committee; Barry Royle, also of the union's district committee; and Alan MacLean, chairman of the thermal engineers' branch of the General and Municipal Workers Union. Some companies have given equipment for these youth centres.

Miss Redgrave made no mention at the Brixton and Liverpool openings of any political purpose. The Liverpool centre even had the backing of the local Labour Party whose secretary, Wally Edwards, told the *Observer*, 'It's meeting a definite social need.' The WRP, he added, had given assurances that the centres would not be used for political indoctrination.

At Merthyr Tydfil, according to the *Observer* of 12 April 1981, 'Youth Training' acquired a 184-year-old former Wesleyan church for its next revolutionary youth training centre. Members of the Merthyr Tydfil English Wesleyan Church decided to dispose of the dilapidated property after merging with another congregation. They sold it for £5,000 to an electrical company called Copsecroft. Mrs Christine Cornell, a church pastor, told the *Observer*, 'When we put our church up for sale, the Moonies were very active here and were interested in the building. We checked out Copsecroft to make sure they weren't a front company. Our solicitor looked them up in the Company Register. All it said was that they dealt in electrical things.'

But in March 1981 the *Merthyr Express* published an interview with Travis Gould, a local member of the WRP Young Socialists, who announced that the church was to be turned into a youth centre. At Companies House, the *Observer* ascertained, Copsecroft was registered as a company with '£100 share capital, which had not filed accounts since its incorporation in June 1979'. One director, Mr David Charles Bruce, was listed as a director of Astmoor Litho, the WRP company which prints *News Line* and other Trotskyist publications. Alex Mitchell, *News Line* editor, told the *Observer* he had never heard of Copsecroft and knew nothing about the details of the Merthyr centre. 'There's a whole lot of them, and Merthyr is one of the places,' he reportedly said. The centres, Mr Mitchell continued, would offer the young a practical alternative to the Government's Youth Opportunity Programme, 'not just picking up bloody leaves'. Courses planned at Beehive Place, Brixton, the national centre, included mechanical engineering, television and radio electronics, dressmaking and hairdressing.

The first youth centres planned by the WRP, apart from Brixton, Liverpool and South Wales, included Glasgow, Newcastle-upon-Tyne and Norwich. In June 1981 the newest areas designated by the Workers Revolutionary Party for youth centres were Consett, Glasgow and Nottingham. As Miss Dixon indicated, the eventual goal is twenty-five, all aimed at 'mobilizing youth and workers up and down the country'. Nevertheless, the WRP continue to maintain they are non-political.

The Party stood sixty candidates in the May 1979 General Election 'and placed our revolutionary socialist programme before the masses'.

The masses failed to respond, with all candidates losing their deposits. WRP members have since been told that the decision to field this substantial force was 'ideologically correct'. But the total cost to the Party was around £100,000, with which I will deal in a later chapter on Trotskyist finances.

The ultimate aim of the Party is a Workers' Revolutionary Government. 'The basic condition for the victory and survival of such a government is that the entire state apparatus must pass into its hands.' But the WRP pays lip-service to democracy. 'The Workers Revolutionary Party rejects totally the policy of individual terror. Socialist revolution is irreconcilably opposed to anarchistic violence', the Manifesto states.

Should it ever attain power, which seems highly unlikely, the Workers Revolutionary Party 'will carry out the complete rationalization and expropriation of big business without compensation and organize the planned operation of industry, banking and commerce under workers' control'. It claims to protect small producers, shopkeepers and professional people from 'complete annihilation from the jaws of the monopolies', with no intention to take over high street shops or one-man businesses. That sounds like a travesty of Little Red Riding Hood.

The WRP also pays lip-service to various shibboleths, such as nationalization of the land and everything else, including food wholesalers and supermarkets, restoration of social services and a complete scientific review of nuclear energy policy. In power, it will also 'have to act at once against all forms of counter-revolutionary conspiracy and violence'. This means disbanding the standing army, the SAS, the police, the Special Branch and the secret police, MI5 and MI6. 'All their secrets will be published without delay.' That, not inconceivably, might prove embarrassing to some WRP leaders.

The Workers' Militia, based on Leninist principles in training, discipline and ideological education, would replace the Forces. The monarchy, Privy Council, the House of Lords and the judiciary would all be abolished, 'along with the hidden "State within the State" and Whitehall's power clique'. Also, 'all capitalist laws would be repealed'. Actors, writers, dancers, musicians, scientists and similar creative and professional workers would be taken care of subject to Trotskyist tenets.

There is much else of this tedious humourless tendentialism, which only people like Miss Redgrave, Mr Healy and obsessed myrmidons take seriously, such as ending secret diplomacy, leaving NATO and the Common Market, abolishing the Stock Exchange, complete control of foreign trade and, more sinisterly, supplying 'arms and weapons and training as well as air and naval support' to foreign revolutionary and terrorist movements, including the Palestine Liberation Organization. Troops would be withdrawn from Ulster before disbandment. Despite unbridgeable ideological enmities, 'unconditional defence' would be given to the Soviet Union.

All these are vain long-term aspirations, pressure-cooked in the self-deluded revolutionary fervour of Mr Healy and his disciples. More interesting is what actually goes on as part of the WRP's efforts to increase its influence by backdoor methods and involvement of unwitting well-wishers and of the politically innocent.

As noted already, the WRP puts great effort into wooing and mobilizing young people. *News Line* regularly carries advertisements for Young Socialists fairs and other special events at which, doubtless due to the prestige and influence of Vanessa Redgrave, the main attraction more often than not is a star actor from television or prominent sporting personality. The Workers Revolutionary Party, in fact, displays a distinct flair for show business.

What is surprising is the number of stage personalities who lend their names and prestige to supporting the Trotskyist cause at these functions. Some, such as the Redgraves and Frances de la Tour, are dedicated activists. Others are fellow-travellers or sympathizers. Others, yet again, are political ignoramuses, or perhaps mistake the Young Socialists for the Labour Party, or will do anything for a personal appearance. What is certain is that some have no idea that they are even associated with a WRP sponsored event.

The list of well-known actors and actresses who have been advertised as attending functions which the Party has sponsored for its own purposes is lengthy. Their appearance is advertised prominently in *News Line* together with photographs and the name of their well-known television show or stage performance. Apart from some individuals discussed below, we have no definite proof that they did attend these functions nor that they even knew of the forum in which their names were advertised. Among those who were advertised as due to appear were Derek Jacobi of 'I Claudius'; Frances de la Tour of 'Rising Damp'; Jeremy Kemp, who appeared in 'The Good Soldier'; Ian Dury, the Cockney pop star; Eamonn Boland from Fox; Natalie Ogle from 'Rising Damp'; Muriel Romanes who plays Alice McEwan in Scottish Television's 'Take the High Road'; Alan Hunter who played Blake in Granada's 'The Spoils of War'; George Harris of 'Wolcott'; Carmen Munro of 'How Do You Do'; and, 'straight from the London Palladium' Windsor Davies and Melvyn Hayes of 'It Ain't 'Alf Hot Mum' with the Peggy O'Farrell Children and Christopher Mitchell.

Other star guests are said to have included Malcolm Tierny of 'L. S. Lowry', Ken Loach, Colin Welland, and Lewis Collins who plays Bodie in 'The Professionals'. The case of Lewis Collins is illuminating. He appeared at a Young Socialists Fair in Islington in February 1979, the purpose of which was to raise cash for the Redgraves' *Observer* Fighting Fund. The Fair was opened by Vanessa Redgrave who, according to *News Line* of 5 February, was with Lewis Collins, the 'star attraction'. It was a 'great success'.

The full-page report of the fair in *News Line* was dominated by a large photograph of Lewis Collins, an 'instant hit', surrounded by young fans. At the bottom of the page was an application form to join the Workers Revolutionary Party.

When I mentioned the name of Lewis Collins (formerly a Territorial

Army paratrooper) in this connection in the *Daily Telegraph*, I received telephone representations on his behalf saying he had never been associated with the Trotskyists and had never met Vanessa Redgrave. I promised to check and sent a long letter to Lewis Collins' father with the above documentary evidence and giving the background to the Workers Revolutionary Party and its Young Socialists. Both Mr Collins and his father were concerned at the damage such publicity could do to his blossoming career. Subsequently, Lewis Collins wrote me a friendly grateful letter, saying he had no Trotskyist revolutionary leanings and had been 'conned' into going to the Fair by an actor working with him on the set of 'The Professionals'. Doubtlessly Vanessa Redgrave had appeared in the morning, and he in the afternoon, so he never met her. I fully accepted Mr Collins' word and assurances; he had done a good turn for a colleague and some young people, little realizing how his presence would be exploited in *News Line*. The clear implication was that if Lewis Collins helps at a Young Socialists Fair, there cannot be much wrong with the Workers Revolutionary Party.

Nor is he the only one to be thus conned. Apart from show business, the WRP and *News Line*, a highly professional paper, make a big thing out of sport. Both Malcolm Allison, the mercurial football manager, and Vince Hilaire, the black Crystal Palace footballer, have written regular columns for *News Line*. They are not alone. Trevor Brooking of West Ham and England has autographed copies of his book at a bookshop in East London. *News Line* has also claimed support for its youth centres from footballers Phil Thompson of Liverpool and England and Mick Lyons of Everton, who were present at centre openings.

I have already cited the disclaimer on behalf of former world boxing champion Maurice Hope. Mick Lyons, Everton captain, said after his attendance, 'No way would I say I was associated with that lot. I did go along to open the centre in Liverpool, but only because there were kids involved. I'd say my politics were totally opposed to theirs. I'm amazed that they would use my name.' Phil Thompson, captain of Liverpool, said he was asked to talk at the opening of the Liverpool centre about his views of the Tory Party – 'I told them I didn't want to be involved in any politics. I was there for the kids. Nothing else.' It would be illuminating to know how many others feel they were conned and exploited. It is noteworthy, however, that the only well-known name to enter a disclaimer after being cited in the *Daily Telegraph* was Lewis Collins. *News Line* and the Young Socialists continue to secure a succession of volunteers to boost their causes. On 30 June 1981 *News Line* announced a new celebrity line-up, 'Meet the Stars', for its Young Socialists summer fair at Peckham Rye junior school on 25 July. Actors due to appear, whose photographs were published, were: Ian Charlesom, star of 'Chariots of Fire'; Brian Murphy, who played George in 'George and Mildred'; Pauline Yates, of 'Keep it in the Family'; and Alun Armstrong, of 'Get Lost'.

But the Workers Revolutionary Party has achieved most notoriety from its Revolutionary College of Marxist Education at White Meadows, a large house with a modern annexe set in spacious grounds in the village of Parwich near Ashbourne, Derbyshire. It was acquired for the Party for £23,000 by Corin Redgrave and, after extensive alterations, opened for full-time indoctrination in August 1975.

Only a month or so later, the bombshell burst when the *Observer* published an account of her two-day stay there by Miss Irene Gorst, an actress, and a WRP member through her association with Corin Redgrave, her former lover. Miss Gorst, who later admitted she 'went with my eyes open', told in the *Observer* and subsequently how she arrived late after missing the WRP minibus in London because a man friend had tried to dissuade her from going. On arrival, she alleged that WRP leaders, including the two Redgraves, had accused her of being a Special Branch spy. She claimed that she had been interrogated for seven hours and when she attempted to leave, after one hour, was pushed back in her chair by Vanessa Redgrave. She could not go to the lavatory, she said, without a man standing outside the door. Finally, after a distressful time, she was allowed to leave with a Marxist admonishment from Gerry Healy.

On re-arriving in London, Miss Gorst reported to Equity, who in turn called in the *Observer*. Before publishing, the newspaper informed Victor Gilbert, head of the Special Branch, of Miss Gorst's allegations. There followed a seven-hour raid by seventy policemen during which the WRP leaders said they were detained incommunicado and unlawfully in a room. In a newly constructed cupboard under the stairs, police found nine .22 bullets during a systematic search.

Mr Roy Battersby, a television producer and College 'headmaster', stated, 'We deny any knowledge of the existence of such bullets.' The College, he said, was a drama centre and place to discuss history, politics and economics. Miss Redgrave in a television confrontation with Miss Gorst said it was all 'lies – a put-up job'. The Party was 'utterly opposed to terrorist violence'. The row and the police raid had considerable repercussions.

On 4 November 1975 Peter Archer, the Solicitor General, said there would be no prosecution over the discovery of the bullets. The Director of Public Prosecutions, he added, had found the find did not justify proceedings. But Miss Redgrave, after failing to get a retraction from the *Observer*, sued for libel together with Corin Redgrave, Gerry Healy, Roy Battersby, Roger Smith, film and television writer, and Michael Hannigan, actor. The two-week hearing opened on 24 October 1978.

In their action, the plaintiffs rejected suggestions that they were people given to violence and nastiness, and claimed the *Observer* report brought them into disrepute. Mr John Wilmers QC said, 'That is really what this case is about', and they were not the violent unlawful lot they were made out to be.

During the hearing, Corin Redgrave, agreeing he had been Miss Gorst's lover, referred to an alleged theatre blacklist of Trotskyist actors, which made it difficult for them to get work. Miss Gorst, he said, had been worried about losing her career and about victimization if she stayed at White Meadows. The statements attributed to her were 'complete invention'.

The case had a curious and unexpected outcome, which proved expensive for the plaintiffs. The jury, after answering four questions from the judge, decided unanimously after a seven-hour retirement that the article libelled the plaintiffs and that not all the words they complained of were true. But it also found that the reputation of the six had not materially altered. In effect, they had lost, failing to prove their entire case, and faced a bill for £70,000 costs.

Interpretations of the verdict, which led to some confusion, were mixed, *The Times* notably concluding the plaintiffs had suffered an injustice. Miss Redgrave stated: 'The decision that it is defamation is very welcome. All the words in the article have been found to be not true – and that in itself is welcome. However, the verdict against us is very distressing.' She added: 'We did not go into this action for money but to clear our own reputation. We proved our case but we lost. An informant can go to a newspaper with a story in which all the words are untrue. The courts can find it defamatory but make the victims pay.' Corin Redgrave described it as a 'very dangerous precedent indeed'.

The actual verdict, however, was based on a section of the Defamation Act, 1952. This states:

A defence of justification shall not fail by reason only that the truth of every charge is not proved if the words not proved to be true do not materially injure the plaintiff's reputation having regard to the truth of the remaining charges.

In a defensive comment, the *Observer* said the verdict had been widely misquoted. 'The jury found that the article was in part true and in part false. The false part was unimportant in relation to the article as a whole.' For this reason, it continued, the *Observer* won and the plaintiffs lost: 'Had the verdict been that all the words in the article were untrue, the result would, of course, have been the other way round.' Subsequently, Vanessa and Corin Redgrave, after deciding against an appeal, launched the *Observer* Libel Fund to offset the costs. Miss Redgrave asserted that for part of the time they had effectively been in the dock and on trial for their political ideas.

White Meadows has been in the news on other occasions. On 19 August 1976 the *Daily Mail* published an account by Miss Shelley Rohde, an able and veteran Fleet Street journalist, of an 'incognito' visit as one of seventeen students. She experienced a week of militant Marxist indoctrination aimed at revolution. Husbands and wives slept in separate rooms and ate at different tables. Children were segregated and cared for by rota. Cleaning, cooking and laundry were done efficiently by daily teams supervised by vigilant group leaders. No smoking was allowed except in the grounds and canteen. Alcohol, drugs and sex were strictly forbidden. 'There was no frivolity, no casual conversation, very little humour, and the summit of distraction for the week was a Party-produced film on the General Strike,' Miss Rohde reported. This was 'loudly translated into German for the benefit of a delegation of fifty Teutonic comrades encamped in army tents in the garden'.

According to Roy Battersby, Miss Rohde recounted, this was the reason for a 'daily flypast of photo-reconnaissance jets'. The 'students' were instructed not to look up at the planes to avoid being 'on record'. The telephone was also tapped, they were warned. Outside phone calls and surreptitious brief visits to the pub were quickly checked. Passing hikers were watched and recorded. No one was allowed to leave the grounds, and 'comrade Gareth', a 'young blond actor from London', was 'hauled out of his tent' for a 'public dressing down', as Miss Rohde reported, for backsliding on chores. Bedtime, after an evening of group discussion or supervised study, was at 11 pm, with lights switched off at midnight by four all-night duty guards.

Reveille was at dawn, with kitchen work at 6.15 am, cleaning at 7 am, or 4.45 am for those detailed for selling *News Line* outside Rolls-Royce or British Celanese in Derby. For Miss Rohde, who admitted to a 'fleeting conversion', workers' reactions, varying from 'Fuck off' to calls for the National Front, were a 'revelation'. When she expressed reservations about the use of violence in response to a direct question from one of the organizers, a former economics lecturer at North London Polytechnic, with a penchant for sandals and corduroys, he reportedly told the class, 'Comrades, there is a nasty undercurrent of liberalism, of humanism, in this group. We are not humanists. We feel no brotherhood. There will be no conversation in our revolution. To use reason against our enemies would be like taking a pea-shooter to a Centurion tank.'

When caught wiping aluminium saucepans with a tea towel instead of leaving them to dry because a second restless sitting of seventy hungry comrades was waiting outside the canteen doors, Miss Rohde was submitted to a 'tirade of four-letter invective' by Comrade Tony, with others being told, 'Christ, we've got a bloody individual here. You are not here to think, but to do as you are told. This is a part of your political education and you must accept it as such. Or you'll be out.' She was refused permission to move from her twelve-bunked room, about twelve feet square, to her thirteen-year-old son who was suffering from a painful gastric complaint. Comrade Steve, a twenty-two-year-old barman from Southampton also fell foul of Comrade Tony, being loudly told, when he said he was only trying to be helpful, that initiative was not a trait required for revolutionaries. Party throughout came before family. Miss Rohde's account of the Trotskyist regimen at White Meadows sounds like *1984* come true.

In February 1977 a fresh rumpus occurred when a group of young people, aged between fourteen and twenty, attended a course at White Meadows. A sixteen-year-old girl in council care at Hackney went with the £10 being met by the local authority. Two other teenagers received £5 towards the costs from the Inner London Education Authority. The sixteen-year-old said all had been searched on arrival. Items such as pen-knives and nail files were removed. They had been given a 'terrible time' with political lectures from morning to night. In the evening, 'light entertainment' was provided by a film of the Jarrow March. The young people, aged between fourteen and twenty, brought back only a hazy message of the need to 'smash capital'. Stephen Cook, chairman of Hackney Social

Services Committee, said, 'We take a dim view of children being indoctrinated in this way.' But, as ever, the Workers Revolutionary Party denied any such aim or activity. Alex Mitchell, *News Line* editor, 'completely repudiated' the allegations. Teenagers attending White Meadows courses, he said, needed signed approval from their parents. They had been searched on arrival because of the previous discovery of the .22 bullets, of which the WRP had denied all knowledge. 'We teach history, economics and discuss general socialist principles,' Mr Mitchell said. Saying that so far, eight hundred people had attended courses there, he added, 'We consider our school a great achievement'.

White Meadows, which several thousand people have attended for Trotskyist indoctrination courses, is still going strong. Its courses now cost around £30. Journalists (non-Trotskyist) are turned away from the door. The 'College of Marxist Education' also runs courses in London and elsewhere. For its 1981 summer season, running from 22 June to 9 October, two courses were offered at a cost of £60.48 for two weeks, including VAT and full board.

Tutor at the first was Gerry Healy, who gave a course of lectures on the origins of Marxism – 'How Marx Became a Marxist' (!) – at the New Ambassadors Hotel, Upper Woburn Place, London WC1. His tutorials included: Dialectical Training; Week 1, Lenin's Theory of Knowledge; Disclosing the 'cell of dialectics'; The source of idealist errors. Week 2 was: From Hegel to Marx; Essential Marxism – Dialectical Materialism; The Hegelian influence on Marx's *Capital*. The second course covered an Introduction to Marxism. Week 1: Man and Nature; Man and labour; Man and thought; Man and society. Week 2: Imperialism; The Russian Revolution; Stalinism; Trotskyism. A deposit of £5 was requested with the order form. How many workers are interested in Hegel, not to mention the rest of the dialectics?

I deal with the WRP's finances and international connections separately with other Trotskyist organizations. But it is noteworthy that it also frequently advertises six bookshops in *News Line*. These are the Paperbacks Centre, 28, Charlotte Street, W1; 10-12, Atlantic Road, Brixton, SW9; 389, Green Street, Upton Park, E13; 96, Magdalen Street, Anglia Square, Norwich; Hope Street Book Centre, 321, Hope Street, Glasgow; Merseybooks, 34-36, Manchester Street, Liverpool.

The Workers Revolutionary Party has signally failed to win support in parliamentary elections, although it regularly fields candidates, notably

Vanessa Redgrave. It continues, however, to maintain an active electoral role, staging numerous meetings throughout the country. It is particularly active in Brixton and Lambeth, the scenes of several 1981 race riots. Lambeth activities are well illustrated in *News Line*'s version of its 1981 Manifesto. So, too, is the Party's active participation in picket-line disturbances in Sheffield. It manages to maintain its daily newspaper without commercial support, and distributes it by its own fleet of eight-ton trucks from Runcorn. Somehow, it continues to secure substantial support in the acting and sporting professions. It can rely on dedicated volunteers to peddle *News Line* in shopping high streets, pubs, outside factory gates and trade union and Labour Party conferences and meetings. It has been reported as having forty full-time paid workers and organizers. Like other Trotskyist organizations, it should not be underrated.

Yet, also like other Trotskyist organizations, the Workers Revolutionary Party would no doubt expire without the drive, flair, organizing ability and discipline of its leading personalities. Mr Healy has been the WRP's driving force. Like a Dostoievskian nihilist, he has never lost sight of his goal nor the ideological 'purity' to achieve his dream of a Trotskyist revolution in Britain. Then there are the Sinhalese Banda brothers, Mike, general secretary of the WRP, and Tony, and Alex Mitchell, a genial well-dressed character, until recently editor of *News Line*. Also worthy of mention is Royston Bull, full-time journalist on *News Line*, and former industrial correspondent of the *Scotsman*. Mr Bull was once a Communist selected for special training in Moscow until he became disillusioned with Soviet education methods. Later, he was granted a year's bursary to study in the United States before turning Trotskyist. Later again, Mr Bull was the only one of a party of British industrial correspondents to be subjected to a full body-search by the East German Communist Vopos at Checkpoint Charlie when entering East Berlin. The reason, it was believed, was the American residence visa in his passport. Such is life.

And of course, there is Miss Redgrave, backed up by her brother Corin, who has been a mainstay of the WRP for many years. Miss Redgrave is something of an enigma. A puritanical Trotskyist, preaching the revolution, she is also much given to litigation. She has stood several times for parliament including Newham North East and Moss Side, Manchester, but only won minimal electoral support. She has financed the Party substantially, and been active in promoting international links in support of the Palestine Liberation Organization. By making the film 'The Palestinian' and appearing as Fania Fenelon, against the lady's wishes, in the film 'Playing for Time' about Auschwitz, she provoked heated protests and demonstrations by American Jews.

Yet Tony Richardson, her ex-husband, said, 'She may have made mistakes, but there isn't a drop of anti-Semitic blood in her veins.' Vanessa Redgrave has also fought in vain over many years to have Trotskyist policies and pro-Palestinian and anti-Israel declarations adopted by Equity. She was regularly defeated by determined opposition.

On 1 September 1980 she claimed at an extreme left-wing anti-Zionist conference that a Red revolution was imminent in Britain. 'It is so close that those people out of the country risk missing it,' she said, according to the *Sun*. Yet she reportedly said on 28 September 1980, 'I was a romantic brought up on Kipling. Churchill sounded so wonderful, but the bomb changed all that. I used to leave well alone – I believe in reason. Emotion alone can't carry you through. Actors are probably prone to schizophrenia' (*Daily Express*, 29 September 1980).

Many might think that Miss Redgrave, who lives at Hammersmith, is extremely emotional about her Trotskyism. Awarded the CBE in 1967, she is endearingly out of the everyday world, and has become one of those eccentric English institutions which contribute to the tradition of this country. Where would we be without Vanessa and her ilk? Perhaps the last word should be with John Barber, the *Daily Telegraph*'s theatre critic. In May 1979, while acknowledging her regal, somewhat ethereal manner, he described her as shy, given to giggles, a low voice and thinking before she speaks. She sounded, he said, like a woman who always worked hard, had been strictly brought up, but remained a romantic.

A final word on the Workers Revolutionary Party. On 30 October 1979, at a Paris auction, it bought Trotsky's death mask for £4,400. It does not seem much to pay for it, even for the faithful. Can there be a moral in that somewhere?

2 The Militant Tendency

The most successful Trotskyist organization in Britain over the past seven years, and the one which most threatens parliamentary democracy and society, is the now notorious Militant Tendency. Thanks largely to Lord Underhill, former Labour Party national agent, much has become known about its activities, which are devoted to penetration of, and influence over, the Labour Party, trade unions, student and other organizations. Militant Tendency is the outstandingly successful practitioner of entryism with its declared aim of eventual control of the Labour Party, and driving out moderates in the process, now being fulfilled.

But none of the publicity has halted Militant's steady advance, although there are increasing signs of resistance with the formation of the Labour Solidarity Campaign, which claims a 4,000 membership, making it the largest group within the Labour Party. Its success in countering the Militant Tendency must wait to be seen. But Militant is already believed, through Labour Party conference voting patterns, to control at least seventy constituency parties and be strong in a hundred. Increasing alarm is felt not only by moderates or right-wingers threatened by re-selection, some of whom have defected to the Social Democrats, but also by conventional left-wingers.

Through persistent 'moling', Militant is not only one of the largest, but certainly the most influential single faction in the Party. With Andy Bevan as Labour's national youth officer, it has long controlled the Party's Young Socialists from which it seeks most of its recruits. Like other Trotskyist organizations, Militant Tendency, itself a Trotskyist term, is extremely secretive, conspiratorial and dedicated to entryism and exploitation of industrial and racial disputes. It is controlled by a small caucus, and exercises iron discipline, including fines for backsliders. Like other leading Trotskyist groups, it also has its origin in the war-time Revolutionary Communist Party and its precursors. Like them too, its origins are partly from abroad.

During the 1930s, the principal Trotskyist organizations in Britain were the Workers International League and the Militant Labour League. Among the South African Trotskyists who arrived in Britain in 1937 to seek more fertile fields was Edward Grant, then twenty-three, a full-time revolutionary who was to found and ideologically guide the Militant Tendency. Soon after his arrival, Ted Grant, now approaching seventy, became active in the Workers International League until it merged with the Militant Labour League in 1943 to form the Revolutionary Communist Party. When this broke up into different factions the 'Grantites' were believed to be the smallest group, as well as the dullest, most repetitious and intellectually unadventurous, a reputation Militant Tendency supporters enjoy to this day.

Already practising Labour Party entryism, they published *International Socialist Review*. In 1956, the group established a connection with the International Secretariat of the Trotskyist Fourth International, which in 1963 became the United Secretariat, then without a British section. A new name was adopted, the Revolutionary Socialist League. The League launched a magazine, *Workers International Review*, which reported in summer 1957 that the League would work for the 'transformation of the Labour Party at ward and constituency level. . . . Our work in the Labour Party', it said, 'will require a slow, methodical and persistent agitation and propaganda around not only such immediate issues but also fundamental ideological questions.' Publication followed from 1958 until 1963 of *Socialist Fight*. But despite surviving, the group showed little growth or progress, and in a paper in 1959, 'Problems of Entrism' (the alternative spelling of 'entryism'), some comrades who had advocated leaving the Labour Party were warned against launching an 'adventure' outside the Party, especially 'after a decade or more of work'. Mr Grant, then working as a night telephonist, admitted to being down to a 'handful of supporters'.

But then came the turning of Mr Grant's fortunes, which led to the Militant Tendency as we know it today. He was joined by Peter Taaffe in Liverpool, who has edited *Militant* since 1964, and is now often regarded as the motor behind the organization. Other groups of supporters were established in Swansea, Bradford (still a centre of virulent Militant Tendency activity), Norwood and Brighton. This last centre was particularly significant because important recruits were made among the first students of the new University of Sussex, who soon controlled the University Labour Club. They included Alan Woods, of Swansea; Roger Silverman, son of the late Sydney Silverman, left-wing Labour MP; Terry Wilson and Bob McKee, of London; and Lynn Walsh, of Basingstoke. Since then, Sussex University has been a hotbed of Ultra-Left activity. At least five of seventeen people identified as members of *Militant*'s editorial board were then at Sussex University. So were six of twenty-five shareholders of Workers International Review Publications, Ltd, the Militant Tendency's master company.

Following this infusion of new energy, the group took off. The Revolutionary Socialist League gradually submerged, and since then Peter Taaffe, Ted Grant and Nick Wilson, a Labour Party Young Socialists' representative on the Party's national executive committee, have denied all connection with it. Mr Taaffe said on BBC Radio 4 on 12 December 1976, 'Militant was founded about ten years ago.... We entirely deny we are connected with any organization called Revolutionary Socialist League, if such an organization exists.' However, the Militant Tendency is regarded as either the League's successor or its front entryist organization. In any case, leading League members such as Mr Grant, Mr Taaffe and Mr Pat Wall moved over to become Tendency activists.

Socialist Fight was wound up in 1963, and the present *Militant* weekly newspaper, 'The Marxist Paper for Labour and Youth', first appeared in 1964, at first as a four-page monthiy until 1971, then an eight-page weekly, and now a sixteen-page weekly, together with the *Militant Irish Monthly* and *Militant International Review*, a theoretical journal. It also publishes an annual policy review, *British Perspectives and Tasks*, various bulletins and much else.

In 1965, the Militant Tendency was still committed to deep entryism into the Labour Party, and when this strategy was abandoned by the Fourth International, links with it were broken. The international Trotskyist mantle in Britain was assumed by the International Marxist Group and the Workers Revolutionary Party. For the next ten years, the Militant Tendency continued to beaver away in constituencies, unions and student organizations, making recruits from the original few hundred to the present 2,000 or so, increasing the sale of *Militant* to its present print of around 10,000 copies and building its secret organization – whose existence it denies – inside the Labour Party and unions.

But its activities had not gone unobserved by Reg Underhill, Labour Party national agent and now Lord Underhill. He set about collecting Militant Tendency documents and other voluminous information about its surreptitious entryist activities, from which he concluded that the Tendency was in contravention of the Labour Party constitution which excludes from the party organizations 'political organizations ... having their own programme, principles and policy for distinctive and separate propaganda, or possessing branches in the constituencies'. Lord Underhill submitted a report to the Labour Party national executive committee in November 1975 in which he quoted *British Perspectives and Tasks 1974* and an additional document referring to a booklet 'Entrism' printed and published by the Cambridge Heath Press, then of 375, Cambridge Heath Road, London E2, printers and publishers of *Militant*. Subsequently, Mr Underhill received a further eight documents of the Militant Tendency, which he also submitted. But in 1977 the Party decided not to publish the documents when its annual conference accepted the advice of a committee of the executive that greater political education was the best way of dealing with the problem.

Lord Underhill, a Labour stalwart if ever there was one, retired from the post of national agent in July 1979. Since then, he has seen a further ten documents issued by the Militant Tendency, one dated 1976, three 1977 and six 1978. Altogether, his twenty documents comprise over four hundred pages of original Militant Tendency material. In addition, Lord Underhill was approached later in 1980 by a number of disillusioned former Militant supporters who recounted their experiences, which he has also published. This followed the brouhaha in March 1980 when Lord Underhill, despairing of national executive action on his report and representations (no real surprise since the left-wing majority on the executive are tacit Militant supporters) published his initial findings, backed by more than four hundred pages of documents.

Lord Underhill, whose report showed that the Revolutionary Socialist League had 'buried itself within our Party in order to change it', said that while he did not believe the Militant Tendency was capable of a complete take-over of the Labour Party, its activities were an electoral liability, and had contributed to Labour's general election defeat in May 1979. He urged the national executive to end its reluctance to tackle the issue head-on, challenged it to expose the Tendency's activities, distance the Party from its policies and call in its leaders with a view to them toeing the Labour line or leaving the Party. He also made it clear he was not seeking a witch-hunt or mass expulsions from the Party as left-wing members of the national executive, such as Frank Allaun, claimed, and suggested that other means could be found of defusing a group which had caused serious difficulties in some constituencies. He did not intend to conduct a 'rip-roaring campaign', but hoped that constituency parties and trade unions, to which he was circulating his report at his own expense, would themselves insist that the executive took action.

Lord Underhill also insisted that the Militant Tendency was different from any other group within the Party. 'This is the first of the Trotskyist organizations which has dropped any activity in its real name and has buried itself within the Labour Party in order to change the Party to its views,' he said. 'It is one thing having pressure groups within the Party. It is quite another thing having a nationwide parallel organization, many of whose meetings are held in secret, which determines activities within the Party.' Lord Underhill said the structure of Militant Tendency posed a direct challenge to the Labour Party's constitution. Its aims conflicted with Labour's commitment to parliamentary democracy. Militant's efforts to form an international movement clashed with Labour's membership of the Socialist International. Its members did not disclose the real name of the movement and it was creating 'embarrassment and difficulties' within the Labour organization. Lord Underhill also said that none of the documents had reached him anonymously as some critics had claimed. In any case, their content was borne out by MPs and party workers who had approached him and who, he presumed, had confided the same fears to national executive committee members. But he would not be drawn on exactly which constituency parties might be controlled by the Tendency. Nor did he suggest that the number was significant, or that any Labour MPs were Militant Tendency adherents. (Since then, it has become more obvious.)

Lord Underhill's submissions fell on predictably stony ground. The Far Left on the executive stressed the need for tolerance. Other members said the issue had already been adequately discussed, while those who wanted it raised again did not believe that much would happen if it were. Ron Hayward, Labour Party general secretary, said the documents revealed little that the national executive committee did not know already and vindicated its earlier decision not to publish the ten papers submitted by Lord Underhill in 1975 and the further ten which he had received recently. Mr Hayward believed the Labour Party was 'mature enough to withstand the inevitable pressures' which the freedom of members to campaign for their own viewpoint aroused. Labour, he added, refused to be diverted from its task by 'undue attention to the small fractions and groups whose activities obsess so much of the media'.

Eric Heffer, MP for Walton, Liverpool and chairman of the Party's organization committee, stressed that the Party had called on all groups within its ranks to answer a questionnaire on their organization, policy and finances. One senior executive member conceded the Party's mistake in not publishing the documents in 1977, but criticized the Militant viewpoint as 'fifth-rate Marxism'. Another member rejected curbs on the

Tendency because its adherents were the 'choirboys and choirgirls of a new church'.

All in all, Lord Underhill did not get very far, at least within the Labour Party, although his disclosures attracted wide attention elsewhere. The Militant Tendency, enjoying considerable influence or sympathy in the ever more left-wing Labour Party, simply carried on. It did, however, reply to the Labour Party national executive's questionnaire, since when little or nothing more has happened, except a continuing spread of Trotskyist influence.

Before examining the present state and organization of the Militant Tendency, however, it is worth examining the full text of its reply by Peter Taaffe, editor of *Militant*, to the questionnaire, which the Labour Party has done its best not to publicize.

On 11 March 1980 the Labour Party national executive committee sent the questionnaire to Militant Tendency posing specific questions on policies, organization and finances. It was answered on 11 April 1980 by Peter Taaffe, but despite representations by Frank Field, left-wing Labour MP for Birkenhead, his submission was not fully published and circulated to every Labour MP and constituency party for comment. A copy was, however, made available for those interested, in the Labour Party library. Mr Taaffe wrote:

1 *Aims and objectives*
'Militant', as its masthead has proclaimed since its first publication, is a 'Marxist paper for Labour and Youth'. 'Militant' aims to support the working class and all exploited people in their struggles in Britain and internationally, publishing reports and articles expressing the problems, demands, and aspirations of working people.

The paper propagates the ideas of Marxism, and campaigns in the Labour Party and in the trade unions to win support for a Marxist programme which would give practical effect to the basic socialist aims of the Labour Party expressed in clause IV, part IV, of the Party's constitution. 'Militant' supports the building of a mass membership for the Labour Party and its youth section, the Labour Party Young Socialists, and the paper campaigns in elections for the return of Labour Party candidates and for a Labour government.

A key plank of 'Militant's' programme for Britain is the call for nationalization of 200 big monopolies, together with the banks, insurance companies, and finance houses, with minimum compensation on the basis of proven need; for nationalized industries and enterprises to be run under democratic workers' control and management; and for a democratic socialist plan of production to develop productive and human resources for the benefit of all working people.

As part of its programme, 'Militant' campaigns for the immediate implementation of the following demands; a job for all workers and an end to unemployment; a minimum wage of £80 for all workers; the 35 hour week for all workers; the reversal of all spending cuts and a massive increase of social spending; and a programme of useful public works to create jobs and provide vitally necessary social facilities.

'Militant' stands for the defence of all democratic rights, the right to belong to a trade union and to take strike action, and freedom of assembly, speech and publication. The paper is fundamentally opposed to the totalitarian, bureaucratic Stalinist regimes of Russia and Eastern Europe. While recognizing the historic gains of the nationalized planned economies, 'Militant' stands for an end to bureaucracy and the establishment of workers' democracy, with the election with right of recall of all representatives and officials, and the creation of independent, democratic trade unions.

2 *Eligibility for membership & 3 Organizational structure*
'Militant' is not an organization but a journal which, like other papers in the labour movement, reflects a current of opinion and sets out to win support for its ideas and policies. There is no organizational structure and no membership.

4 *Names of elected officers and part-time workers*
The Editor of 'Militant' is Peter Taaffe (a member of the Labour Party since 1959), the Assistant Editor Lynn Walsh (LP member since 1964), the Political Editor Ted Grant (LP member since 1950). Other members of its editorial and administrative staff are: Keith Dickinson (LP member since 1958), Clare Doyle (LP member since 1964), Roger Silverman (LP member since 1960) and Brian Ingham (LP member since 1968). Together with other journalistic, administrative, secretarial, print, distribution and sales staff, 'Militant's' staff totals 50 workers.

5 *Offices and premises occupied*
The 'Militant' occupies offices at 375, Cambridge Heath Road,

London E2 9RA, and offices and factory premises at 1, Mentmore Terrace, London E8 3PN.

7 *List of publications*

'Militant' is published weekly with 16 pages, and from time to time with larger issues. It also publishes a quarterly journal, 'Militant International Review', together with a large number of occasional pamphlets on general political issues, trade union issues, and historical and theoretical subjects.

6 *Accounts and sources of finance*

'Militant' is funded exclusively from the contributions from supporters in the labour movement. It receives no money whatsoever from any sinister source, either in Britain or abroad.

In view of the clear evidence, on the other hand, of sinister funding from sources hostile to the labour movement for right-wing groupings and journals in the Labour Party, 'Militant' considers it necessary to state categorically that it has never received any funds from bankers or businessmen, from any private trust or foundation, or from any capitalist government or government agency. 'Militant' has never received funds or any form of support from the American Central Intelligence Agency, from the North Atlantic Treaty Organization, from British Intelligence Services or their front organizations or from any other capitalist organization opposed to the fundamental aims and aspirations of the labour movement. 'Militant' has never received any funds from Russia, and although the absurd allegation of 'Moscow gold' has been made against the 'Militant' by the millionaires' gutter press, anyone with the slightest political understanding knows that the Russian bureaucracy and its secret police hate the supporters of Leon Trotsky's ideas even more violently than they hate their capitalists [*sic*] opponents.

Unlike the capitalist press, moreover, 'Militant' has no revenue from commercial advertising and cannot rely on commercial wholesalers for its distribution. It relies entirely on activists within the labour movement to build up the paper's resources and staff.

Money comes to 'Militant' in three ways.

Firstly, 'Militant' receives cash from the sales of the paper, the 'Militant International Review', and 'Militant' pamphlets. 'Militant' also has a relatively small income from commercial printing, which it undertakes mainly for organizations of the labour movement. This 'commercial' source of cash seems to have been completely ignored by our right-wing and Fleet Street critics.

Secondly, 'Militant' receives cash from contributions made to the 'Militant' Fighting Fund. These come from individual readers, supporters, and well-wishers together with organizations of the labour movement which from time to time make donations to the paper.

Money also comes to the Fighting Fund from fund-raising activities. Full details of our Fighting Fund income are published weekly in the paper. Last year, we raised over £80,000. Previously, we raised £66,000 in 1978, £47,000 in 1977, etc.

Thirdly, 'Militant' has benefited from a series of loans, amounting to over £148,500 over three years from WIR Publications Ltd. to the Cambridge Heath Press Ltd., the 'Militant's' publisher and printer.

The two separate companies, Cambridge Heath Press Ltd. and WIR Publications Ltd., were set up on advice from lawyers and accountants. This arrangement was considered to be in the best interest of the thousands of workers who contribute their pennies and pounds from their hard-earned wages to further the cause of socialism.

WIR Publications Ltd. acts as a 'collecting box'. As its Memorandum of Association states, the company exists 'to aid and further the interests of the international working class', and its income is derived solely from the donations of active members of the Labour Party and trade unions who, in addition to occasional donations to the 'Militant' Fighting Fund, are prepared to make regular contributions to develop the support for Marxist policies within the labour movement.

The accounts of both Cambridge Heath Press Ltd. and WIR Publications Ltd. are prepared, audited by chartered accountants, and deposited in accordance with Company law at Companies House, where they may be inspected by members of the public.

I have quoted the full text of Mr Taaffe's reply for several reasons. It is significant, apart from the reluctance of the Labour Party national executive to publish it, for several particulars. Mr Taaffe, anxious to establish Militant Tendency's credentials according to the Party's constitution, denies it is an organization, only a band of like-thinking people within the Labour movement whose views are expressed in *Militant*. There is no organization as such, no members, only supporters. That, as will be shown, is clearly misleading. Mr Taaffe is less than forthcoming about Militant Tendency's finances, with which I deal in a separate chapter. But his memorandum is particularly noteworthy because he acknowledges that supporters, or members, of the Militant Tendency and its weekly paper are 'supporters of Leon Trotsky's ideas'. Is that why the Labour Party, now riddled with members of the Militant Tendency, was reluctant to publish?

Militant Tendency has always sought to remain as secret an organization as possible. But despite its denial that it exists, it has found it impossible to prevent those actively seeking facts to establish much about its framework and affairs. The key lies in the two companies named by Mr Taaffe, WIR Publications and Cambridge Heath Press, together with an offshoot, World Books, publishers of books and pamphlets. They operate from their printing works in Mentmore Terrace in a decayed area between Hackney and Bethnal Green.

WIR Publications was incorporated, on 23 June 1973, with Edward Grant, described as a journalist, and Keith Dickinson, also a journalist, as directors. Patrick Marshall Craven, a prominent Militant activist, was secretary, to be succeeded by Elizabeth Clare Doyle. Nominal capital was £100 in £1 shares.

The memorandum of association said the objects of the new company, which was to act as the funding organization of Cambridge Heath Press and the Militant Tendency, included:

3 (A) (1) To acquire by purchase gift or any other lawful means real and personal property of any kind and every description and whether involving liability or not and to apply both capital and income thereof and the proceeds of the sale or mortgage thereof for or towards all or any of the objects hereinafter specified.

(2) To aid and further the interests of the international working class generally and for that purpose to do and carry out or assist in doing or carrying out all such matters and things as are likely to promote the interests of the international working class and in particular to assist pecuniarily or otherwise any socialist or working class society, union, club, committee, bookshop or organization now existing or hereafter to exist and to render such aid, pecuniary or otherwise, to labour or socialist candidates in parliamentary, municipal or other elections, to persons charged with political or other offences and to any person who has in the past now or hereafter carried out assisted in doing or carrying out matters and things in the interests of the international working class.

Other detailed provisions give the company virtual *carte blanche* over the conduct of its financial affairs, including granting of loans and credits and giving guarantees to other companies, promoting, financing and assisting them for the purpose of acquiring all or any part of their property rights and liabilities and to pay any person, firm or company rendering services in any manner.

In January 1980 WIR Publications, after a reshuffling of its shares, reported that its twenty-five shareholders were: Raymond Apps, a member of Labour's Parliamentary panel of candidates and candidate for the national executive committee; Brian Beckingham, a member of Bristol SE constituency Labour Party; Muriel Browning; Patrick Craven, former secretary and director, Cambridge Heath Press; Keith Dickinson, a director, and partner in World Books; Elizabeth Clare Doyle, secretary of both companies; Peter Doyle, former member of Labour's national executive and former president of Gateshead Trades Council; Robert Edwards, an employee of *Militant* and member of Harlow constituency Labour Party; Robert Faulkes; Edward Grant, director, and partner with Keith Dickinson in World Books; Peter Hadden; Terence Harrison; Robert Jamieson; Robert McKee, assistant editor of *Militant*; Edward Mooney; Anthony Mulhearn, a candidate for the European Parliament; Michael Newman; Robert Reeves, a partner in World Books; Patrick Wall, a candidate for Labour's national executive and former president of Bradford Trades Council; Lynn Walsh, a journalist employed on *Militant*; Thomas Ward; William Webster; Terence Wilson; Alex Wood; and Alan Woods.

The Cambridge Heath Press, which publishes and prints *Militant*, was registered on 16 August 1971 with nominal capital of £100 as a commercial printer's.

A number of people have been identified as being or having been members of *Militant*'s editorial board. Apart from Mr Grant, past editor, now political editor, Mr Taaffe, editor, and Mr McKee, assistant editor, they are: Ray Apps, Jeremy Birch, Nick Brooks, Patrick Craven, Keith Dickinson, Clare Doyle, Bob Edwards, Brian Ingham, Mike Newman, John Pickard, Bob Reeves, Roger Silverman, Lynn Walsh, Pat Wall and Terry Wilson.

Altogether, about sixty-three people are now employed full-time by *Militant*. About half of them are at Mentmore Terrace, others as full-time newspaper sellers-cum-organizers in strategic centres. These include East and West Wales, Merseyside, Humberside, West, North and South Yorkshire, the West Midlands, centred on Birmingham, and Scotland, not to forget Dublin. The staff includes political, technical, international and regional field workers as well as paper sellers. The Militant Tendency's national organization, which is not supposed to exist, includes new supporters, contact workers, full members, trained cadres to work in various Labour Party and trade union organizations where numerous caucuses have been established, area committees and organizations, local district and regional editorial boards. It runs readers' meetings, Marxist discussion groups, cadre training schools, and organizes baby-sitting rotas, crèches and much else. It is clear that the Militant Tendency, apart from being well-funded, is nothing if not highly organized.

How does it recruit? That more than anything else illustrates the sinister and conspiratorial nature of its activities. In 1970 Militant Tendency supporters gained a majority on the national committee of the Labour Party's Young Socialists, numbering 3,500–5,000, and have retained it ever since. In 1972 a change in the Party's constitution enabled the Young Socialists to have a representative on the Party's national executive, since when that member has always been a Militant supporter. Later came the much-criticized appointment of Andy Bevan as the Party's national youth officer.

Andy Bevan, a Welsh-born Bristol University graduate, was a heating and ventilation engineer aged twenty-four when, as chairman of the Labour Party Young Socialists, he was appointed youth officer of the Labour Party at a salary of £4,000 in autumn 1976. He had already been active in the Militant Tendency and in the campaign against Reg Prentice in Newham North-East.

There were twenty applicants for the post, including six Labour agents, and Mr Bevan was selected by the vote of Ron Hayward, general secretary, from a shortlist of three. The appointment, which was opposed by Mr Callaghan as Prime Minister, led to bitter opposition from the National Union of Labour Organizers, initial 'blacking' of Mr Bevan by other Transport House staff which led to his short suspension on full pay and other controversy. But Mr Bevan's appointment was confirmed in January 1977 by the national executive by eighteen votes to nil, in the absence of Mr Callaghan. Mr Bevan weathered the storm, and is still going strong today. On 23 June 1981 the *Daily Mail* reported from the Transport Union conference at Brighton that at the end of the union's seventy-five-strong branch meeting of Labour Party staff on pay, when only thirty-six members remained, Mr Bevan succeeded in getting a vote in support of Mr Wedgwood Benn's candidacy for the Labour Party deputy leadership. Mr Nick Sigler, its delegate, was mandated to support Mr Benn at the

Brighton conference. Neither Denis Healey nor John Silkin, the other two candidates, was nominated.

Mr Bevan has a long-standing link with Mr Benn. When the controversy over his appointment was at its height, Mr Benn issued a personal statement in his support, saying he had first met Mr Bevan in the 1974 general election campaign when he proved a keen worker in the Bristol SE Labour Party, Mr Benn's own constituency.

Since Mr Bevan's appointment, the Young Socialists, whose members' addresses can be easily obtained from records, has been a main recruiting ground, together with Labour Party meetings and trade union activities, particularly in industrial disputes. Lord Underhill, in research following up his earlier submissions, has collated evidence from disillusioned former supporters of Militant and minutes of a Militant branch over two years to September 1980.

Recruitment is systematic, highly organized and selective. When a likely recruit showing interest is spotted, contact is made with him or her by a Militant Tendency activist assigned for the task. The new contact is given a copy of *British Perspectives* to read. This is followed up later with other documents, including *International Perspectives*. Militant activists have regular political discussions with the contact, informing him or her of the Tendency's programme. If the contact continues to show encouraging interest, he or she is invited to *Militant* readers' meetings and also to a Marxist discussion group. If progress continues, the contact is told of the Militant organization, the local group and its role of entryism in the Labour Party. Next step is an invitation to a Militant branch meeting. Later, the contact may be told the branch has decided to accept him or her into membership. There does not appear to be any requirement to sign an application form.

All this process can take many months, or even up to a year. Various Militant Tendency branch members are allocated different tasks in treatment of the new contact: setting up discussions, delivering *Militant*, ensuring attendance at branch meetings and asking for financial support. Every step and all progress is logged in detail in weekly minutes, which only use initials, with regular progress reports.

Contacts are seen weekly, if possible, to prevent them drifting away. Backsliding, such as failing to turn up for a discussion or meeting, is noted, and the reasons, such as domestic problems, investigated and recorded. Lack of active commitment is a black mark.

Only when the potential recruit is judged to have been effectively brainwashed is he or she accepted into the Militant Tendency. But from then, the pressure is on. The recruit is expected to make regular monthly financial contributions of at least £3-£5, to sell the paper, attend branch meetings, a *must*, and help in contact work. He or she must also attend Labour Party constituency and union meetings to support and vote for Militant motions and candidates. But the new recruit, like other Militant supporters, should not seek office, particularly such posts as chairman, secretary, social secretary or treasurer, where it would mean too much work. They are instructed to exercise political influence and control from the sidelines, reserving their time, energy and talents for Militant objectives.

The branch whose minutes were passed to Lord Underhill told its Militant entryists: 'Generally, members must be wary of taking positions which involve a lot of work. However, members must take political positions and tasks, for example, sub-committees or canvassing. It is important to give a political lead, with resolutions through branches and the general management committee. We must have a presence at every meeting and sell the paper as well as collect money. Re the GMC we cannot win any existing delegates – there is no need for a strong presence, we can rotate delegates.'

Altogether, more than sixty persons were approached by this branch in two years. Some were given up after the first contact, at least four eventually accepted into membership and others expressing willingness to join were subjected to further regular discussions.

Because of the demands made on members and Militant's dreary ideology and tactics, many recruits do not remain members. They become disillusioned or fed up or just drift away. Tom Forester gave an account by an ex-Militant Tendency member, 'David James', a thirty-nine-year-old manual worker, who had been a member of the central London branch. It strongly bears out Lord Underhill's findings.

'David James' told Tom Forester that because of his proletarian status, he gained rapid promotion, and attended committee meetings. Weekly branch meetings reviewed each comrade's progress, examining how many copies of *Militant* had been sold and how many contacts made. Backsliders were 'interviewed'.

At his work in a large West London industrial plant, he said:

I would begin softly and then I would steer people round to Trotskyism. Workers recruited to Militant are basically brought in by Militant to be used by Militant. They take great care over it. They do a good job on people. They give people a very good grounding in theory. They take an interest in you and encourage you. They get loyalty because they make people feel they have a role to play. During strikes we were put on alert and sent in to make contact with the leaders, saying we were from the Labour Party.

I disagreed with this elitist approach to workers and I also had differences with them over their lack of tolerance towards people. A lot of them are book socialists, and I began to realize what living in a Marxist-type society would really be like. There would be less freedom than there is under capitalism. There would be more dissidents in prison than there is in Soviet Russia. It would be a one-party state....

The end came for me when I stopped going to branch. A bloke came one night and said I should have applied for permission to take leave of absence. They wanted to interview me. I told 'em to stuff it. Now they ignore me at union meetings and they've got the poison grapevine working against me. You'll never stop these people. They are working away all the time.

They are all programmed to say the same things. They've got the knife into MPs, councillors and most of the NEC. People underestimate Militant. People think that if you don't worry about them, they will go away. But they're wrong.

Considerable local as well as national attention is given to the Young Socialists – wooing new members with a weekly meeting, preparing lists of names and addresses, organizing public meetings under their name, chasing Young Socialists to attend, inviting them to cadre schools and pushing them into 'days of action'. The Militant Tendency also devotes much energy into other youth work. In its summer bulletin, 1979, and *British Perspectives, 1979* the Tendency reviewed at length work by its youth organization, both among industrial workers and students. Both progress, such as the hope that another fifty new branches should have been established (albeit with only a dozen branches claiming regular attendance of more than twenty), and reverses were recorded. Setbacks included a greater preoccupation by students with actual study to improve job prospects. However, some quotations aptly illustrate the Tendency's activities, based on expectations of growing anger over Tory government policies.

Consequently, the prospects for growth are tremendous. Public activity is the prime necessity. Unless we go out and reach young workers we will not build.

Each area must plan out regular visits to sell and leaflet at factories and workplaces using the office and shift workers, the unemployed and the students who can all participate in the early morning and lunchtime sales. Shop stewards and convenors should be visited and persuaded to put youth material round the factories. They should also be asked to order copies of the youth paper for distribution.

Regular sales in the evenings must be arranged around the pubs, youth clubs, discos, ice-rinks, football matches, anywhere the youth are to be found. At a later stage perhaps even the youth organizations outside the movement such as the Boys Brigade, Girl Guides, Young Christian Workers etc. can provide fertile recruiting ground.

Outlining campaigns, the summer bulletin says:

Unemployment, housing, racial discrimination, education, cuts in services and police harassment will all be explosive issues. ... The possibilities for youth organization intervention in industrial disputes were demonstrated during the strikes of the bakers, firemen and local authority workers.

It quotes Trotsky's advice of May 1929:

We must tighten up on matters of organization; the keeping of minutes in books, the recording of funds and membership and the payments for the youth paper. Failure to do so not only hinders the growth of the branches but can also prove to be our achilles heel – a marvellous pretext for the opposition to demand investigations and closures.

'Every member of the Opposition would be obligated to have under guidance several young workers, youths from fourteen to fifteen years of age and older; to remain in continual contact with them, help them in their education, train them in questions of scientific socialism, and systematically introduce them to the revolutionary politics of the proletarian vanguard.

Oppositionists who are themselves unprepared for such work should entrust the young workers they have recruited to more developed and experienced comrades. We don't want those who are afraid of rough work. The profession of a Bolshevik revolutionary imposes obligations. The first of these obligations is to win over the proletarian youth, to clear a road to us to win over the proletarian youth, to clear a road to its most oppressed and neglected strata. They stand first under our banner.'

Thus is Militant's wooing of youth based on Trotsky's precepts. Other advice, in which Lenin is also cited, includes:

Weeks of collecting names of potential members can be wasted through a failure to follow up, weeks of work on a few individuals can suffer due to them not being involved in any activities and shown how we work, over-ambitious (i.e. ill-thought out) campaigning activities can lead to cynicism and confusion when a campaign comes out and goes without comment. Even worse the periphery of the youth organization fails to get the constant visits and reminders about meetings, activities and socials.

It is our belief that the youth organization paper is a tremendous improvement on the past efforts and can now be used as an organizing weapon for each branch. Regular monthly sales to youth organization members and those on the periphery should keep the organization with a network in each area of young people ready to pass on names of individuals, raise and give money and inform on local issues of discontent amongst the youth.

On students, the bulletin reviews penetration tactics in the National Union of Students, successful intervention in and control of the 'SO [Student Organization] national event' - 'We applied enormous pressure on the student "official", and must continue to do so' - and progress in further education and technical colleges and polytechnics. Main areas of continuing work would be:

1 To intervene in the industrial disputes, using the C's [cadres?];

2 To fully integrate every comrade into the youth work; The campaign on grants for 16-19 year olds in education is an excellent opportunity to do this. Student comrades should also be involved in all youth activities, drawing C members into this;

3 To follow up and integrate student contacts;

4 To build the C's, and ensure they remain active, and build up new C's particularly in the FE and Technical Colleges;

5 To organize regional activities around the SO and C's we control;

6 To continue to build in the NUS.

The review concludes: 'Despite not controlling the SO, we have built a strong position amongst students, and can look forward to the future with confidence.'

Like other Trotskyist organizations, the Militant Tendency sees racial, and particularly black and Asian discontent, as fertile ground for recruitment and exploitation. As *British Perspectives, 1979* acknowledges, however, progress has been limited. But in the light of the Brixton riots of April 1981, in which white Trotskyists and foreign revolutionaries were identified as having been at least on the fringe, its comments are illuminating.

Describing blacks as generally having the worst and lower-paid jobs, their high unemployment, inadequate housing, health conditions and schooling, with which few would disagree, Militant notes that: 'A majority of black workers live in the industrial conurbations of the country, mainly in England. ... Their conditions of life are such as to make them susceptible to revolutionary ideas.' The bulletin adds that the percentage of industrial workers among this strata (*sic*) of the population is far greater than in the population as a whole. 'Because of their freshness to industrial life – many have peasant origins – they have been drawn into the cities and been flung into the cauldron of industrial life.' (Blacks might be intrigued by the thought that Militant Tendency regards them basically as peasants.) Union organization among blacks, the bulletin claims, is greater than among whites.

> Because of all these circumstances they are more susceptible to the ideas of Marxism and to support for the labour movement. However, whilst they have been massively organized, large numbers do not participate actively either in the Labour Party or in the trade unions. In the coming period they will more and more be compelled to take up positions as shop stewards and become active in trade union branches.
>
> At present only a small minority are integrated in this way in the working class movement. ... In a healthy way they have entirely rejected the ideas of sects who advocated organizing independently in the unions and in the Labour Party as black factions, or black caucuses. Living in the industrial conurbations, they occupy a strategic position in the inner city areas of the country.

Militant Tendency does not elaborate what 'strategic position' really means, but its obvious connotation is urban violence and disruption of local government, and ultimately of the State. Well based for revolution, it might be thought.

When won over, the bulletin continues, blacks 'could carry these ideas to their mates in the workplaces. But only the ideas of Marxism can win them to understand the need to participate actively both in the trade union movement and in the labour movement. ....' The proportion of black readers of *Militant* should be greater. 'They will be responsive to the ideas of Marxism when these are put forward in a sufficiently skilful and diplomatic way', which could be of 'enormous importance to the immigrants'.

Militant must take up housing, job discrimination, unjust arrests and so on. 'Where organizations such as Indian workers' associations, the Pakistani workers' associations, the Bangladeshi and the West Indian Youth are in existence, efforts should be made to link these organizations to the labour and trade union movement by affiliations, by joint activities and in joint work. The field is open for an expansion in the influence of the ideas of Marxism.'

While Militant Tendency's dialectical approach to the issues of immigrants varies from those of other Trotskyist organizations, these basic considerations apply to all of them. Blacks, Asians and other minorities, not omitting homosexuals, feminists and nuclear opponents, are all there to be exploited for the Tendency.

During the riots of summer 1981, fighting, looting and burning took place on a huge scale. After the events at Toxteth, Liverpool, over the weekend of 3-4 July, David Alton, Liberal MP for Edge Hill, drew attention to leaflets distributed by the Labour Party Young Socialists, which named as a contact Terence Harrison, Labour candidate for Liverpool Edge Hill, and a journalist on the board of *Militant*. The leaflet, entitled 'Sweep Them Out Now', blamed provocative police action, years of unemployment, and bad housing for the violence, and called for withdrawal of the police and all charges against those arrested. It was disowned by many notable figures in the Labour Party, including Eric Heffer, MP for Walton. Clare Doyle, now a full-time worker for *Militant* for nine years, was also revealed to have travelled from London to Liverpool to hold a meeting immediately after the riots to advise those arrested. She denied such meetings were fomenting the trouble.

But the Militant Tendency's main area of operation, and where it is most dangerous is in the Labour Party, although it is now, not without success, striving to broaden its base in the unions. Reg Prentice, MP for Newham North-East, was the first Militant scalp. Compulsory re-selection of MPs has gone through, threatening many more. The Social Democratic Party has been formed from Labour dissidents from Ultra-Left domination, and more defections are likely. Anthony Wedgwood Benn, who has admitted, though not too specifically, his sympathies with Militant ideas, has enjoyed its full backing in his bid for the deputy leadership, and ultimately, the leadership of the Labour Party.

What is particularly worthy of note, certainly by all moderate Labour Party members and MPs, whether right or left of centre, is that Militant Tendency, like Hitler in *Mein Kampf*, spelled it all out in advance in its 1979 *British Perspectives* and previously. Moreover, as late as October 1979 Militant Tendency stated: 'Whittled out piecemeal from the Parliamentary Labour Party, the Neanderthal men will become convinced that there is no hope for the Right in the Labour Party.... In one way or another, the heavy ballast of Neanderthal men will be removed, either by jumping overboard themselves, or more painfully by the process of reselection of councillors and MPs. ... The ideas of Marx, Engels, Lenin and Trotsky will become the ideas of the Labour Party. This process is already shown by the regional conferences of the Labour Party in the aftermath of the election....'

While not predicting the coming course of events in the Labour Party entirely accurately – by overrating the possible success of the right wing and underrating the left wing – the bulletin said: 'The right wing would be ousted from leadership and the Left would become the leadership of the Labour Party.... Right-wing MPs will be removed in one constituency after another....' If the right wing were defeated at the Labour Party conference, it was possible that they 'will abandon the attempt to regain control of the Party.... They would split away from the Labour Party to organize a so-called Social Democratic Party, a right-wing rump perhaps of 20, 30 or even 50 MPs. They will not move towards the Tories because the political climate will be unfavourable. The unpopularity of the Tories will reach new heights. They may try to make an arrangement with the Liberals, forming a "centre" party. On this basis they could hope, if not in the present Parliament then possibly in the next, to attract the "left" wing of the Tories.'

Such a split was not impossible, but 'such an organization would be doomed to disintegration. ... In the early days it would have secret links with the Heath wing of the Tory Party, but only in the event of a crushing defeat of the Tories would the so-called "liberal" Tories move over to such a party.'

Not bad predicting so far, one might think. Militant also foresees an 'extremist' Labour Party winning hundreds of thousands of supporters, with many right-wingers either dropping out of politics or moving 'in the direction of reaction'. That is more wishful thinking, where the Militant Tendency has proved disastrously inaccurate in the past.

But Militant Tendency marches on, originally by stealth, but now coming more and more into the open as its power and influence increase. It imposes fines on members, unless they quit, when they may be subjected to direct intimidation. Like other Trotskyist organizations it too appears as an obsessed, termite-like world, dreary, conformative and disciplined, communicating in a jargon foreign, if not entirely incomprehensible, to outsiders. It is difficult, indeed, if one is a normal person, however efficient and devoted to one's job, to comprehend that every thought and all spare energy of these 2,000-plus activists, not to mention rival Trotskyists, is locked up and devoted to what appears political, pathological mental obsession.

But as with other fanatical movements, it is there, it exists, and is working with appreciable success to undermine parliamentary democracy through the Labour Party which, it must be assumed, would normally some time win another general election. It is a frightening prospect, and one not to be discounted.

Already, not only right-wing or moderate Labour MPs are running scared, threatened with re-selection, but orthodox left-wingers also. John Silkin (Deptford) is under attack. So is Frank Field, Labour MP for Birkenhead, champion of child poverty, low pay and other deprived causes, who sees himself, however, as a democratic left-winger. At Birkenhead, he told me, he had worked hard for two years to build up what he had found to be a weak Labour constituency organization. 'There was already a Militant presence there. They work hard, but they all work in one group. They would canvass separately.'

Mr Field, who thinks it 'double-talk' for Labour to preach open democracy but not have published Mr Taaffe's reply to Labour's questionnaire, said on the issue of a party within a party: 'It seems to me that is precisely what is happening locally. Militant don't have "organizers", they have newspaper sellers. These are mere euphemisms for what is going on. They come to meetings almost as if a magnet has gone over their brains. They all speak the same, have a set line. Nothing you say is relevant. They are totally closed to reason. I am not asking for a personal witch-hunt. Every Militant member has a right to belong to the Labour Party. But they do not have the right to dual membership, to use the Party to organize. Because Militant has been successful, other revolutionary groups are coming back in. Seeing Militant, they see more success from entryism than working from the outside.'

Mr Field and Mr Silkin are not the only MPs threatened by Militant's long-prepared purge. Peter Hardy, a teacher and MP for Rother Valley, has beaten off the attempt to oust him under re-selection backed by Arthur Scargill, Marxist president of the Yorkshire miners and a Militant supporter. But in Bradford, where Bradford College is a nest of left-wing activity, three MPs are threatened: Ben Ford (North), Tom Torney (South) and Edward Lyons (West). Others threatened include: Eddie Wainwright (Dearne Valley), Albert Roberts (Normanton), and in the North-West, Ken Marks (Manchester Gorton), Eric Ogden (West Derby) and James Dunn (Kirkdale). In London Michael O'Halloran (Islington North), George Cunningham (Islington South and Finsbury) and Ron Brown (Hackney) also face challenges. There are many more. In May 1981 the Rank and File Mobilizing Committee published a 'death-list' of 150 Labour MPs who opposed Mr Wedgwood Benn's programme. They were those who signed a statement after the special Wembley conference in January 1981 opposing the Parliamentary Party only having 30 per cent representation in the new electoral college. The list was published in the Committee's bulletin as 'a service to our readers'. It included eight shadow Ministers: Albert Booth, Roy Hattersley, Gerald Kaufman, Roy Mason, Merlyn Rees, Peter Shore, John Smith and Eric Varley. Also named were thirteen members of the Tribune group, including Frank Field, Jack Straw and Arthur Davidson. The list was entitled 'Gang of 150'. The message was clear – targets for re-selection.

Already more Militant Tendency candidates are being nominated for constituencies. In Brighton Kemptown in February 1981, Rod Fitch was chosen as its parliamentary candidate after a stormy meeting at which moderates tried to stop his nomination. He was nominated by thirty-one votes to thirty. Mr Fitch will be lucky if he is elected; the seat has been held by Andrew Bowden, Conservative, for eleven years and he got a majority of 8,008 votes over Labour. In 1964 Labour won the seat by only seven votes after seven recounts. Mr Fitch, according to the *Daily Mail*, said: 'My views are in line with the views of the Labour Party today. The Party is returning to its working-class base. The Social Democrats have dictated Labour's policies in government time and time again, and they have always failed'. Selection of Mr Fitch, a Brighton bricklayer, was said to have followed a fifteen-year battle for control of Brighton Labour Party. Moderates were frustrated as Militant supporters, backed by Sussex University students, took over local ward parties and sent their own delegates to the constituency party's general management committee, a process duplicated in Bradford, with Bradford College, and elsewhere. Tom Forester, a Brighton councillor and Labour activist, estimated there were only twenty-five Militant Tendency supporters in the town. The decision, said Mr Forester, whose Hanover Ward had fought strongly against Militant penetration, was 'plain barmy, just plain stupid. It is utterly ridiculous to put up a Trotskyist sloganizer in one of the few seats in the South that Labour has ever had a hope of winning. A party which allows itself to be taken over by these nutters is in deep trouble.'

Also in early 1981 Militant Tendency succeeded in winning the selection of Terence Harrison, one of its leading activists, as Labour candidate for Liverpool Edge Hill. Kurt Weisskopf, retired economic editor with Reuters news agency, feared that Britain would not survive a Trotskyist take-over. He appealed in the *Daily Mail* to his 'personal friend', Eric Heffer, left-wing MP for Walton, Liverpool, and the orthodox Labour Left, to take action. 'Some day I hope that Eric Heffer, who has contempt for Trotskyists, will wake up. He might still be able to rally support against them.' Mr Weisskopf said his own Brighton ward of Moulsecomb had been taken over by Militant supporters. 'They pursued their aims with religious fervour,' he said. 'They moved in at a time when ward membership was growing older and older – it was turning into a geriatric ward. Most were students from Sussex and local polytechnics. They moved in as lodgers, got on to the electoral register, and launched a classic campaign of entryism. They would extend meetings until they were adjourned, then they would come back the following week when no-one else was there and push through their own policies.'

In Brighton's Pier Ward, the 'bed-sit Trots' elected three Militant supporters to represent the ward at a meeting attended by fewer than ten people. They captured all three delegation seats by six votes to two.

Where does Michael Foot, Opposition Leader, stand in all this? The answer is not very clear. Mr Foot, who disappointed many by not taking a more active role at Labour's 1981 Wembley conference, which ended in a triumph for Mr Benn's supporters, said before the conference that he would discuss further a major complaint about infiltration of party organizations by the Militant Tendency. Although he was not in favour of expulsions, he said, he thought the Tendency's activity should be highlighted and their methods denounced. He said he would also do everything he could to help any MPs over the re-selection process. On leadership election moves, he quoted Daniel in the lions' den. The lions were tame and not searching for blood, he said naïvely.

But since Mr Foot's words, nothing appears to have happened so far as the Militant Tendency is concerned. A veteran Labour MP of the old sort said to me, 'Whatever he says, Michael Foot is a prisoner of Militant. He has adopted their policies. They are much bolder than before, coming out into the open. Benn runs with them.'

So the questions remain. Whither the Labour Party as the Militant Tendency grows ever stronger, not only in central but in local government?

3 The Socialist Workers Party

The Socialist Workers Party is one of the largest Trotskyist organizations in Britain, with a membership probably approaching 4,000, and also the best known, although it is fast being overtaken in this respect by the Militant Tendency. It is also regarded by some observers as the most professional, particularly in industry. The Socialist Workers Party is also notably active in education, in journalism, particularly Fleet Street, local government and the Civil Service, among women's libbers, the immigrant community and fringe movements.

It is prominent in the self-styled Anti-Nazi League, whose activities have even upset the Jewish community, and also runs the Right to Work Campaign. Those who have attended TUC or Labour and Conservative annual Party conferences will be only too familiar with the screaming hordes of largely juvenile, often 'punk', Right to Work campaigners, wearing their standard-issue orange plastic jerkins, waving pre-printed placards, and chanting pre-rehearsed slogans. The Right to Work campaigners are a politically exploited rabble, for whom one can only have genuine pity, jobless and without prospects as they are.

The Socialist Workers Party, however, has a strong middle-class and intellectual content. Now eschewing entryism, it seeks to project itself as a political party in its own right, seeking a broader appeal than the smaller, narrowly revolutionary and ideologically obsessed sects. It professes open debate within its ranks and has been subject to internal ideological differences, leading to splits and expulsions. It is also an extremely prolific publisher of pamphlets on all kinds of issues, including 'Rank and File' movement sheets for specific industries, apart from its major publications.

These are: the weekly *Socialist Worker*, with a claimed sale of 30,000, but probably 20,000; *International Socialism*, a monthly dialectical journal; *Flame*, an SWP publication for the black community (not to be confused with *Big Flame*, see p. 89); *Chingari*, published in Urdu for the Asians, and *Women's Voice*, the Party's monthly women's magazine, well produced with a glossy two-tone red and blue cover.

Women's Voice – like other Trotskyist groups – is both an organization and a magazine. It also suffers from the common disease of ideological differences. In October 1979, before the Women's Voice conference, the Socialist Workers Party internal bulletin contained an extensive debate on the organization's role and on differences with the Party. As with black members, not all Women's Voice members wanted to be dominated by the Trotskyist centre. In the event, *Women's Voice* is still described on its cover as 'Women's magazine of the Socialist Workers Party'. In April 1981 it gave advice to readers on how to produce a good leaflet using duplicators, stencils and illustrations. 'A Women's Voice leaflet may be the first contact an unsuspecting member of the public has with our organization.' It is good advice, telling how to write concisely, choose short and apposite headlines, how to type and the need to include an imprint by law. 'Never put one of the WV members' home address on a leaflet. If necessary use the national address, PO Box 82, London E2.' However, *Women's Voice* is quite happy every month to print phone numbers of 'contacts' throughout the country.

Women's Voice stands for equal pay, free abortion and contraception, maternity leave and child-care provision and the right to work. It is 'against all forms of discrimination on grounds of sex, sexual orientation or race.... Women's liberation can only be achieved by linking its struggles to those of the working class and overthrowing the capitalist system.'

Like other Trotskyist organizations, the SWP traces its origins to the war-time Revolutionary Communist Party, of which Tony Cliff, now leader of the SWP, was a member. Tony Cliff was born Ygael Gluckstein in Palestine in 1917 when it was still part of the Ottoman Empire. He married his wife Chanie Rosenberg in Tel Aviv in 1946, and came to Britain via South Africa after the war. An Israeli by birth, he is still not a British citizen. Chanie Rosenberg is a Hackney schoolmistress and leading Trotskyist activist in the National Union of Teachers.

Already in 1947, ideological differences were developing which led to the break-up of the Revolutionary Communist Party in 1949. It was in 1947 that Tony Cliff advanced the theory that the Soviet Union is not a true Marxist state, but a form of state capitalism, a view frequently expressed by Trotskyists. Following the Revolutionary Communist Party's dissolution, Cliff, like others, embarked on entryism of the Labour Party, as part of 'The Group'.

But in 1950, his 'tendency' left, or was expelled, from the British section of the Fourth International over its view that the Soviet Union was not a true workers' state. While remaining in the Labour Party, the Cliff tendency, the Socialist Review Group, started publishing *Socialist Review*. For the next decade, it moled away like rival Trotskyist factions, becoming slowly but steadily stronger.

By the early 1960s, the Cliff group was working, like the future Workers Revolutionary Party, in the Labour Party Young Socialists, to be purged by Harold Wilson in 1964. The group started a new publication, *Labour Worker*, re-named in 1968 as *Socialist Worker*. In 1962 it reorganized and re-named itself as the International Socialists. But as Labour Party policies became more unpopular, the International Socialists became disenchanted with entryism and withdrew its members. Henceforward, it set out to establish a separate identity as a political party, concentrating its efforts on recruitment of students in competition with the International Marxist Group as Ultra-Left student unrest spread, notably in France and West Germany. Some student recruits made then now constitute much of the present SWP leadership.

Ten years later, having consolidated the gains of the late 1960s the International Socialists turned their energies to the trade unions and shopfloor with appreciable success, publishing a wide range of 'rank and file' bulletins. These were disclosed in the *Daily Telegraph* on 7 March 1975 when it published the contents of an internal seventy-five-page bulletin. They totalled sixteen up to March 1973. Some still exist.

The approximate balance sheet including some pamphlets on which it took longer to get the money back, was:

	ISSUES	TOTAL WORK (£)	TOTAL PAID (£)	% OF BILL PAID	BALANCE (£)	LATEST PRINT ORDER
Carworker	9	1,105	515	45%	715	6,000
Collier	6	465	153	33%	411	5,000
Hospital Worker	7	740	467	60%	273	6,000
Platform	3	130	60	50%	70	3,000
Textile Worker	1	25	nil	nil	25	1,500
Case Con	4	815	775	95%	40	5,000
Journalists Charter	4	204	120	60%	84	2,000
NALGO Action News	8	715	665	98%	50	6,000
Rank and File Teacher	13	2,725	1,162	42%	1,500	10,000
Redder Tape	4	370	210	57%	235	3,000
Scots R. & F.	3	145	20	15%	125	2,000
Tech Teacher	4	725	250	30%	475	2,500
Dockworker	12	830	825	99%	80	5,000
GEC R. & F.	5	650	385	60%	265	8,000
Building Worker	6	400	111	27%	289	2,000
Electricians' Special	3	135	38	15%	197	2,000

I deal with both SWP trade union activity and the Party's finances separately. But this table gives a fair indication of the measure of the Party's activities on the shopfloor. At the time, Mr Cliff talked of the prospect of recruiting 20,000 industrial worker recruits in the next few years. The document disclosed that total membership was 3,310, with the aim of achieving up to 5,000, including at least 2,000 manual workers, by the end of 1973. This aim has failed. Average branch membership was only seven, but all were dedicated activists. Work among black and Asian minorities was already a top priority. The International Socialists' national committee was then forty strong, but a woman organizer was badly needed. Organization was good in the Black Country, and strong among journalists.

The full list of the forty national committee members in 1975 is also of interest. Successful candidates in the order of voting were: Jock Wright, Jimmy McCallum, Larry Connolly, Nigel Harris, Tony Cliff, John Deason, Martha Osamor, Steve Jefferys, Gerry Jones, Ian Gibson, Willie Lee, Roger Cox, Frankie Drain, Rab Jeffrey, Duncan Hallas, Les Kay, Gordon Poters, Paul Foot, Frank Henderson, Tommy Douras, Ken Appleby, Chris Harman, Steve Ludlam, Micky Fenn, Jimmy Rule, Jim Nichol, Steve Abbott, Carol Douras, Eddie Prevost, Gerry Walsh, Mike Healey, Tommy Healey, Roger Griffiths, Alice Murray, Andreas Nagliatti, Mike Atkinson, Ross Pritchard, Laurie Flynn, Anna Paczauska, Neil Davies.

Unsuccessful candidates included Chanie Rosenberg, Dave Peers, until 1974 national secretary, and John Palmer, then business editor, and now European editor, of the *Guardian*. Publication of the details in the *Daily Telegraph* led to an announcement in *Socialist Worker*, then edited by Paul Foot, and now by Chris Harman, on 22 March 1975 that they 'demonstrated beyond dispute the need for much tighter security'. Smarting from attacks in the Workers Revolutionary Party's *Workers Press*, the IS national committee unanimously agreed to stop publication and circulation of the minutes of leading committees. 'In future only political documents will be circulated and, as far as possible, they will appear in *Socialist Worker* or *International Socialism*. A clear distinction was drawn by the national committee between political discussion material, which should be freely available, and administrative, financial and other confidential matters which will not be divulged at all.'

Although 1975 is six years ago, it marked a milestone in the Party's development. It had reached a peak membership of about 3,500, but with a high turnover of up to 50 per cent, a characteristic of Trotskyist organizations which persists today, since many recruits, both among the young and on the shopfloor, quickly become disillusioned. A sale of 35,000 was also claimed for *Socialist Worker* during the February 1974 general election.

But fresh ideological differences had already set in. In early 1974 Tony Cliff called for a re-styling of *Socialist Worker*, with shorter articles, exposures of the 'ugly face of capitalism', much of it written by workers, and aimed at achieving a sale of 70–80,000 among workers largely without labour movement tradition or experience. In 1971 a faction broke away as Workers' Fight to base itself in Manchester. In 1973 another group, the Revolutionary Opposition, the 'Right Faction', was expelled from the International Socialists and, in 1974, formed the Revolutionary Communist Group aimed at recovering abandoned 'revolutionary traditions'. This, again, spawned the Revolutionary Communist Tendency in 1976.

The debate about policies and organizational methods continued, with the International Socialists leadership adopting an increasingly doctrinaire attitude. Probably the most important split was the expulsion in 1975 of formerly prominent members who had already been demoted for criticizing Mr Cliff's optimism and changes in policy. They formed the Workers League, which now publishes *Socialist Voice*, a monthly journal formerly known as *Workers News*. With an initial strength of about 140, largely based round Birmingham, prominent members are said, with their pseudonyms, to have included: Jim Higgins (Robert James), John Palmer (John Anthony), Roger Protz, now editor of *What's Brewing*, journal of the Campaign for Real Ale, Harry Wicks and John Connolly. Remaining close in ideology, they disrupted IS activity, particularly among engineering workers, teachers and women's libbers. They are also active through *Engineering Voice*, and have collaborated with the International Marxist Group.

Another small group expelled in October 1975 formed the Workers Power Group, which publishes *Workers Power* and was active in 1981 in the Ansells brewery dispute at Birmingham. Another split involved about 100 members based in Liverpool and active at Fords of Dagenham, known as Big Flame.

In January 1977 the International Socialists changed its name to the Socialist Workers Party. It also changed its tactics. Co-operation with other Trotskyist organizations, notably the International Marxist Group, was ended in student activities. The SWP founded the National Organization of International Student Societies (NOISS), members of which run for office in the National Union of Students. The Party had started the Socialist Worker Youth Movement in 1976, but had little success. Its successor today is Red Rebel. It also controls the leadership of the National Union of School Students, founded about 1970, whose chairman, Hardy Desai, is an SWP member. By January 1980, it was claiming a membership of about 8,000; in that month links with it were severed by the National Union of Students, which had previously supported it with funds and facilities. The reason was that it had been taken over by left-wing extremists.

Other policy changes included a decision to stand candidates for parliament, not in the hope of winning seats but in the hope of recruiting members and establishing the Party's separate 'alternative' identity. It had minimal success at the polls, and the move led to further resignations because the SWP refused to associate with the Socialist Unity campaign backed, in particular, by the International Marxist Group.

Nevertheless, the SWP made its own sporadic bids for Far Left collaboration. In 1973 it tried unsuccessfully to penetrate the Communist-backed Liaison Committee in Defence of Trade Unions. Its failure led to the Rank and File Movement, later resulting in the Right to Work Campaign. In July 1977 the SWP proposed joint work on the industrial front and racialism with the Communist Party, but was rebuffed.

Today, the Socialist Workers Party presents a formidable range of activity, wider, probably, than other Trotskyist organizations. It nevertheless remains more prone than others to the sort of relatively open internal debate that would be inconceivable, for example, in the Workers Revolutionary Party, and to internal ideological differences, which can be deep, far-ranging and questioning of the leadership. The Party, still led by Tony Cliff, its veteran creator and ideological guru, is based at Corbridge Crescent, London E2, where *Socialist Worker* is printed by the Larkham Press – treasurer of the Party is John Larkham.

The Party is run by a national committee of forty, chosen at its annual conference, which in turn elects a full-time executive committee of ten. Its national secretary is Jim Nichol, its industrial organizer Steve Jeffery and its women's organizer Lindsey German. It has branches throughout the country, which hold numerous local meetings. It also has district committees and full-time district organizers. It runs 'fractions' and 'caucuses' in the Civil Service, local government (NALGO), railways, the Post Office and British Telecom, and many other areas. It also co-ordinates speeches and voting intentions at union annual conferences. It runs a number of bookshops, of which one was burned out early in 1981 in Birmingham. Chairman of *Socialist Worker* is Duncan Hallas. The editor is Chris Harman, whose predecessors include Paul Foot, now a *Daily Mirror* columnist, and Roger Protz.

In 1978 Mr Harman, who four years earlier in collaboration with Mr Foot had ousted Roger Protz as editor, only to oust Mr Foot later, himself faced a challenge. In an ideological clash with Laurie Flynn, the paper's industrial reporter, he attempted to fire him, but failed after Paul Foot added his own backing for Mr Flynn. He was later reinstated, first as political editor, but later as editor. Mr Nichol and Mr Foot resigned from the paper. Mr Foot ended up at the *Daily Mirror* after doing a notable stint at *Private Eye*.

Behind the clash is said to have run a dispute on the nature of *Socialist Worker*. Mr Foot, it has been said, wanted simple words, short paragraphs, large photographs and *Private Eye*-style exposés, of which he is a master. Mr Harman wanted a less popularized paper, more political, with in-depth analyses of strikes and political guidance. He attacked Mr Foot savagely at the 1978 SWP annual conference. Today, Mr Harman is still editor, and Mr Foot is happily employed by the capitalist Press.

Mr Harman, the victor, wrote in an SWP internal bulletin of August 1979, 'The party paid a heavy price for such mistakes, as the circulation figures for SW show'. The paid sale figures were: November 1974, 18,250; November 1975, 14,910; November 1976, 16,170; November 1977, 17,190; November 1978, 13,550. Mr Harman commented that while the November 1977 figure was not typical, the circulation had fallen 'quite considerably' during 1975, slowly recovered in 1976 and 1977, but 'fell right back again' in 1978 despite a 'year of much higher class struggle'. He added, 'The "popular paper" of last year cost us two or three thousand sales a week. That is a cost which our party is still paying for. It is the price we are paying for political disagreements within the leadership which were not clearly argued out.' A sale of only 13,550 in 1978, however, hardly bears out current claims of a 30,000 sale.

Today, *Socialist Worker* spells out 'Where We Stand'. It advocates 'independent working class action' apropos of which it adds: 'The workers create all the wealth under capitalism. A new society can only be constructed when they collectively seize control of that wealth and plan its production and distribution.' It advocates revolution under the heading 'Revolution Not Reform', saying: 'The present system cannot be patched up or reformed as the established Labour and trade union leaders say. It has to be overthrown.'

Spelling this out, it continues, 'There is no Parliamentary Reform'. This means:

The structures of the present parliament, army, police and judiciary cannot be taken over and used by the working class. They grew up under capitalism and are designed to protect the ruling class against the workers. The working class needs an entirely different form of state – a workers state based upon councils of workers delegates and a workers militia. At most parliamentary activity can be used to make propaganda against the present system. Only the mass action of the workers themselves can destroy the system.

In a ragbag of miscellaneous aims under the heading 'Internationalism', it says:

The struggle for socialism is part of a worldwide struggle. We campaign for solidarity with workers in other countries. We oppose everything which turns workers from one country against workers from other countries.

We oppose racialism and imperialism. We oppose all immigration controls. We support the right of black people and other oppressed groups to organize their own defence. We support all genuine national liberation movements. The experience of Russia demonstrates that a socialist revolution cannot survive in one country. Russia, China and Eastern Europe are not socialist but state capitalism. We support the struggle of workers in these countries against the bureaucratic ruling class. We are for real social, economic and political equality of women. We are for an end to all forms of discrimination against homosexuals.

The policy declaration concludes:

The Revolutionary Party. To achieve socialism the most militant sections of the working class have to be organized into a revolutionary socialist party. Such a party can only be built by activity in the mass organization of the working class. We have to prove in practice to other workers that reformist leaders and reformist ideas are opposed to their own interests. We urge all those who agree with our policies to join with us in the struggle to build the revolutionary party.

The policy declaration deserves some comment. The SWP has not been outstanding, unlike some other Trotskyist organizations, for international links. It has also been criticized for not being over keen on women's rights. Like the others, it is out to exploit all minority grievances, such as homosexuals - they have no keener protagonists than the Ultra Left - blacks and the Irish. But the declaration makes no bones about the fact that the SWP is Trotskyist and revolutionary, devoted to overthrowing democracy and order in our society in return for a *1984*-style revolutionary, proletarian dictatorship.

In some areas of its more recent activity, however, the Socialist Workers Party has achieved large propaganda and mass support successes. They are principally in the Anti-Nazi League, the Right to Work Campaign exploiting the unemployed, and in black and Asian causes.

The Anti-Nazi League must surely be one of the most successful left-wing front organizations ever launched in Britain. It was a brilliant idea appealing to completely laudable sentiments of a wide range of society, recruiting many thousands of people, some household names, and most of whom knew very little about Nazism. It also formed an ideal vehicle for Far Left organizations from the Trotskyists to the Communists, as a popular movement of mass demonstration and protest against a basically insignificant enemy. As its street action became more violent, it became steadily more discredited. But above all, it was and is very much a tool of the Socialist Workers Party. So much so that one can only wonder why left-wing trade union leaders, who know the political score as well as anybody, even today remain associated with it.

The motive is abhorrence of Nazi ideology and racialism. As one who for eight years reported German war crimes trials, and who has stood in the gas-chamber at Auschwitz, apart from visiting other concentration camps, I share those sentiments. Unlike the great majority of Anti-Nazi League supporters, the grisly details and sheer brutal facts of what the Nazis did, a litany of sadism and death, will remain imprinted on my soul till the end of my days. But the purpose of the Anti-Nazi League was blatantly overt political exploitation and opportunism. Even worse, it has itself been racist, and its street tactics, aimed at the police rather than 'Nazis', reminiscent of the role of the sa in Berlin during the early 1930s.

The Anti-Nazi League was formed at a meeting in the House of Commons in November 1977 between Peter Hain, erstwhile Young Liberal leader, and since recruited to the Labour Party; Ernie Roberts, left-wing Labour mp for Hackney North, a former assistant general secretary of the Amalgamated Union of Engineering Workers; and Paul

Holborrow, a teacher and member of the SWP who later became the League's only full-time official. Also present was Neil Kinnock, left-wing Labour MP for Monmouthshire, and the Party's education spokesman.

The purpose was to organize opposition to the National Front following alarm at increasing cases of racial violence. Mr Hain told the *Daily Telegraph* on 25 April 1979: 'I was concerned at that time at the way in which anti-Nazi factions were going. They seemed to be just throwing bricks or bottles or being entirely impotent. We felt the need for a more dynamic company which involved people of all political persuasions.'

The Anti-Nazi League was on its way. Mr Holborrow was appointed organizing secretary, Mr Hain Press officer and Mr Roberts treasurer. In the first instance funds were provided by a Jewish businessman. A steering committee was formed, including four left-wing Labour MPs, Mr Kinnock, Audrey Wise (Coventry South West), Martin Flannery (Sheffield Hillsborough) and Dennis Skinner (Bolsover). Other members included: Mr Hain; Mr Roberts; Simon Hebditch, a former chairman of the Young Liberals who defected to the Labour Party with Peter Hain; Nigel Harris, a university lecturer also an SWP member; Bill Dunn, a Communist; Miriam Carlin, actress; and the late Maurice Ludmer, editor of *Searchlight* magazine.

The League, like the Workers Revolutionary Party, had the bright idea of enrolling the support of well-known, but often politically naïve, personalities. Soon it claimed 30,000 members in about 320 local branches. This number excluded many associated groups, such as Firemen Against the Nazis and Rock Against the Nazis. By 1978 its income from private and trade union donations amounted to about £175,000. Contributions ranged from £250 from a trade union to a £1 postal order from a private citizen plus £2,400 from the Rowntree Trust. Unions giving backing included the TGWU, ASTMS, the CPSA and NALGO.

As organizing secretary, Mr Holborrow, former East London organizer of the SWP, was diligent. Paid £600 a quarter by the Rowntree Trust, he set about issuing internal bulletins to the League's 320 branches and about 200 other sympathetic political, religious and other groups, organizing a mailing list of 500 sympathizers, and issued details of National Front meetings. Some were marked for 'local cover', others merited the mobilizing of thousands of supporters for mass demonstrations. In the first year, the League spent £8,000 on postage, £1,500 on telephone bills and another £1,500 on British Rail parcel services for distribution of propaganda. Travel expenses accounted for another £5,000. Thousands of leaflets were distributed earlier this year by 150 supporters outside

West Ham football ground, a popular venue of skinheads and other National Front sympathizers. Printing alone accounted for £68,000, with five million leaflets prepared for the 1979 General Election campaign alone. In reply to criticism of SWP involvement, Mr Holborrow said: 'The main reason that the SWP is involved in the League is that the problem of the National Front and racism can only be defeated by having a large involvement of people ... most of the other anti-racist organizations are fairly moribund. We have emphasized actions rather than committee meetings.' Mr Hain and other League leaders denied that the SWP was in control or that they were being manipulated. But despite minor policy differences, such as the SWP not advocating immigration controls, there is little doubt who gained most from the populist approach. The SWP had achieved through the backdoor a mass appeal.

As it turned out, the National Front, the prime target, was well past its peak. But the League, organizing pop carnivals with punk and rock bands, which in April 1978 attracted 80,000 people, soon won 150 national sponsors, including more than thirty Labour MPs, academics, stage personalities, journalists, writers and sportsmen. But soon disillusion set in.

The League itself had been planned by the SWP since 1974 when it published a pamphlet, 'The New Nazis – Organize Against Them'. In 1976 followed 'The National Front and How to Smash Them'. Even Tariq Ali, leader of the International Marxist Group, who also tried to join in, acknowledged, 'Hats Off to the SWP!'

But a leopard cannot hide its spots. Soon, the Anti-Nazi League was actively involved in street disturbances, throwing bricks at Lewisham in 1979, the precursor of riots at Brixton and elsewhere, ostensibly against the National Front, but with the real target the police, the crucial guardians not only of law and order but of democracy. Among the first to be disillusioned were the Jews, victims of Nazi extermination. The Socialist Workers Party had attacked Jewish student organizations. Mr Hain had written in *Free Palestine*, an organ of the Palestine Liberation Organization, an article attacking Zionism. In reply to a letter in *The Times* on 27 October 1977, he wrote on 11 November, 'I believe Zionism to be a racialist creed.' Jewish students at the London Polytechnic led a walk-out. The Jewish Board of Deputies were particularly concerned over the unexpected Far Left commitment. Dr Jacob Gewirtz, head of research, said he was convinced the League was the brain-child of the SWP, and the Party 'has other fish to fry'. He also recalled the two-year planning of the League by the SWP, which, he said, 'exercises tight control over the leadership'. While the Jewish Board of Deputies had no doubt that the League was opposed to the growth of Fascism, the SWP, which dominated it, was 'one of the most virulent and aggressive anti-Zionist, anti-Israel movements in the world'. The decision by the leaders of British Jews to dissociate themselves from the Anti-Nazi League coincided with the similar departure of the Federation of Conservative Students, with 16,000 members. Its chairman, Edward Longworth, said the League was not the broadly-based organization it said it was.

But the biggest exodus came from prominent personalities who realized they had been conned into supporting what appeared to be a worthy cause. Michael Parkinson, celebrated television interviewer, soon pulled out. His decision followed the fifth issue of the magazine *School Kids against Nazis* (SKAN). This included four-letter words and featured a competition showing young people throwing missiles at the National Front, with a prize for indicating where the missile landed – 'Spot the Brick'. Another article said, 'We have to wipe out fascism, but to make sure it doesn't come back, we'll also have to wipe out capitalism.' Mr Parkinson said, 'If the League believe in all that, I just don't want anything to do with them. In my view, they are just as bad as the people they are opposing. There is no sense in meeting a lunacy with another kind of lunacy.' Another 'defector' was Jack Charlton, then manager of Sheffield Wednesday football club, who said, 'It now seems to me that the League has set itself up as an organization that intends to meet force with force – and I'm just not going along with that sort of thing.'

Another who went was Labour Life Peer and writer, Lord (Ted) Willis, who said: 'I resigned because of some of the methods they have been using, and some of the propaganda they have been putting out. It is almost as bad as the National Front.' Others who lent their name to the League, but sooner rather than later had second thoughts included Henry Cooper, former British heavyweight boxing champion, Brian Clough, the more than articulate football manager, and Dave Allen, the Irish comedian. Other early sponsors included: Dame Peggy Ashcroft; Alfie Bass, the comic actor; Iris Murdoch, the novelist; Lee Remick, the American film actress domiciled in London; and Tom Stoppard, the playwright.

Since then, the Anti-Nazi League has staged more confrontations, always with the police as the main target rather than the skinheads of the National Front. The most notorious was that at Southall in April 1979 which led to the death of Blair Peach, the New Zealand teacher member of the SWP, whose skull was cracked fatally by the police when tackling street rioters. Little more needs to be said about the Blair Peach affair, except to note that like Horst Wessel for the emergent Nazi Party, he was to prove a potent propaganda theme, mainly for the Socialist Workers Party, but also for all the fringe of the Far Left, including the Communist Party. Blair Peach, in fact, only died because of the Anti-Nazi League decision to oppose violently a National Front demonstration, itself deliberately provocative and reprehensible. Once again, the Far Left matched the Far Right with tragic results. But who was to blame – the police, the popular scapegoats? Hardly. Today, the Anti-Nazi League is largely discredited. But it has served its purpose.

The Right to Work Campaign remains active, thriving on growing youth unemployment. Its columns of marchers and screaming, serried-rank demonstrators converge every autumn on Brighton and Blackpool. In 1980 it organized a march from South Wales to Brighton to demonstrate outside the Conservative Party conference. The march itself was a thin straggly affair. But the demo was different, met by massed policemen, many mounted, on the Brighton front. Organizing the march, the Campaign, led by Mr John Deason, a veteran Trotskyist who has been involved in clashes with the law over his revolutionary activities, said its aim was to 'help highlight the need for a sustained fight against unemployment' and a campaign of defiance against the Employment bill. The march, it claimed, would mainly comprise unemployed school-leavers and steelworkers. But a letter signed by himself and Ernie Roberts, MP, as honorary treasurer, made no mention of the Socialist Workers Party.

By the end of July forty-two Labour MPs had agreed to sponsor the march, together with three constituency Labour parties and fourteen Labour Party wards. Trade union sponsors included the South Wales area executive of the National Union of Mineworkers, six other NUM organizations and more than 150 other trade union organizations representing workers in engineering, steel, construction, transport, education, retail distribution, the Civil Service, Inland Revenue, printing, the National Health Service, the railways, fire brigades, Post Office and local government. Boilermakers, public employees, metal mechanics, actors, musicians, white-collar workers and students were also represented. Another twenty-three trades councils and seventeen joint shop stewards committees were also among the sponsors. No doubt they were inspired by concern over unemployment, particularly in stricken South Wales. But the beneficiary was the Socialist Workers Party. In the end, however, the march was a flop.

Preparing for its members' conference in December 1980, the SWP issued a number of internal bulletins aimed at clarifying its position on the major issues in which it was involved. They included 'united front' work with the Labour, Communist and other parties, aimed specifically at increasing SWP size and influence, to attract 'people to the SWP on the basis of our activity and ideas, on the basis that we are the best, most serious fighters as an organization and not simply as individuals'.

The bulletin on the Right to Work Campaign said:

> The Right to Work Campaign was our earliest substantial and sustained attempt at a general united front.... Denounced as an 'SWP front' by the CP ... the problem for us was to promote the activity ... which depended on our members and sympathizers, whilst fighting very hard to broaden the union support and establish a credible base which was clearly within the SWP periphery. This persistent struggle has obviously borne fruit and has played a real role in establishing the credibility of the SWP.

So much for those big-hearted but naïve union and other organizations who believe everyone has a right to work.

On the Anti-Nazi League, the bulletin said:

> The ANL had a different origin to the extent that it proved possible to involve more than a token number of Left reformists at an early stage.... As with the RTWC our comrades did the donkey work, but the block was able to attract forces well beyond the drawing capacity of either component on their own. This is an important characteristic of an effective united front.
>
> A feature of the ANL was that we felt it essential to retain a sizeable influence on the 'machine' because of the need to prevent the whole operation being derailed by the Ultra Left phrasemongers or 'constitutional' opportunists. The decision was absolutely right in the circumstances.

Seldom has Trotskyist cynicism been more frankly admitted.

With all Trotskyist parties, a prime aim is to undermine the State and its organs of law and order. At mass demonstrations, the target is less the National Front than the police. It is therefore illuminating to read guidance in the SWP bulletin on 'Strategy and Tactics against the State' by three Oxford members, Xavier Duffy, Giles Ungpakorn and Lenny Coleman.

After some discussion of likely police and court responses, they turn to tactics.

> When we do have mass picketing we shall have to work hard to make them bigger than just a bunch of 'Lefties'. . . . The police learn from Lewisham, Leicester and Grunwicks. We should learn too. We can only outmanœuvre the police by keeping one step ahead of them. The elements of surprise will win the day. Since one of the police's main tactics is to saturate with numbers, unless we can get 20–30 thousand (or more) people to an event we will not have the numbers for face-to-face confrontation. Even if we do we will pay a high price in sentences.
>
> SWP stewarding must be efficient and well planned at events. We should use all kinds of tactics to avoid arrest. It is not possible to discuss these in print but branches should discuss tactics and pool experiences. Attempts to break police lines should not be encouraged unless they can gain something definite. If it is necessary to do so it should be done properly so that people follow through the gaps and do not hold back.
>
> Physical fitness also helps. Apart from this tactical withdrawals of certain people/groups should be considered. Dressing and personal conduct on pickets and demonstrations should be part of basic training. Certain clothes can be used against you as 'offensive weapons' in court; others cause increased chances of arrest.
>
> Rather than shouting slogans and having speeches where comrades thump a few chests, the audience at demonstrations should be given the chance to hear some of our political arguments, phrased in a short, sharp manner. Any rallies should be kept to periods when the action has finished, not used to draw people away from it.

The three authors then turn to fund-raising.

> Since crippling fines are going to be the order of the day, we must become experts in raising money. It is easier to raise money from trade unionists if you win the political arguments *first*. Fund raising must be viewed as being part of the mobilization/picket activities. Experiences about ways of raising money should be pooled (and a handbook produced?). Fund raising should also be a continuous part of our work.

An SWP legal department is suggested.

Advice given to people should include: How to plead, how to get witnesses and legal representation (lists of good lawyers should be drawn up), how to prepare statements and how to answer questions in court. Tactics on being arrested should also be advised (given different circumstances). New members should attend sessions in magistrates courts (as the police do). The legal department could be made up by pooling our law students, graduates, solicitors, lecturers and social workers etc. Its work would also be very much concerned with the Workers Information Service. Thus it would advise on up-to-date aspects of the law concerning picketing, occupations, rights at work, claiming benefits, abortion etc. . . . It should also be responsible for advising on the setting-up of Defence Committees. We should campaign, together with 'Civil liberties' groups to defend the few rights that we have, e.g. union legislation, the right to remain silent when arrested, police powers etc. . . .

Finally, the trio urge:

It might be in our future interest to encourage more decentralization of the organization in order to counter any State repression and also build the confidence of the comrades in the various localities. We must, of course, not sacrifice our democratic centralist politics as a result. Finally we call ourselves the embryo of a revolutionary party. It is time we showed the faintest glimmer of the ability to *organize* as revolutionaries. Our periphery will not be too impressed if they see that we cannot even organize on pickets and street mobilizations efficiently.

So much for 'spontaneous' demos. Mass mobilization on the streets, planned attempts to break police lines, physical fitness and the right clothing, legal follow-up on arrest, that is the planned Trotsykist strategy behind any well-staged march or demonstration.

Perhaps because it has a major middle-class and intellectual content, the Socialist Workers Party has more breast-beating and frank admission of failure than other Trotskyist organizations. In its internal bulletin of October 1979, its central committee, while concentrating on activity in industry (see Chapter 7), thought the political climate a 'very healthy one for us to build our Party in. We have to establish our credibility as the best anti-Tory fighters. . . .' But, it admitted, 'The last five years have taken a toll on our organization.' The Party had suffered indirectly from demoralization and lack of generalized struggle.

But things were not all that bad. After detailing its progress in a wide range of industry and white-collar unions, the committee claimed, 'Our membership is now predominantly working class', but 'with usually just two or three comrades' in 'workplace units', although their total was higher. 'Rank and File' papers were better established. Triumphantly, it concluded, 'The SWP is now nationally known. We are *the* reds under the beds.'

Reflecting differences over what *Socialist Worker* should be, it quoted Tony Cliff as saying 'the paper must smell of the workers' vodka' [*sic*]. It must not be written by professional writers, but by workers, 'able to influence tens of thousands of workers outside its own ranks'. The paper 'must contain propaganda against capitalism'. For these reasons, in a dig at the Workers Revolutionary Party, *Socialist Worker* did not 'reproduce great slabs of Trotsky'. Citing Communist efforts to sell the old *Daily Worker* in the thirties and weakened efforts on behalf of its successor, the *Morning Star*, the committee conceded, 'Over the past few years our paper sales have relatively declined.' The paper must be used to organize supporters, the key role of Trotskyist publications. Later, the central committee says on race, 'The Socialist Workers Party has, thanks to its role in the Anti-Nazi League and its opposition to immigration controls, the reputation of being *the* fighters against racialism.' But experience had taught that 'it is very difficult to recruit and hold Asians and Afro-Caribbeans'. Nevertheless, Mrs Desai, the central figure in the Grunwick strike in which the SWP played a major role in organizing violent demonstrations against the police, is prominently featured as a 'heroine' in the fight for Asian and women's rights.

But not all runs smoothly in Trotskyist attempts to exploit the blacks. The Socialist Workers Party runs a 'Black Caucus', as well as publishing *Flame* for the black community. In its pre-conference internal bulletin of October 1979, it published the 'amended versions of documents presented to the Black Caucus of the SWP' in the previous September.

The Black Caucus, it stated, rejected the general line of the central committee on race work. After the document was read out, eighteen voted for its rejection, seven against and four abstained. Changes were made, particularly over geographical or local organization of groups. A total of thirty-five black members of the SWP attended the weekend conference.

'Obviously, the political credibility and confidence of the SWP/Flame members *depends* on the political attitude of the SWP as a whole to Flame. The more hostile it is to Flame, the less credibility we in Flame have. (Passed 21 for, 2 abstentions).' It continues, 'At the moment the exact working relationship between Flame and the SWP is uncharted.' It goes on to mention lack of historical examples on which to work and joint campaigns. Flame is an 'independent black revolutionary organization.... It attempts to inject into the black communities and workplaces revolutionary socialist politics....' Its aim is a multi-racial revolutionary party. 'We believe that the SWP is the embryo of that party. That is why we are the sister organization, with definite organizational links to the SWP but with our own membership groups and able to make our own decisions. Support of the SWP and of its full programme is not a condition of Flame membership. (Passed 20 for, one against).' But while black workers were highly organized in unions, this was not reflected in the number of black shop stewards, union branch and other officials. 'Flame needs to pay attention to "winning its spurs" inside the black community. We need to pay much more effort to building links with the community, finding out the mood, issues arousing anger, etc. Local agitation, consistent local work paying attention to contacts, building links with youth clubs are all preconditions to building a successful Flame group.'

The SWP bulletin adds: 'The second generation of black youth are clearly far more militant than their parents.... Amongst black students there are far more "thinking" youths than elsewhere. In many ways they represent the advance guard of the black youth movement. Witness the number of FE colleges run by black students (and black student societies). The student movement has now to deal with an aggressive, confident black student organization. Work inside the colleges is clearly important: film shows, dances, meetings can be organized inside the FE colleges if Flame goes into them confidently.' Increased attention should also be paid to agitation among black women.

Another contributor, however, Swapan Dasgupta, also underlined differences between Flame and the SWP central committee, referred to the 'obvious lack of sales (recruits) in the black department', alleged the Party regarded Flame as 'their new subsidiary company', mentioned a charge by 'a leading member from Brixton' that the central committee were 'socialist Dr Beechings', and said 'the unity of the Black Caucus was merely illusory'.

Similar attention was given to Trotskyist work among Asians. The bulletin recorded increasing militancy among Asian women, pictures of whose demos appear frequently in all Trotskyist publications. Even more striking was militancy among Asian youth, both in major concentrations such as Southall, Bradford and Birmingham, and in colleges and student unions. Here again, however, dissatisfied Asians do not always respond to the activities of white revolutionaries. In Southall, one Pete Alexander reported, Flame members worked closely with Peoples Unite, a community-based organization 'dominated by Afro-caribs' which included the Misty reggae band. Apart from a branch of fourteen members and supporters, including seven Asians, four whites and three Afro-caribs, 'more significantly we now have three Asian cadres'. Mr Alexander claimed SWP credit for instigating 'The Riot' which resulted in the death of Blair Peach, using the Anti-Nazi League: 'Most of our mobilizing had been as ANL.' After the riot, 'we agreed that our main orientation had to be towards Asian workers. We accepted that the best vehicle for this work was *Socialist Worker* with the possibility of direct recruitment to the party.' The SWP had produced five special Southall editions, sold up to 900 copies in one week, selling most from door to door by twenty comrades. Other publications had also been sold, thousands of leaflets in Punjabi as well as English distributed, and nearly 1,000 special pamphlets sold. Mr Alexander details much agitation on industrial issues. Sales of *Socialist Worker* were four-to-five times higher when headlines related to Asians. But only about £20,000 towards a target of £70,000 had been raised for the Anti-Nazi League – 'the response of the Left in general has been atrocious'.

This account of SWP activity at Southall gives a fair picture of how legitimate immigrant grievances are exploited with considerable effort. Another major area of activity by all Trotskyist groups has been Brixton, one scene of the 1981 riots. Not only does the Workers Revolutionary Party advertise a bookshop in Atlantic Road, a centre of the disturbances, but the Revolutionary Communist Tendency, a minor faction, is based there. After the summer of 1981 riots SWP leaflets were found in the streets. So long as immigrant grievances are allowed to fester, they will provide fertile ground for Trotskyist activity.

Dreary though much of it is, not all the deadly serious Trotskyist theorizing is without its humour. In the October 1979 internal bulletin, Dick Naylor, of Swindon, gives 'A Layman's Guide to Flyposting'. It explains all on how those slogans, bills and defacing graffiti originate.

In Swindon, Mr Naylor says,

If nothing else, our tiny branch has at least succeeded in keeping the SWP in people's minds through our frequent nocturnal forays armed with bucket, brush, poster and paste. We are fortunate in Swindon insofar as the central area has numerous back alleys for us to materialize from and vanish into. I can appreciate the problems of flyposting in, for example, Oxford which has none. Anyway, here are some tips on flyposting, an important aspect of our work and one which we modestly claim to have elevated into an art form.

1. Be imaginative when filling in blank posters, and do so with a permanent marker for obvious reasons. Amongst our most popular slogans were the following: Crime Pays – Ask any Tory; Watch Out, there's a Fascist about and Airey Neave didn't escape from Colditz. He's so Right Wing the Nazis Let Him Out. Keep the message brief and simple.

2. Red print on posters fades very quickly when exposed to the elements. Trace round these words with a permanent black marker, so the complete message remains intact.

3. During the summer flypost in the late evening as soon as it gets dark. Most people are at home or still in the pub at this time, yet there are still sufficient people around for you not to be too conspicuous. During winter early evening is out – do it in the early mornings (I'm on my way to work, Officer!).

4. If on foot two is an ideal number, although one is less conspicuous.

5. Use 'Solvite' paste, it's easily the best, if not as good as the advertisements claim! Put the solution in the smallest possible bucket inside a carrier bag.

6. If you have only a few posters, fold and wrap them them inside a newspaper.

7. Choose your targets carefully so as to minimize public outrage. Empty shop premises, bus shelters and junction boxes are ideal. Posters hold well on existing posters, although it is well to remember that advertisements are quickly replaced. Small advertising boards are better. It makes our posters look 'official'. Occupied houses and shops are out. Use your discretion with public buildings.

8. Blanket coverage is better than the odd one here and there, which, unless they are in prominent spots, tend to be ignored.

9. Paste the chosen spot first, slap the poster on, then seal it with

more paste. Place the posters as high up as possible to make it harder for them to be removed, or defaced.

10. Carry bogus ID with you in case you are apprehended. You will not be conveyed to the Police Station if you can produce 'evidence' of your identity.

Use a membership card with a genuine name and address on it – preferably of someone you don't like! (When I was collared putting up anti-racist posters I produced an ANL membership card with the name and address of a local Fascist on it.)

Remember, flyposting is only an offence against the bye-laws, and you have (in theory at least) to be caught actually putting a poster up. Much to their chagrin, the police cannot nick you for intent to fly-post. If you do get stopped, don't push your luck, abort mission.

That's it, comrades, everything you ever wanted to know about flyposting but were afraid to ask. Sorry to be so brief. I've got to go and do a bit of flyposting!

So, if you see a furtive figure, armed with a carrier bag containing a newspaper, small bucket and brush, vanishing into and emerging from dark alleyways, that is your local Trot on his nocturnal or early-morning mission. Should you get a visit from the local police or a summons, he had taken the precaution of putting your name and address on his 'ID'.

Following the Toxteth riots, the *Sunday Telegraph* reported that Tony Cliff said at a meeting of supporters in Liverpool that he 'regretted' the Party's failure to gain control of and organize youngsters in Liverpool, Manchester and London. He reportedly said, 'The riots and looting have been fantastic. But they have not gone far enough. Because they have not been organized, the kids have attacked shops when they should have been attacking factories.... We must teach them to take the bakery not just the bread.'

Mr Cliff also said, significantly, that it was only extensive television coverage that had spread rioting throughout Britain. 'I wish it was true that we had organized a national revolution, but I am afraid that cannot be said. The young have provided the steam, and now we must provide the engine for that steam to drive.... This is an exciting time for Socialists. But it would just not be true if I promised that the revolution was just around the corner.' The SWP, however, claimed to have two hundred members in Liverpool. Party members said they had sold several hundred copies of *Socialist Worker* and distributed 1,000 leaflets in Toxteth attacking the police, in an attempt to maintain disorder there. The SWP is placing increasing emphasis on agitation in industry. If it expended as much energy in its indoctrination of workers as it gives to its endless pamphlets and theoretical debates it might become an even more powerful threat.

4 The International Marxist Group and smaller organizations

Tariq Ali, Pakistani turned Briton, former president of the Oxford Union, son of a wealthy Punjabi businessman and landowner, one of the most prominent leaders of the students' revolt in the late 1960s, activist in the anti-American Vietnam movement, London School of Economics sit-ins and many other causes, is now half-forgotten.

But despite talk at one time of returning to Pakistan, Tariq Ali, now on the threshold of middle-age, is still with us and alive and well, said by gossip columnists to enjoy the good life. He remains a leader and ideological motor of the International Marxist Group, the fourth of Britain's major Trotskyist factions, probably about 1,000 strong, academically orientated and with a strong middle-class element. As with Gerry Healy, of the Workers Revolutionary Party, Tony Cliff, of the Socialist Workers Party, and Ted Grant, of the Militant Tendency, the IMG would hardly exist without Tariq Ali.

Tariq Ali came to Britain in 1963, but did not take out a British passport until 1973. After coming down from Oxford, he soon became a leader of the Vietnam Solidarity Campaign, which resulted in the 1969 riot outside the United States embassy in Grosvenor Square when a policeman was grievously injured, the first of many such casualties. Other activities included demos at the West Germany embassy, visits to Belfast, China, North Korea, France (from which he was later barred), Bolivia, Belgium, Denmark, Sweden and Cuba. Arrest for obstructing the police and a fine came in 1973.

But 1963 is significant, for it marked the beginnings of the International Marxist Group. A group of dissident Socialist Labour League members formed the International Group, or Nottingham Group, publishing *The Week*, edited by Ken Coates. Various attempts were made until 1965 at joint organization with the Revolutionary Socialist League. By 1965 the International Group changed its name to the International Marxist Group, and supplanted the Revolutionary Communist League as the British organization of the United Secretariat of the Trotskyist Fourth International, although it did not become a full section until 1969.

Entryism in the Labour Party continued as did publication of *The Week*. But in 1968, yet another ideological dispute arose, and Ken Coates departed to concentrate on the Betrand Russell Peace Foundation and the Institute for Workers Control, a favourite cause of Tony Benn. *The Week* was replaced by a theoretical journal *International*, and, despite losing support in the trade union movement and elsewhere, the IMG hoisted its colours as an openly Trotskyist movement. Leader of the Party was then Pat Jordan, a veteran revolutionary.

As the international revolutionary student movement developed, notably in France and West Germany, the international Trotskyist movement saw a new field for agitation. It was at the ninth conference of the United Secretariat Fourth International in April 1969 that the International Marxist Group became the official British section, withdrawing from the Labour Party. It also decided to concentrate on recruitment and propaganda in the working class.

In May 1968, the IMG started publication of *Black Dwarf*, aimed largely at young people, and edited by Tariq Ali from a Soho office from 1969. Previously, he had been a founder member of its editorial board. At lectures at universities, he was reported as attracting 'vast audiences'. But by early 1970 came another split in the *Black Dwarf* editorial board, and Tariq Ali and five others left to set up *Red Mole*, of which they claimed to have sold 8,000 copies in five days. They had a new headquarters in Pentonville Road and their own printing press. Among the six was Robin Blackburn, who had been sacked as a London School of Economics lecturer for his activities.

The cost of the operation was reported in the *Sunday Times* on 19 April 1970 as being: the house in Pentonville Road, £10,000; refurbishment, £3,000; a Solna 125 printing press, £5,000; photographic equipment, £2,000; weekly wages and costs, a mere £125. Only the printer, Roger Hunt, and typesetter Felicity Trudal, were paid full wages. One editorial member, David Kendall, got only £5 a week. A new recruit was Teresa Hayter, daughter of Sir William Hayter, a former British ambassador in Moscow, who later wrote a revolutionary book.

International changed to become an ideological journal. Facing growing competition from the International Socialists, the IMG and Tariq Ali worked through minority protest movements, such as the Black Defence Committee in 1971, the Irish Solidarity Campaign and School Students Alliance in 1972, the National Union of School Students and the National Union of Students. In 1969, it founded a youth movement, the Spartacus League. It also started *Socialist Woman*, successful among women's libbers. As the ideological emphasis continued to shift up to 1974, *Red Mole* was rejigged, as journalists say, in mid-1972 and became *Red Weekly* in May 1973, with a parallel withdrawal from youth revolution and increased concentration on the labour movement. In 1976 the International Marxist Group with other Trotskyist factions split from the Rank and File Teachers movement, the front organization of the International Socialists/Socialist Workers Party. It set up the Socialist Student Alliance.

A group of Scottish Labour Party entryists was expelled from the SLP in October 1976 and became the Scottish Socialist League, allied with the IMG, which it agreed to join in October 1977. In June that year, *Red Weekly* was changed into *Socialist Challenge*, of which Tariq Ali was editor and which continues today. Some notoriety was attracted in July 1977, when the paper published the *Gay News* blasphemous poem about Christ being crucified, giving the explanation, 'We printed it to express our solidarity with *Gay News* and with the gay people of this country.' In fact, members of the National Graphical Association refused to assist in printing it, and photocopies were run off as a supplement by Tariq Ali. Like other Trotskyist activists, he was interested in exploiting homosexual aims. In October 1977 came another furore. Sir Richard Dobson, then chairman of British Leyland, referred at a private lunch to 'wogs', and his post-prandial address was secretly tape-recorded. The transcript was published in *Socialist Challenge*, and Sir Richard resigned. Soon afterwards, The Other Bookshop, in Upper Street, Islington was firebombed, allegedly by Column 88, the extreme neo-Nazi organization.

The IMG, led by Tariq Ali, sought in 1979 to broaden its appeal in alliance with Big Flame, the International Socialist Alliance, the Asian Socialist League and other groups through the front organization, Socialist Unity. They had moderate success in local elections. In April 1979 Tariq Ali was arrested at the race riot in Southall, Middlesex, and later fined £150 for obstructing a policeman. In May 1980 he was a sponsor of the Socialist Campaign for Labour Victory.

In May 1980 the IMG held a founding conference of yet another youth organization, Revolution Youth. It would, it claimed, be 'independent'. But IMG members would 'argue for political solidarity with the IMG and the Fourth International within the youth organization'. About fifty young people took part in a protest march against youth unemployment in Wales in April 1980 which was organized by the IMG.

On 27 June 1981 the International Marxist Group celebrated the first anniversary of Revolution Youth at a rally at Caxton House, Archway,

North London, with 'international youth speakers' from Grenada, Nicaragua, El Salvador, Ireland and 'French revolutionary youth'. Advance publicity stated: 'Revolution Youth sees its role as building support for liberation struggles wherever and whenever they take place.... Revolution Youth is building an organization of young women, young workers, young blacks and all young people who want to fight against the sort of future that the Tories offer us.' Also held was a conference on ways of 'fighting for socialist policies in industry' and 'building a party of worker revolutionaries'. A principal aim was to organize support for Anthony Wedgwood Benn in his bid for the Labour Party deputy leadership, particularly in the engineering and transport unions.

In early summer 1981, the International Marxist Group through *Socialist Challenge* promoted a new badge, 'Tony Benn for Deputy', with a sheriff's star in gold or silver colours on which 'deputy' was printed. It was described as the 'fastest-selling badge' on the People's Job March from Liverpool to London in May, and was advertised as a 'hot property' costing 'just 20p (plus 11.5p postage). Give-away bulk rates are available from the Islington Research Group, PO Box 50, London N1', stated *Socialist Challenge* on 25 June 1981.

Three days later, the *Sunday Telegraph* reported that *Socialist Challenge* had provided £779.80 plus VAT for 15,000 such badges in support of Mr Wedgwood Benn's campaign for Labour's deputy leadership. John Silkin, also a candidate, and who had already challenged Mr Benn over the cost of his campaign, saying such expenses should be published and submitted to the Labour Party, commented, 'If something similar had been done for me, I would have told them this was not to be.' He appealed to Mr Benn to hold a 'democratic British election, not a Mafia-type jamboree'.

Socialist Challenge said Mr Benn had neither sought support nor been consulted, but they had sent him a badge. Phil Hearse, editor, described his paper's policy as 'to the left of the Communist Party'. On the possible profit, the IMG said: 'We will be happy if we just break even. The motive was a political one. It was not to make money. We sold the first lot in bulk at around 9p or 10p each when they cost us 7p or 8p. Local Labour Party groups and trade unions can buy them in bulk. If they make money, that is a good thing. If we do make a few pounds, the money will go back into running the newspaper. It will not be used for Mr Benn's campaign.'

The badges were produced by the Universal Button company, of

Bethnal Green. Alan Clayton, a director, said they printed 500,000 badges a week, 'We are apolitical'. He added, 'We made "Love Maggie" badges at the time of Mrs Thatcher's birthday.' Clearly, badges are a booming business, involving considerable enterprise. But the episode illustrates how Far Left groups have both supported and exploited Mr Benn's candidacy and, by implication, how he has tacitly accepted such support. He has also given regular interviews to Far Left publications.

Over the years, the IMG has made repeated efforts for alliances with other Trotskyist groups, including the Socialist Workers Party, the Workers Socialist League and the International Communist League. I have one long bulletin by 'Landis' of the ICL on such a merger move in summer 1980, 'Fightback and Women in Action: The Facts'. It says:

> The IMG approached us before the June conference with a merger proposal. *Women in Action*, by the way, is purely a front, one-off magazine that those women in the IMG who were keen on it couldn't get the IMG to support financially. Though nowhere in its pages is the IMG or *Socialist Challenge* mentioned, and the thing is presented as a very broad, bland effort, we have seen no evidence of anyone beyond the IMG being involved....
>
> At the beginning, they stressed how difficult they found bringing out a paper, but that they didn't just want to disappear without trace into WF. We suggested the banner would include 'incorporating Women in Action', and they seemed pleased to be offered that much. Since that stage, they have become bolder and bolder. At the SC meeting ... we were unable to have such a full discussion because they already had someone planted in our camp....

The bulletin continues with an intricate description of Trotskyist infighting. 'This "broad meeting" (26 July) was attended by some dozen IMGers.... In the meantime their hand had been strengthened with an order from NUPE for 2,000 WinA.... [Women in Action] We did our most blatant cave-in that afternoon....' The merger was turned down. 'What would have been the gain from the merger? We had planned some sort of "unity" razzamatazz, a rally with various notables speaking on a women's newspaper [*sic*]. It might have made it easier to get TU orders, and we might have got some of their orders (hopefully including the big NUPE one) transferred to the joint paper. Without all that, and faced with a barrage of slanderous stories about "Workers Action dominating the campaign" etc., life will be harder. But we're in a far stronger position than they are to carry on.... They might try to get some broadsheet out as a gesture of defiance and to kid people that they are still alive.'

But the IMG has also had its problems with rebels and infiltrators. On 21 May 1981 Steve Potter, its national secretary, announced:

The leadership of the International Marxist Group has discovered a secret plot by the international Spartacist tendency to smash the IMG as a 'counter-revolutionary organization'. The IMG political committee on 16 May expelled from the organization the so-called 'Communist Faction'. A majority of this faction's membership were secret members of the Spartacists. The faction was unanimously expelled for disloyalty after refusing to characterize the IMG and the Fourth International as revolutionary organizations, implying that it was necessary to build a separate party to the IMG and FI.... [Fourth International] From investigations undertaken by the IMG leadership, incontestable evidence was presented to the political committee that at least nine members of the 'Communist Faction' had joined the Spartacists, some as early as the summer of 1979. They had joined by signing a secret contract describing the IMG/ FI as a 'counter-revolutionary organization which had to be smashed' and the Spartacists as 'the only revolutionary organization in the world'. The national commitee of Revolution Youth took similar action last weekend and expelled three Spartacist infiltrators.

On 18 May 1981 the so-called Communist Faction published a weighty brochure entitled 'Documents of the Communist Faction of the IMG Part II: Purge in IMG'. It contains seventy-one pages of vituperative correspondence on such topics as: 'Should Mandel be expelled from the USFI?'; 'Warning! – Disarmament slogans only disarm the working class!'; 'Exchange on Arnot'; 'Letter from Cannon to Harney'; 'Letter to comrade Khalid from executive committee'; 'IMG leadership statement on the "events in Manchester"'; and 'Resolution in defence of comrade Khalid'.

The rebels stated that the Communist Tendency in IMG, which later became the Communist Faction, was formed in January 1981. They accused the IMG leadership of methods being 'culled from the Stalinist school'. They added: 'The expulsion of the Communist Faction (and any other serious opposition to liquidation into the Labour Party) is the tribute offered for full membership in the Tony Benn supporters' club.'

Comrade Khalid lives in Hemel Hempstead and the mysterious Comrade Arnot appears to be based in Birmingham.

Some of the dispute arose over proposals to merge the IMG with the Socialist Workers Party – 'immediate fusion'. Some of it covered how to exploit the Campaign for Nuclear Disarmament. 'We can no more recruit revolutionaries out of CND by adopting CND's pacifist disarmament politics than we could regroup with the SWP, Big Flame, the ISA etc., by dropping all mention of our differences.' Well laced with quotations from Trotsky and others, few documents better illustrate the underworld politics of the Far Left.

Today, like other Trotskyist groups, the International Marxist Group continues, campaigning on the IRA and Troops Out, and backing such causes as the occupation of the Lee Jeans factory in Scotland, which its owners had decided to close down because of a slump in sales. It was active in the 1981 TUC's 'People's March for Jobs'. Other concerns are gettting Mr Benn elected as deputy Labour leader, Grenada, the Campaign for Nuclear Disarmament, El Salvador, and all the rest of the ragbag of opportunist Far Left causes. Tariq Ali tends to keep a low profile. But he still operates, both with middle-class academics and the shopfloor, and should not be forgotten by those who are interested, since he has a habit of bouncing back.

Apart from the International Marxists, Socialist Workers Party, Workers Revolutionary Party and Militant Tendency, there are a number of smaller equally virulent sects, some eccentric offshoots, others important, in Britain. They include:

The Workers Socialist League

Alan Thornett, now in his forties, has acquired a certain fame over the years, not quite a legend but a certain revolutionary charisma which causes his name always to be noticed. He is the Oxford 'mole', so nicknamed not for any MI5 or MI6 penetration like more distinguished Oxbridge predecessors, but for his Trotskyist digging as a British Leyland shop steward and Transport and General Workers Union activist.

Mr Thornett, who in spring 1981 appeared to be making a comeback, has had his ups and downs. He has been threatened with dismissal and barred from recognition as a Transport Union shop steward by British Leyland and been disciplined by the union. He has also been the subject of legal proceedings instituted against him by Vanessa Redgrave.

The Workers Socialist League, largely based round Oxford, was formed in the mid-1970s after the expulsion of about two hundred members from the Workers Revolutionary Party. Alan Thornett had argued that the WRP was giving up the Trotskyist Transitional Programme and becoming sectarian. Pursuing entryism in the Labour Party, the WSL soon set itself up as a force in its own right. It began publication of *Socialist Press*, a weekly publication. It also started in 1976 the Campaign for Democracy in the Labour Movement. It has its youth wing, the Socialist Youth League, as well as a women's section with its own paper.

Membership of the Workers Socialist League has been estimated at only four hundred. But its influence through the motor industry is wider. One of the best accounts of its activities was published in the *Daily Mail* in summer 1980. The WSL is based at 63, Bartlemas Road, Oxford, a large detached house with at least five bedrooms, a darkroom and a £3,000 printing press in the basement. Curtains, it was reported after a doorstep visit, were kept drawn. Ownership was disputed between the League and the Workers Revolutionary Party, which claimed it owned the lease. But Alan Thornett, despite his involvement with legal proceedings, and also his divorce, retained possession.

Several other WSL supporters lived nearby. Also close, on the Blackbird Leys estate, was Redefield School, a modern establishment, where the League holds revolutionary summer schools. It has widespread international links with which I deal in Chapter 11. Living at the house were not only Mr Thornett, but other prominent members, Tony Richardson, another British Leyland shop steward, and Ian Swindale, a full-time Workers Socialist League employee and joint editor with John Lister of *Socialist Press*. Other activists incuded Terry Eagleton, an English tutor at Wadham College. Mr Eagleton's tasks included writing political analyses for internal consumption only. Despite being a Wadham Fellow, he has also been active in strike action at Reading, and hired rooms at Wadham on 10 June 1980 to assist a servants' strike at Pembroke College. His explanation was that this was on behalf of the self-styled Oxford Students Trade Union Liaison Committee, not itself a Workers Socialist League front organization. But it was set up by another prominent WSL member, 'Red Ted' Heslin, and Pat Lally, another WSL activist, to rally support from the trade union Ruskin College and Oxford Polytechnic students for a strike at Blackwell's bookshop in 1976.

In December 1977 Mr Thornett was, as often happens in the Far Left movement, involved in a curious episode. According to *Socialist Press* of 23 April 1980, a 'highly sophisticated' day-time burglary was made on his house in Oxford. A total of two hundredweight of documents covering twenty years of activity were stolen, including trade union files, a filing cabinet full of personal correspondence and other material. At the time, Mr Thornett was being proceeded against on disciplinary grounds by the Transport and General Workers Union.

The correspondence taken included other interesting items, such as documents on the expulsion of himself and two hundred others from the Workers Revolutionary Party in 1974 and formation of the Workers Socialist League. There was also a letter dated 16 January 1976 to Mr Thornett from Dr G. Picton-Davies, of the Police College, inviting him to take part in an instructional television film, to which no reply was made. Two and a half years later, a facsimile of the letter was printed in WRP's *News Line* with the suggestion that Mr Thornett's faction was trying to invoke a police raid on the WRP. The mystery remained how the original letter, or a photocopy of it, came into the hands of *News Line*. It was also used on the cover of a pamphlet.

'Red Ted' Heslin has achieved prominence on another score. He was expelled from membership of Oxford Labour Party for his Trotskyist activities. But on appeal his expulsion was rescinded by the left-wing dominated national executive of the Labour Party. The issue of Mr Heslin is a continuing bone of contention between orthodox Labour Party members in Oxford and the Party's national leadership. In the IMG's *Socialist Challenge* of 25 June 1981, Mike Picken, of the local party, complained that the issue was still unresolved after a visit by Eric Heffer, chairman of the national Party's organization committee and David Hughes, the national agent. The national executive had written to the Oxford party saying they would accept Heslin back if the organization committee would interview him, seeking assurances that he would not repeat the actions or his critical statements against the Labour Party.

'But even this backtracking was not enough for the Oxford right wing,' wrote Mr Picken. 'The Oxford party will only accept Heslin back on the understanding that he will refrain from the actions for which he was expelled – "i.e. supporting the WSL, selling its paper and distributing its literature". The NEC will now have to interview Heslin and decide what to do about the conditions. Socialists in the party should be campaigning for no restrictions on the membership of Heslin and for unconditional reinstatement by the NEC.' But this would involve a conflict with the right-wing majority in the Oxford party.

This surely is a graphic illustration of where the Labour Party is going. Meanwhile Mr Heslin, with Mr Thornett, Mr Swindale and Mr Lister, remains in the inner, decision-making caucus of the Workers Socialist League.

International Communist League

The International Communist League, whose internal bulletins, penetration of Labour fringe organizations and links with *Socialist Organiser* I cite elsewhere, is a small, secretive group of perhaps not more than 100 members. Its national secretary is Sean Matgamna, and its publications include *International Communist*, a theoretical journal. The League also supports *Workers' Action* and *Left Action* aimed at Labour Party Young Socialists.

Its complex origins go back to 1967 when members of the Socialist Labour League and the Militant Tendency formed Workers' Fight. A year later, an alliance was formed with the International Socialists and the Trotskyist Tendency created, only to be expelled from the International Socialists in 1971. Workers' Fight reappeared, until in 1975 it merged with another group of IS expellees, Workers Power and some former members of the Workers Revolutionary Party to form the International Communist League.

Since then, further ideological differences and splits have followed, but the League continues to practise Labour Party entryism, exercising strict discipline over its members.

League for Socialist Action

The League split from the International Marxist Group in 1974-5. They voted to rejoin the IMG early in 1980, but still remain a separate organization. The sect publishes *Socialist Action*, practises entryism, and works in the National Abortion Campaign, women's liberation, black power and Ireland movements.

Revolutionary Communist Group

This group, which despite its title is Trotskyist not Communist, was founded in 1974 from part of the 'revolutionary opposition' or 'right faction' expelled from the International Socialists in 1973. Devoted to restoring revolutionary traditions, it is small in number and publishes an ideological journal, *Revolutionary Communist*, as well as *Hands off Ireland!* Leading members include David Yaffe and Robert Dornhorst.

In the past, it has concentrated on gaining influence inside the Communist Party, the Chile Solidarity Campaign, women's rights, and the Anti-Apartheid Movement, which led to the expulsion of a large minority of members in 1976 for attacking the Communist Party. The expellees formed the Revolutionary Communist Tendency.

Revolutionary Communist Tendency

This small splinter group from the Revolutionary Communist Group publishes *Revolutionary Communist Papers*. It has itself experienced further ideological splits.

Revolutionary Workers Party

Another minor organization which adheres to the tenets of Posadism. Posadism takes its name from Juan Posadas, a Latin American Trotskyist who founded the International Secretariat of the Fourth International (Posadist) in 1962, which aimed at fomenting guerrilla movements. Practising entryism, the fraction favours centralized planning and control, and for this reason, supported the Russian invasion of Czechoslovakia in 1968. It publishes *Red Flag*.

Socialist Charter (Chartists)

The Chartists were formed in 1969-70 as the Socialist Charter Group from members of the Militant Tendency, International Marxist Group and the Workers Revolutionary Party as an entryist organization aimed at committing the Labour Party to a revolutionary programme, and other Trotskyist causes. For a time, they were also known as the Revolutionary

87

Communist League. Publishing *Chartist* and the quarterly *Chartist International*, the group takes its name from a 'charter' of Far Left demands.

Full control was achieved by the Trotskyists in 1972, and in 1973 the organization called for rebuilding of the Fourth International. The Chartists have been active, too, in the Labour Party Young Socialists. Peter Shipley comments: 'It has been able to engage in a form of open entryism – admitting its Trotskyist faith while continuing in the Labour Party – in a manner that would have been unimaginable a decade earlier.'

Spartacist League

This small group is the British link of the International Spartacist Tendency, formed in the United States in 1964 after an ideological split in the American Socialist Workers Party. It opposes work in front organizations in favour of independent revolutionary action, and is at odds with other Trotskyist organizations. Until 1978 it collaborated with the Workers Socialist League. It publishes *Spartacist Britain* and also distributes American Spartacist journals.

Workers League

This League, only about 120 strong and very active in Birmingham, was formed in 1975 by leading members expelled from the International Socialists. It publishes *Socialist Voice*, a monthly journal formerly known as *Workers News*. In rivalry with the SWP, it has competed with it among engineering workers through *Engineering Voice* and teachers, where it co-operated with the International Marxist Group in founding the Socialist Teachers Alliance. Among original members are said to have been Jim Higgins, John Palmer, Roger Protz, Harry Wicks and Larry Connolly.

Workers Power

Workers Power, which publishes a journal of the same name, was formerly another left-wing faction of the International Socialists, now Socialist Workers Party, who were expelled in October 1975. Its members joined with Workers' Fight to form the International Communist League in December 1975, but split again and formed the present organization in

September 1976. Differences had arisen over tactics inside the Labour Party and trade unions, with Workers Power urging agitation among shop stewards. Early in 1981, when its membership was estimated at only around 100, it attracted prominence for its violent role in the Ansells brewery strike in Birmingham, with which I deal in Chapter 7.

Ideological differences among the many Far Left groups, which constantly split, re-form and proliferate, are as complex as in any other theology, and except for main trends, as difficult to define and comprehend by outsiders. Indeed, the intellectual divisions over obscure tenets seem a passion, almost a *raison d'être* in themselves, were it not for the active agitation and disruption which are their practical manifestation. But some other Marxist organizations are worthy of mention.

Big Flame

This movement, which publishes *Big Flame*, described as the 'paper of the revolutionary Socialist organization, Big Flame', is about 100 strong and based in Liverpool and Clerkenwell. It is also active at the Dagenham plant of the Ford Motor Company. Big Flame originated in ideological differences in the mid-1970s, and combines to fight elections under the banner of 'Socialist Unity' with the International Marxist Group. For those interested in Trotskyist theory, it published in April 1977 'The Revolution Unfinished? A Critique of Trotskyism' by Paul Thompson and Guy Lewis. It claims branches in Birmingham, Cambridge, Coventry, Leeds, Liverpool, London, Manchester, Norwich, Nottingham, Oxford, St Albans and Sheffield, and 'members throughout the UK'. Most branches have regular separate men's and women's meetings as well as mixed ones – rather like a sauna. Like other Far Left movements, Big Flame pushes every domestic and international cause. In March 1981 it published a letter from the late Bobby Sands, speaking on behalf of the 'Republican Socialist Prisoners of War'. Other contributions covered the Claimants Union in Sheffield, 'where we managed to organize a very effective campaign against the Department of Health and Social Security fraud officers employing voluntary snoopers', 'Repression of Gays in Moss Side Special Hospital: 6:5 Special' and the anti-nuclear campaign.

Communist Party of Britain (Marxist–Leninist)

Contrary to its title, this party of only a few hundred members is not Communist in the accepted sense, but Maoist. Publishing *The Worker*, it was founded by Reg Birch, former executive councillor of the Amalgamated Union of Engineering Workers.

Reg, if I may allow the familiarity since I have known him for many years, became disillusioned with the orthodox Communist Party when it chose to back not himself but Hugh, now Lord, Scanlon, who had left the party in the mid-1950s, for the Engineering Union presidency. Some commentators have depicted him as a dangerous revolutionary, leader of Britain's Maoists, a visitor to Peking and Albania. Those who know Reg well hold him in general affection, and know differently. They also have a very high opinion of his intellectual quality and negotiating abilities, also his honesty.

Something of a maverick, Reg's negotiating abilities have been gladly acknowledged by employers desperate for a break in the deadlock. Once, the Ford Motor Company found Reg was in France and sent the company plane for him. Ford bosses will never forget one of those protracted negotiating sessions when they were interrupted by a rapping under the boardroom table. 'What's that?' they asked nonplussed. 'It's my members who have passed on,' Reg replied laconically. 'They want to know if the death benefit is backdated.'

5 The Communist Party

No account of the Far Left would be complete without an account of the Communist Party of Great Britain, founded on 1 August 1920 in the repercussions of the Russian revolution and the capitalist attempts to suppress it.

Its formation followed the initiative by Harry Pollitt, later to be its first general secretary, but then a boilermaker in the London docks, in leading a campaign there as part of the 'Hands Off Russia' movement which culminated in the refusal of dockers on 10 May 1920 to coal the *Jolly George*, loaded with munitions for Poland.

From the start, the Party sought affiliation to the Labour Party, but met bitter resistance from Ramsay MacDonald, Arthur Henderson and other leaders. In 1924 all individual Communists were excluded from Labour Party membership. That wooing goes on today.

Passing verdict on the Communist Party is difficult. Some dismiss it, others present it as a 'bogey'. While the various Trotskyist sects make much of the running as the partisans of the revolution, Communist Party members remain legionaries, much more important as union office-holders and with a disciplined purpose. Communists feel contempt for Trotskyists, noting their rapid turnover of young adherents and frequent splits.

Yet all is not well for the Communist Party. It is ailing. Its membership, as announced on 15 July 1981, stands at 18,458, a fall from 20,590 in 1979. This compares with 15,000 in 1941, the previous lowest after the Nazi-Soviet pact of 1939, a rise to 55,000 in 1942, and a fall to 26,000 after Russian suppression of the Hungarian uprising in 1956.

Full-time staff of the Communist Party in 1980 totalled twenty-two at the centre and twenty-eight in the provinces on a standard wage of about £70 a week.

Membership has suffered for many reasons. For militants, the Party appears almost staid compared with Far Left rivals. Like them, too, it makes considerable financial and other demands on members. But worst of all, it has long been identified with the Soviet Union in the public mind. When Russia invaded Czechoslovakia and Afghanistan, it did not help the British Party at all.

As a result, it has in recent years sought to distance itself, like other Euro-Communist parties, from purely Soviet policies, advocating 'socialist democracy' as a way of reform in Britain, rather than revolution. On 1 March 1981 Gordon McLennan, general secretary, publicly criticized Russian intervention in Afghanistan at the 26th Soviet Communist Party congress in Moscow. He was one of the few foreign Communist representatives to tell the 5,000 delegates of fraternal unhappiness.

Mr McLennan said:

The independence and sovereignty of each Communist party is the essential basis for relations between our parties, vital to the principles of internationalism and to mutual solidarity between Communist parties. Differences can and do exist in the international Communist movement on certain questions, including that in Afghanistan.

Our views on these questions are well known, as is the proud internationalist tradition and record of our party. We will continue to express our views within the international Communist movement while conducting the militant struggle in union with brother Communist parties for peace, against imperialism and for socialism.

Mr McLennan was given a 'courteous but unenthusiastic' hearing. Signor Giancario Pajetta, Italian delegation leader, was not even allowed to voice similar remarks. But when it came to reporting Mr McLennan, TASS, the Soviet news agency, omitted the key passages from what it claimed was the 'full text'.

The Communist Party has its converts and defectors. A rather surprising member of its national executive, of whom the Party is proud, is Irene Brennan, a former nun who is described as a practising Roman Catholic. It also has its Asian and black protégés. Its defectors include Jimmy Reid, the Upper Clyde work-in leader, who went to the Labour Party, and Des Warren, the jailed Shrewsbury picket, who became a Trotskyist. It still has two members on the TUC General Council, Ken Gill, general secretary of TASS, the technicians' union, and an impressive speaker, and George Guy, a lesser light, leader of the Sheet Metal Workers. It is reckoned to muster around 100 delegates, about one-tenth of the total, to the TUC annual conference, and has scored some policy successes. Through Mr Gill and others, it manages to get its voice heard on television.

The 36th annual congress of the Communist Party in autumn 1979 was attended by 319 delegates, comprising 250 men and 69 women. The number of branches recorded in the credentials report was: 114 factory branches, 33 student branches and 624 local branches. As regards trade union membership, there were twenty delegates from the Engineering Union, nine from TASS, its technical section, one from its foundry section and seven unspecified AUEW members. At the 35th congress two years earlier, there had been thirty-six. Other union representation included twelve from UCATT, the construction union, and no fewer that thirty-four from the TGWU. Electricians numbered ten, National Union of Journalists two, APEX, the clerical workers union, sixteen, NALGO thirteen, Mineworkers eight, Teachers eighteen, Higher Education Teachers (NATFHE) ten, National Union of Students sixteen, ASTMS, eighteen.

There were twelve delegates from print and publishing, six from the Post Office, ten clerical workers, eleven from distributive trades, twenty-one from local government, eight from the Health Service, fifteen professional and technical, twelve full-time trade union officials, eighteen full-time Communist Party workers, five housewives, four unemployed and eight retired. This breakdown gives a fair idea of where the Party's strength in the unions and elsewhere lies.

At Labour Party conferences, there has been criticism of, for example, how Mick McGahey, former Party chairman and Scots miners' leader, can sit in the lobby bar at Brighton or Blackpool, master-minding how the vote should go. Such activity led Michael Foot, as new Opposition Leader, to warn in vain before Labour's special Wembley conference that proposed electoral changes could prove a 'system which allows Communists to vote, a system which deals in smoke-filled rooms'.

Nor was Mr Foot alone in condemning such activities. In October 1980 when Joe Gormley, NUM president, was abroad, Mr McGahey was able to advise the miners' delegates on how not to vote on the Labour Party leadership. Mrs Shirley Williams, before leaving the Labour Party, said, 'I am bloody well not going to have the Communist Party in a situation where it can determine the leadership of the Labour Party.' In the event, the attempt at a last-minute delegation meeting at Blackpool town hall to persuade the miners, with their 244,000 votes to abstain, failed.

Early in December 1980 Mr McLennan made a further bid for closer relations with the increasingly left-wing Labour Party. He suggested in the *Morning Star* that a merger of both parties might be in prospect in the form of 'more developed forms of Labour-Communist unity, including the electoral field' and the 'possibility of future (Communist) affiliation to the Labour Party'.

The suggestion was rebuffed. John Cartwright, MP for Woolwich East and a former Labour Party national executive member, said, 'If there were any closer links between the Communist Party and the Labour Party, Labour would pay a very high electoral price.' Eric Heffer, chairman of the Party's organization committee, declared, 'It just isn't on. It's not a starter.' He had never heard of informal talks between Communists and some members of Labour's executive. 'I have never heard of any such talks, official or unofficial. Neither are there likely to be any. If there were unofficial talks, I would like to find out who was involved.' Norman Atkinson, left-wing MP for Tottenham and Party treasurer, said the only way the Communist Party could make itself organizationally acceptable to Labour was if it formed itself into a 'Fabian Society'.

These overtures, which continue, could be construed as a change of direction. The Communist Party has not won a parliamentary seat since post-war days. It has little appeal to youth, with membership of the Young Communist League down to 954. It loses 10 per cent of its membership every year, according to Mr McLennan, and although it needs to recruit between 2,000 and 3,000 annually to make up for natural wastage, only secures between 1,000 and 1,500. It acknowledges that persons join for quasi-religious reasons, a wish to change society and its injustices. But as with other religions, converts are fewer.

Apart from Jimmy Reid, apostates have included Sue Slipman, first woman president of the National Union of Students, who in February 1981 joined the Social Democrats. She gave as her reason for resigning from the Communist Party the 'sterile policies' of the Far Left. Despite being a CP member, Ms Slipman, an education officer of the National Union of Public Employees, had been regarded as a moderate left-winger who had dropped out of student politics in 1978. She said: 'For about the past three years, ever since I left the NUS, I have been more and more worried about the trends within the Left which I believe are moving towards more and more sterile policies, an approach which I do not feel is compatible with democracy. My politics have not changed – I have not become a right-winger.' Mr McLennan said that Ms Slipman, who joined the Party in 1969 and served on its executive for four years until 1979, had taken a wrong decision based on a mistaken understanding of the Party's aims. Others will think she was an honest woman.

The difficulties faced by the Communist Party in achieving general appeal, including the problem of a general ageing of stalwarts – the days of Claude Berridge, Joe Scott, George Caborn, Peter Kerrigan, J. R. Campbell and others have gone – led to a major ideological reassessment in 1979. In effect, it resulted in a major personal victory for Mick Costello, now in his mid-forties, successor to Bert Ramelson as national organizer.

Mr Costello is a likeable, honest, but formidable character. Son of a New Zealand diplomat, educated not only at a minor British public school but for five years in Moscow (he is a bi-lingual Russian speaker), he defeated Anna Ford for the presidency of Manchester University Students Union in the early 1960s. His concentration on political activities later led to him leaving without a degree. After being active in Communist student politics, he became industrial correspondent of the *Morning Star*. He again showed outstanding energy and ability. Mr Costello had a major ideological controversy with Dave Cook, Communist Party national organizer, both within the Party leadership, and in its theoretical journals, such as *Marxism Today*. In a major article in June 1979, headed 'The Working Class and the Broad Democratic Alliance', he argued that the Party should switch its emphasis from unsuccessful political work to concentration on industry, building factory branches, issuing a flood of union-orientated propaganda.

He said of Mr Cook: 'I should like to express sharp disagreement with him. . . . Comrade Cook's interpretation of the "new" puts it in contradiction with the "old" and would give the impression that the 1978 edition of the *British Road to Socialism* was the founding document of a new party that was writing off its roots in the labour movement.' Also, about 'workers' battles', that 'the importance of their battles is not appreciated by Comrade Cook'. Mr Costello went on in much lengthier Party jargon, but his basic argument, as he said, was: 'For Communists, agitation is a matter of winning workers to engage in struggle for demands which objectively advance the cause of the working class.'

Mr Costello won the ideological argument. The subsequent Party congress approved concentration on industry and building factory branches, including one at that bastion of capitalism, the *Financial Times*. It appointed younger officials, and a larger number of new executive members came from industry. The Broad Left alliance in the union movement, including the Engineering Workers (AUEW), the Electricians, the National Union of Seamen, the Construction Workers (UCATT) and among teachers and printers was strengthened. The Party was proud that Mr George Jerrom, an able union negotiator, became the first full-time Communist official of the key print union, the National Graphical Association. Derek Robinson, 'Red Robbo', of British Leyland,

Longbridge, was finally sacked, but his place as chief shop stewards' convenor was taken by Jack Adams, also a Communist. Further successes were registered in shipbuilding, the aerospace industry, steel, cars and road haulage, although the Party was badly hit by factory closures, lay-offs and the recession.

Mick Costello has his critics, both inside the Communist Party and outside. Some say he lacks the common touch of Bert Ramelson, a view I do not share. If I could hazard a prediction, I think Mr Costello will one day be the leader of the Communist Party of Great Britain.

On 17 July 1977, when ideological differences were reaching a peak, Sid French, secretary of the Party's Surrey district committee, announced the formation of the breakaway New Communist Party. It was regarded as Stalinist, after defending the Russian invasion of Czechoslovakia, opposing the Party leadership's condemnation of this action and calling for an end to defensiveness about the Soviet Union's actions against dissidents and more active participation in the world Communist movement. The New Communist Party published a pamphlet stating its case from 188, High Street, Colliers Wood, London sw19. It also began publication of the *New Worker*.

Nevertheless, the tribulations of the Party continue, not least in its finances and maintenance of the *Morning Star*. The Party has always denied receiving subsidies from Moscow. No one has ever been able to produce evidence, let alone prove it. As with possible foreign funding of other Far Left organizations, funding could be done with no proof being possible. All that would be necessary is a car or taxi-cab to collect a suitcase full of money.

But partly because of financial difficulties, and also because it was an inefficient rabbit-warren of an office, the Party sold its historic King Street headquarters in 1980. No details were published, although the deal was handled by a firm, Rodell Properties, whose directors included Tony Chater, editor of the *Morning Star*. But the price received for a valuable site, being redeveloped in 1981, was estimated at between one and two million pounds. The Party headquarters has since moved to Clerkenwell, a short walk from the *Morning Star* and the Marx Memorial Library.

The principal purpose was to raise capital to fund the paper and the industrial campaign more soundly. Sales of the *Daily Worker*, which it was once my duty to read at 7 pm every evening in 1956 to identify the latest defectors for publication in the *Daily Telegraph* next morning, were more than 100,000 in 1950. By 1962, circulation was down to 60,000, and by 1968 to 50,000. In 1981 sales in Britain of its successor, the *Morning Star*, are down to less than 20,000, plus another 14,600 copies sold abroad, almost all to the Soviet Union. There, apart from being the only British newspaper on general sale, it is distributed to schools and colleges for English language instruction. A plane-load leaves for Moscow every night.

According to *Morning Star* executives, these copies are paid for at normal commercial rates. But critical observers have wondered whether this is one way for Russia to subsidize the Communist Party. The paper, they say, has suffered deficits every year except in 1943, and no commercial undertaking could thus survive. What is true is that almost half the nightly print of the paper goes to the East bloc.

The *Morning Star* is published by a co-operative society and is nominally independent of Party control. In mid-1980 its finances began to be seriously undermined. It launched a special appeal for £80,000, which was achieved by July, to which trade unions contributed £20,000. The Transport Union, under the leadership of Moss Evans and on whose executive Communists had significantly increased in strength, made a controversial gift of £5,000. The National Union of Public Employees gave £3,000. Other contributions included: National Union of Mineworkers, £1,867; UCATT, £1,731; Engineering Workers, £1,129; TASS, £923; NALGO, £760; NUR-ASLEF£665; NATFHE (higher education teachers), £552. Other receipts including conference collections included: CPSA, £506; National Graphical Association, £425; Furniture Trades, £356; Seamen, £352; SOGAT, £352. But it was noted that rank-and-file collections were not so large. The big union gifts led to resignations and complaints. The total received from unions was only one-quarter of the target.

Despite this appeal, however, difficulties have continued. By the end of 1980, the *Morning Star*, which sought £10,000 a month from its 'fighting fund', now run by Peter Pink, was still hoping to avoid a £97,000 deficit, which had arisen despite raising the price to 16p, ending its eight-page edition and paying its journalists only £81 a week from which they made covenanted repayments.

In January 1981 the editor, Tony Chater, launched a fresh appeal to boost sales. He warned a special meeting of the Party's national executive that the paper was 'facing the most serious crisis in its history. At stake is the very survival of the paper.' Only an increase in sales of several thousand copies a day could save it. It was a mandate on which Communists had to succeed at all costs. The People's Press Printing

Society, nominal owners, had decided to seek quick economies of £50,000 following a fall in sales of 1,232 copies during 1980. These later included ending the second edition and raising the price to 20p. Mr McLennan, urging a campaign of meetings to boost sales, not only said that 8,000 Party members had not yet renewed their membership cards, but 1,000 of them did not read the Party paper.

But the tribulations of the *Morning Star* have continued. When the management committee announced on 20 February 1981 that the second edition would be suspended on 16 March, financial estimates showed that despite the price rise to 20p, the paper still faced a deficit for the year of £100,000. Ending the second edition, 'the biggest single saving that is immediately open', would save about £22,000. The monthly fighting-fund target was raised to £12,000. But sales continued to drift down.

Early in 1981 the Party launched a national appeal for another £75,000 during a five-week fund-raising campaign. On 26 March 1981 it announced that only £62,971.37 had been raised, £12,030 below the target, despite nine districts including London and the West of England having met their targets in full for the sixth year in succession. But further steps and economies would have to be considered. One economy was the closing in March, after sixty years, of *Labour Monthly*, the Party's Marxist journal once edited by Palme Dutt, a leading CP ideologist. 'Despite drastic economies and price rises to meet soaring costs, the financial problems have made closure unavoidable,' its editorial board stated.

On 8 June 1981 the People's Press Printing Society, in which nearly 30,000 individuals and organizations hold shares and of which share capital in 1980 totalled nearly £140,000, held its annual meeting. Tony Chater, editor, again warned: '... we have got to face the fact that the *Star* is confronting the most serious financial crisis in its history. Its continued existence is at stake. It needs an increase in daily sales of 3,000 copies to take it out of the danger zone.'

But sales continued to drop, with the danger of a 'catastrophic drop of a thousand or more by mid-August'. More shares had been taken out by the ASLEF executive, led by a Communist, Bill Ronksley, and the London NATSOPA machine branch. But the meeting heard that the overall loss of the Printing Society and the Morning Star Co-operative Society over the year was £140,652, reflected in the drop in reserves. Cuts included ending of the 'market', which sold such things as Russian radios, and a reduction of four in the editorial staff, which in 1980 comprised 30-40 journalists earning £81 a week, and 100 production workers on agreed union rates. It was hoped to save £50,000 in a full year. But by July there was speculation in Fleet Street that the *Morning Star* might be forced into weekly publication.

Other aspects of Communist activity deserve mention. It has always been strong on front organizations, until 1973 proscribed by the Labour Party. Since that ban on dual membership of Labour and Communist front organizations ended due to left-wing influence, that left-wing penetration has increased. The number of such organizations is large though not all are worthy of mention. Also noteworthy are those non-Communists who lend their names to such causes and whose names appear, too, as sponsors of a number of such organizations.

There is, for example, the Marx Memorial Library at Clerkenwell Green, an organization which played an active part in conversion of left-wing students at Cambridge University and elsewhere in the 1930s. Nothing more needs to be said about Burgess, Maclean, Blunt *et al*. The Marx Memorial Library has a close link with the Marxist–Leninist Institution in Moscow. It is run by a fifteen-member committee, the most important of whom are Communist Party members. In 1980 it launched an appeal, as a registered charity, for £50,000 to extend its premises to accommodate more than 20,000 books and 30,000 pamphlets and other reference works. Sponsors of the appeal included: Norman Atkinson, MP; R. Bellamy, lecturer at Leeds University; Lord Asa Briggs, Chancellor of the Open University; Ray Buckton, general secretary of ASLEF; Richard Clements, editor of *Tribune*; Lawrence Daly, general secretary of the NUM; Jonathan Dimbleby, television journalist; Douglas Grieve, then general secretary of the Tobacco Workers Union. Other notable sponsors were: Michael Foot, Opposition leader; Ken Gill, TASS general secretary, an avowed Communist and member of the TUC general council; George Guy, his Communist colleague who leads the Sheet Metal Workers; thirteen assorted professors, Stuart Hall; Royden Harrison; E. J. Hobsbawm, Arnold Kettle; Ralph Miliband; Joseph Needham; George Rude; John Saville; Brian Simon; E. P. Thompson; Raymond Williams; Bob Williamson, and Christopher Hill. MPs included: Neil Kinnock; Stan Newens; John Maxton; Joan Maynard; Dennis Skinner; and Stan Thorne. Also on the list was Lord Wedderburn, of London University and under the Labour Government, a much-used industrial arbitrator.

Most are not Communists, nor even Marxists. But they lend their names to perpetuating an institution linked to Marxism.

Another front organization is the so-called World Peace Council, which

Mr Attlee once condemned as an 'instrument of the Soviet Politburo'. It was first banned from Paris and then from Vienna, when the Austrians secured their neutrality. It is now based in Helsinki under the presidency of Romesh Chandra, an Indian Communist, supported by twenty-three vice-presidents. British supporters have again included Labour MPs and trade unionists.

Yet another Communist front organization which has enjoyed growing support is the self-styled Labour Research Department, not to be confused with the Labour Party. While some of its reports on capitalist undertakings are well done, it is not an independent research organization as its name might imply. The same names appear among its sponsors.

Nor would any account of the Communist Party of Great Britain be complete without a reference to ex-Communists. They are legion. They could well outnumber present Party members. They include Denis Healey, deputy Labour Party leader at the time of writing, who, however has long been opposed to the Far Left and now faces the challenge of Mr Wedgwood Benn. They also include Len Murray, TUC general secretary. And Lord Briginshaw, former general secretary of NATSOPA, who was asked by a QC in the early 1950s whether he really could not remember visiting Moscow about fifteen years earlier, and who, since being given a Life Peerage by Sir Harold Wilson, has dropped out of public life.

Indeed to list former members of the Communist Party would fill a double index of this book. They include prominent politicians, public servants, Fleet Street journalists and many others. But one thing they should know. They are all on a card index at Communist Party headquarters, just as all former members of the Nazi Party are on two indices, in West Berlin and Washington. No doubt they are also on other card indices.

One can only be glad never to have joined the Communist Party or the Young Communist League. Many are inclined to dismiss it as a youthful peccadillo, not to be taken seriously. But no doubt in Moscow, too, there is also a list of former comrades.

Finally, any discussion of Communist activity in Britain must also encompass the Russian connection.

The TUC still does not invite Russian 'fraternal delegates' to its annual conference. But there is always a strong Russian presence of both diplomats from the Soviet Embassy and journalists, not obtrusive but constantly on the move in the conference bars and in the headquarters hotel lobbies at night. Some are better than others at making contacts. The more convivial do very well. Clive Jenkins is unlikely to forget, although he took it in very good part at the time, the *Daily Telegraph* photograph of him in absorbed private conversation with Klimov, the Soviet labour attaché, who was among the hundred or so expelled from Britain in the early 1970s for being a KGB agent.

Over the years one recurrent Russian visitor has been Boris Averyanov, former head of the international section of the Soviet Trade Union Federation, but now based in Prague as a senior official of the Communist World Federation of Trade Unions. I must admit to having sorely persecuted Mr Averyanov on his annual visits to the TUC congress at Brighton or Blackpool. Not so much from malice, but as a joke, although British humour is unlikely to be appreciated in Moscow.

Some years ago, I arrived back at the Imperial Hotel in Blackpool at about 2 am in the company of a foreign diplomat. Sitting in the lobby with a beautiful Italian lady trade union leader, whom I had previously met in Brussels, was Mr Averyanov, a heavy, squat, bull-necked figure with a brush haircut. He looked like a character from James Bond. I was told he was really a KGB colonel, although it could not be proved. I suggested we have some fun, and join the foreign observers. I soon had a high respect for Mr Averyanov, who had travelled the world on behalf of Moscow, spoke perfect English and never stopped talking for forty minutes. He had sized us up, and we could hardly get a word in edgeways.

Next day I checked Mr Averyanov out with the TUC. He was only present as a self-invited observer. I was also informed that he visited the Scottish TUC and had been observed sitting at the head of a table of all the Communist delegates present. I put over a diary paragraph to the *Daily Telegraph*, but within twenty minutes had to make a minor correction. Subsequently, a friendly colleague informed me that Mr Averyanov had been following me and listened over my shoulder while I telephoned the correction. My professional respect increased.

Next evening things started to happen. Mr Michael Ivens, of what was then Aims of Industry, now simply Aims, a right-wing pressure group, issued a statement saying this alleged KGB colonel should be expelled from Britain. Every industrial correspondent except myself was called from the spare ribs of the Electricity Council to ask Mr Averyanov whether he was a KGB colonel, which he denied. Subsequently, in later years, we met again. In 1980, after the Soviet invasion of Afghanistan, a question arose whether Boris had applied for a British visa and whether it would be refused. He was given one, after some delay. Boris Averyanov will be back again. But by now, however much he and his British comrades protest that he is not a KGB officer but merely one of their observers (which is probably true), he is aware that his activities are watched.

In the end, the Communist Party will always be with us as a dedicated fighting-force. It has its trade union legionaries, its academics in influential professorships, its fellow-travellers, also, it has been alleged, its crypto-Communist members among Labour MPs, senior civil servants and elsewhere. It would be libellous today to name those who clearly support the Soviet cause, who are frequent guests at the Russian and other East bloc embassies. But by their sponsorships, support of appeals and speeches, they identify themselves. Were they Mosleyites, they would be subject to obloquy. There are many who loudly condemn, with justification, Far Right regimes, such as Chile and other juntas. But as has often been noted, they do not publicly criticize the Soviet Union. The Communist Party should not be overrated, but certainly never underestimated. That statement, as I know, will be warmly acclaimed by Communists themselves.

6 Finances

Finance, as much as fanaticism, is vital to the Far Left. It is the oil which keeps the all-important printing presses going, ensures production and distribution of propaganda, pamphlets, broadsheets and special bulletins, and maintenance of bookshops. It also provides subsistence when needed for comrades on picket lines, travelling expenses, staging of conferences and membership and affiliation fees for Labour Party and other fringe organizations.

When in money, Trotskyists and Communists are expected to contribute a tithe of their earnings, preferably by banker's order, and make other payments to the party and its causes. They have their perpetual fighting-funds and special appeals, a maw which is never satisfied. Their organizations are for ever proclaiming crisis or poverty. Yet when disaster seems imminent, and they seem to have suffered like everyone else from the economic recession with a reduction in cash flow, they suddenly recover funds and keep going, with cash for further expansion. Their total income, in fact, is substantial.

But what is mysterious – and it has puzzled all who have taken a close interest in Far Left funding – is, apart from supporters' contributions and constant fund-raising efforts, where all the money comes from. New printing plant and delivery lorries are purchased, new enterprises opened and others expanded, with evidence of the injection of large sums from undisclosed sources. Evidence on financial affairs, particularly of Trotskyists, is scant. There is widespread belief that some of the funds come from abroad, that there are other unidentified benefactors, or that money is kept outside the orthodox accounts. Certainly, with the exception of the Militant Tendency, most parties show no evidence of more than minimal profits, if not losses, and no receipt or flow of substantial funds. Nevertheless, the various factions keep going. Money seems an occasional short-term, but not long-term problem.

Take the Workers Revolutionary Party, which publishes the daily *News Line*. This is a highly professional production, the only daily Trotskyist paper, able to produce not only yesterday's news, but illustrate it with colour pictures, something still beyond Fleet Street with its old technology and infinitely larger circulations. On 10 August 1981 it raised its price to 12p, and 14p on Saturdays. Its predecessor, the *Workers Press*, the first Trotskyist daily paper, appeared for the first time on 27 September 1969 after almost five years' preparation. According to *News Line* eleven years later, 'We owe an enormous political debt to the Young Socialists. It was they, above all, who provided the political and financial muscle for the daily paper.' But in due course it ran into trouble. 'We will admit, however, to severe financial crisis early in 1976. . . . We were in danger of bankruptcy if we continued to lose money at the rate we were losing it. We had no choice but to close down *Workers Press* and fulfil our creditors and staff redundancy commitments. We admit to living through a few anxious weeks, but once again the Party (now the Workers Revolutionary Party) rallied its strength as never before, and on 1 May 1976 we appeared as a 16-page tabloid newspaper, the *News Line*.'

This was achieved by the quick establishment of a new printing firm, Astmoor Litho, Ltd, in a development area at Runcorn, Cheshire. It had a nominal share capital of £100 divided into five ordinary shares of £20 each, one held by Raymond Efford, the printer, one by David Bruce and three by Sheila O'Regan, both of Clapham. Directors were Mr Efford and Mr Bruce, who was also secretary and manager. Over the years, as its Companies House records show, it has operated only as a minor printing firm, with minimal profits. In 1979 the WRP again reported an 'acute financial crisis' developing at an 'alarming rate'. Its political committee announced in *News Line*: 'It is the worst we have experienced for well over a decade and unless prompt action is taken it will be necessary to reduce our full-time professional staff in addition to introducing cutbacks in areas of vital expenditure. We may have to cut back to 12 pages in *News Line*.

'Briefly the problems are as follows. The fourth congress of our Party meeting in February correctly decided to stand 60 candidates in the General Election incurring a total estimated expenditure of £100,000. So far we have received £52,000, leaving £48,000 still to come in. But meanwhile we have had to pay the total costs for the 60 candidates, hoping that in the near future the Fund will be completed.

'But such hopes have to be realized in hard cash and meanwhile we have had to borrow £35,000 at an exorbitant interest rate, leaving the balance of £13,000 for the Party to pay. In short we are in debt up to our eyebrows with our slender cash reserves totally depleted. Now to crown our difficulties the monthly *News Line* £4,000 Fund for May which should have been cleared first post by June 1 has fallen behind by £2,000.' The committee hoped this could be made up by the same day. 'We are confident our Party can swiftly overcome the financial crisis. . . .'

Within three weeks of the closing date, appeals stopped and only after a few months was successful conclusion announced. No explanation was given. But substantial contributions from individual members are made to WRP funds, apart from systematic area collections and, it is suggested, a levy of 15 per cent on members' net pay. In 1978 it was reported that Vanessa Redgrave was giving the Party a £40,000 film fee. Commenting on this in an attack on me, *News Line* said on 2 April 1981: 'He finds this quite shocking! [Not at all, then or now.] It is inconceivable to someone like Mr Baker that there are professional workers who believe in a political career and are willing to contribute towards it, sacrifice for it and perhaps even give their life for it.' In other words, *News Line* tacitly confirmed the contribution.

On 1 May 1980 the WRP launched a fresh £50,000 expansion fund, half to be raised by 31 May and the rest by 31 July. It had previously announced conclusion of a £30,000 fund on 31 March 1980, half of which was placed at the disposal of the Young Socialists for acquiring adequate premises for revolutionary youth centres. The remaining £15,000 went towards improving circulation, transport and distribution of *News Line*. Of the next £50,000, another £5,000 was earmarked for the Young Socialists, and £30,000 to buy 'three long-distance, eight-ton vehicles with specially-designed bodies for transporting and distributing *News Line* to our agents' network in different parts of the country. The cost for each vehicle on the road will be in the region of £10,000. They will be part of a fleet of six and will be incorporated into the mobile system of distribution which came into operation in our branches earlier this year. The final £15,000 will be handed over to the trustees of a special Education Memorial Fund to be launched towards the end of May. It will be in commemoration of important leaders of our party who have died over the past 30 years.' Names followed.

'The Education Memorial Fund will start with £15,000 and will be used for assisting Young Socialists and Workers Revolutionary Party cadres to undergo long-term basic educational training at our Marxist College of Education. It is hoped that the fund will eventually contain £20,000, which will be kept at this level each year by annual appeals. These proposals our readers can see are signs of the growing strength and political maturity of our party.'

By 4 August 1980 *News Line* was able to announce that the expansion fund had closed at £54,270.50, a 'splendid response' and 'surprise of surprises. . . . Magnificent, well done, comrades. It is important to understand that our Fund was an Expansion Fund and not money that is immediately used up in some Party or *News Line* deficit. *News Line*, to be sure, faces the rigours of almost runaway inflation. But up to date, we clear our commitments from sales revenue and the monthly Fighting Fund', despite having fallen behind that month.

'Immediately, our Expansion Fund is split three ways: £15,000 to the Robert Shaw Memorial Education Fund; £5,000 to the Revolutionary Youth Centres Campaign (which makes a total of £20,000 the Party has donated to this fund so far in 1980); £30,000 will be used in the purchase of three eight-ton vehicles for the transportation of *News Line* daily into the main areas. Here is *real expansion* and it could not come at a more appropriate time.'

In autumn 1980 the Party appealed for another £11,000 to finance colour printing equipment for *News Line*, now in operation to considerable effect. Early in 1981 the Party launched yet another development fund for £60,000. But there were growing signs that contributions to its monthly £4,000 fighting-fund target were flagging. Despite claims of increased sales, members were warned: 'The future of *News Line* is at stake. If our Fund does not arrive, we will be forced to put up our prices. ... To keep a colour edition every day needs extra resources. ...'

Despite all the fund-raising, speculation has persisted whether the Workers Revolutionary Party is subsidized by Arab money from Colonel Gaddafi, the Palestine Liberation Organization and other causes to which *News Line* gives such prominent publicity. In September 1980 Alex Mitchell, *News Line* editor, reviewing the history of *Workers Press*, which, he said, Tony Cliff, leader of the Socialist Workers Party, had wagered £500 would not appear, said: 'Then it was "mystery" money which made it possible. Later the "mystery money" became "Arab gold". All lies from beginning to end.'

In his book, *Left, Right; The March of Political Extremism in Britain*, John Tomlinson, a former Labour junior Foreign Office Minister, raising the same possibility when reviewing the funding of the WRP and other groups, states:

Nevertheless, it is difficult to see how many of these groups which often produce well-presented and voluminous publications on a regular basis could possibly finance their considerable efforts without equally considerable subsidies. The Workers Revolutionary Party, as has been noted, is the only party Left of centre in Britain, excluding the Communist Party but including the Labour Party, which is able to produce a daily paper. *News Line* is a sixteen-page tabloid with regular colour features which sells at 10p a copy. The chances of so ambitious a project financing itself are slender. But on the other hand, its unremitting idolization of Colonel Gaddafi and Yasser Arafat hints strongly at two possible sources of subsidy.

Less is known about the finances of some other groups, although they run a sizeable operation involving publishing houses, bookshops and distribution of their publications throughout the country. All this requires a large permanent staff and substantial funds which are clearly available despite periodic appeals pleading necessity.

For the November 1979 annual conference of the Socialist Workers Party, fees of £35 per delegate, one delegate per thirty members, were payable in advance by districts, not by the individual delegate. The money was to cover the registration fee, a pooled fare and loss of earnings. 'Fares will be paid, but comrades are asked to travel by the cheapest method possible, i.e. by car or bus. Loss of earnings will be rated at £12 a day for money actually lost. Where possible comrades are asked to take days' holiday with pay.'

A pre-conference financial report was given by John Larkham, treasurer, under the heading, 'Finance – Arming Ourselves for the Struggle'. Mr Larkham said the rapid increase in inflation and the need for an increase in national political propaganda 'presents problems for the central financing of the organization'. Not only were they faced with quite steep increases for telephones and printing costs, but would have to 'sharply increase the amount, and improve the quality of the propaganda we produce. At the same time, some of the machinery at our print-shop is in need of replacement. The most urgent requirement is the purchase of new type-setting equipment to replace the worn-out, breakdown-prone machinery that we bought four years ago.'

Mr Larkham announced the launching of a £10,000 appeal, to be completed by the end of the year, for these main purposes. 'We need to pay the deposit on the £20,000-worth of type-setting equipment that we so urgently require.' Regular breakdowns had caused some *Socialist Worker* articles to be type-set by outside companies 'at a lot of expense and inconvenience. Because of the way in which the print-shop helps to subsidize the costs of our publications charging minimal costs for party printing, it inevitably means that the print-shop's finances cannot always stretch to the replacement of machinery.' Mr Larkham added that much of the SWP rank-and-file propaganda was produced by their second, smaller print-shop S.W. Printers, who had in the past produced *Rank and File Teacher* pamphlets and Anti-Nazi League leaflets, as well as badges and stickers. This firm, too, needed new equipment, but has, in fact, since gone into liquidation. Remaining funds would make possible a 'marked increase in our national propaganda' with regular production of national posters and leaflets.

On raising the money, Mr Larkham was more specific. Each branch and district would be set a target. Collection sheets would be issued before October 1979 when income-tax rebates were due. It should be possible for some comrades to take workplace collections in the week the rebate was paid. 'Many members will receive in excess of £70 refund – some will be able to give a lot and others perhaps only a few pounds. With the ideal opportunity presented by the rebate, we should be aiming to raise a substantial proportion of the target in the week in which it is paid.' Other steps included a national raffle, fund-raising parties, 'socials' and Christmas bazaars, 'which can raise a lot of money when properly organized'. Branches should book halls well ahead.

Mr Larkham then turned to contributions and tithes on members' earnings. It was over a year, he said, since reintroduction of a system of subscription payments 'based on a sliding-scale of earnings and paid, wherever possible, by banker's order to the national Party account. The result of the change has been to increase and stabilize the resources of the party, particularly because of the banker's orders, which virtually guarantee a set amount of money at the beginning of every month.' But since then, earnings of most comrades would have risen without them necessarily having increased their banker's order or weekly subs in line with their wages. 'It is very important that comrades re-assess what they should be paying in national subs. All treasurers have been issued with special forms which allow comrades to increase their existing banker's order.' They would also provide the necessary form to make a banker's order if they did not have one.

Mr Larkham also gave a table of desired contributions for 'single comrades with no unusual financial commitments'. This ranged, for the lowest paid, from a monthly contribution by banker's order of £1.40 for those with weekly take-home pay of under £30, rising to £10 for those taking home £56–60 a week, £20 for those between £71 and £80 a week, and for those between £91 and £100 a week no less than £40 a month. These are very substantial contributions to demand from a member of a political party – of the order of 10 per cent of net earnings – which no church, for example, would realistically expect save from the most devout.

Mr Larkham made a last, and, ironic for a Trotskyist, appeal: 'Finally, it was mentioned in a National Secretary's letter last month that occasionally a comrade has had the misfortune of inheriting money/stocks/shares etc and that we ask these comrades to contact the National Office with the view to a meaningful relationship.'

From these observations, and taking into account that many SWP members are middle-class academics or professional people earning relatively high salaries, quite apart from good earnings in industry, it seems clear that the Socialist Workers Party has an assured, regular high income by banker's order from its 3,000 or so members. Tony Cliff is himself believed to have been wealthy on arrival in Britain. Despite Socialist Worker Printers being compulsorily wound up in 1977 and its successor, the Larkham Press, making losses, the SWP does not seem seriously deterred by any shortage of finance.

Other Trotskyist groups experience passing financial difficulties or make special appeals. In mid-1980 the International Marxist Group, also a substantial organization with its own printing, publishing and sales facilities, asked for £6,000 for an emergency fund to cover the cost of leaflets, bulletins and organizers during the steel strike. The Workers Socialist League launched a special fund of £3,000. Most Trotskyist publications in any case attract practically no commercial advertising revenue.

For some smaller groups, the cost of agitation is considerable. *Socialist Organiser* 'Info 9' reported on finance: 'The delegate meeting heard that although the inflow of paper money has improved a bit, and so has the inflow of supporters' contributions, practically no money is coming in from fund-raising. We budgeted for £500 a month from fund-raising. So we're in real difficulties!

'Don't just think of fund-raising in terms of big events like jumble sales or Christmas bazaars (though we should have those too). A comrade from Glasgow reported that he had had much more response than he expected when he made [*sic*] a collecting tin to use when selling the paper. Even people who would not buy the paper would give a small contribution. Comrades everywhere else can do that without a huge extra effort. You can ask regular *SO* readers for donations. And please take a collection every time you have a meeting.'

Socialist Organiser 'Info 11' of 23 December 1980 painted a blacker picture. 'We are in a bad way. We budgeted for £500 a month from fund-raising and £500 from supporters' contributions. In fact we have got about £100 or £200 from supporters' contributions and practically nothing from fund-raising. Most supporters are being very slow and unreliable about sending in their contributions. In addition, a lot of local groups are building up sizeable debts for their paper sales money.

'It has now come to the point of a real crisis – just at the same time as we have to bear a lot of extra expenditure for the Longbridge struggle. So: (a), We are asking for a voluntary levy of £5 a head from SO supporters to get over the immediate crisis; (b), We are asking local SO groups to open group bank accounts and get a regular standing order for their supporters' contributions.' An International Communist League bulletin, incidentally referred to a separate bulletin outlining the financial position of S*. All comrades had a special responsibility to take a leading role in helping it.

A further appeal in *Socialist Organiser* of 10 January 1981 said a special broadsheet had been rushed out at Longbridge, meetings had been called, and comrades from other areas had gone there to help. 50,000 leaflets were printed for distribution throughout the country. 'All this has cost money – a lot of money. And at a time when *Socialist Organiser* funds were running very low anyway. The effort had to be made – and we have made it. But only at the cost of a severe financial crisis. *Socialist Organiser* is now running on borrowed money.' Total cost of producing another new *Socialist Organiser* pamphlet aimed at gaining new recruits was about £600, which also added to the crisis. But if each SO supporter took six, 'we will break even on it', and if it were twelve, selling eleven a head, 'we will make £450 profit'.

As with other Trotskyist organizations, *Socialist Organiser*, the publication, masks a rapidly developing organization of 'supporters' and readers committed to entryism in the Labour Party and trade unions. It appears at times to be further Left than the Militant Tendency. Other Trotskyists, such as Alan Thornett, of the Workers Socialist League, and Sean Matgamna, of the International Communist League, feature regularly in *Socialist Organiser* pages.

But most interesting and puzzling of all, since they are registered at Companies House, are the finances of the Militant Tendency as contained in the accounts of the Cambridge Heath Press, printer and publisher of *Militant*, and WIR Publications, which is the funding company. Affairs of both companies overlap.

In his letter to the Labour Party executive, quoted in full in Chapter

2, Peter Taaffe, editor of *Militant*, said it was funded exclusively from contributions from supporters in the labour movement, received no money whatsoever from 'sinister sources', either in Britain or abroad, had never received funds from Russia and had no revenue from commercial advertising. Money came from sales, a 'relatively small income from commercial printing, fund-raising activities and the *Militant* "fighting fund", which raised over £47,000 in 1977, £66,000 in 1978 and £80,000 in 1979'. Finally, *Militant* benefited from a series of loans from WIR Publications to the Cambridge Heath Press, which totalled £148,500 from 1975 to 1978.

The two separate companies, Mr Taaffe added, were 'set up on advice from lawyers and accountants. This arrangement was considered to be in the best interest of the thousands of workers who contribute their pennies and pounds.' He continued: 'WIR Publications, Ltd acts as a "collecting box". As its Memorandum of Association states, the company exists "to aid and further the interests of the international working class", and its income is derived solely from the donations of active members of the Labour Party and trade unions who, in addition to occasional donations to the 'Militant' Fighting Fund, are prepared to make regular contributions to develop the support for Marxist policies within the labour movement.

'The accounts of both Cambridge Heath Press, Ltd and WIR Publications, Ltd are prepared, audited by chartered accountants, and deposited in accordance with company law at Companies House, where they may be inspected by members of the public.'

Full accounts of both companies since their inception in 1973 have been subjected to detailed analysis by other chartered accountants. These analyses show over the years changes in accounting policy, which were legitimate, discrepancies from time to time, and from year to year in the accounts of each, and both when compared with each other, and other obscurities. These cover the sources of income; when, from a calculation of bank interest received, it came in; whether cash was held in outside bank accounts; loans by WIR Publications not immediately obvious in the accounts and not, apparently, to Cambridge Heath Press; and donations received and given. Although this is not required under company law, there is no indication of how much was spent on payments to full-time or other staff, or other items of running expenditure. I must also emphasize that there is no suggestion whatever of improper auditing by the firm involved, who have themselves expressed reservations to which I will refer.

One analysis of the accounts was made for Charles James, a Labour lawyer, who first drew attention to oddities in Militant Tendency finances, but before Mr Taaffe's letter and before more became known, for instance, about the £148,500 loans by WIR Publications to Cambridge Heath Press. Another was made by a chartered accountant of the *Daily Telegraph* early in 1981 from a full copy of all accounts for my series of articles in March–April.

While differing on some details, they agree on essentials. Mr James pointed out that although Cambridge Heath Press did not start trading until 1 April 1973, it was incorporated in 1971 when it was already publishing *Militant* with a capital reserve of £6,279. From its trading figures, including bank interest received of £350, he deduced it had much more bank interest in its account at the beginning of the year than indicated from trading figures. My accountant did not agree with this, but had other things to say about bank interest in later years.

Mr James raised questions over the legality and nature of £6,140 donations paid in the first year. Although the company said these were part of a fund-raising scheme, and therefore not political, such a scheme was not mentioned in *Militant* at the time. Figures on donations made and received in the public accounts were also wrong from information given by the accountants.

Mr James queried how *Militant*'s presses were destroyed in a fire in February 1975 and replaced quickly after an appeal at a cost of £6,547. In fact, this item appears in WIR accounts, but not in those of Cambridge Heath Press. So presumably the presses are owned by WIR and not Cambridge Heath.

Substantial donations were received by WIR Publications, incorporated in June 1973 with initial capital of £7,113. These amounted to £18,079 in 1973–4; £30,332 in 1974–5; £42,112 in 1975–6; £60,802 in 1976–7; and £77,738 in 1977–8. Mr James comments: 'The published donations in *Militant* exceed the actual donations, but not by enough to account for income at this level. ... So where does the money come from?' He asks whether there could be a secret organization with branches in the constituencies. In fact, as I have made clear in the chapter on the Militant Tendency, it is now obvious that such an organization exists, which both costs money but also raises it.

Mr James said close links between *Militant* and similar newspapers in seven other countries was an indication of an Internationale. In either case, membership of such an organization or of a secret organization in Britain was a disqualification for Labour Party membership. He again suggested that in 1974 not all the income of WIR Publications and Cambridge Heath Press was kept in the bank accounts of either company, but somewhere else until late in the financial year. 'Someone was holding Militant's money who was neither Cambridge Heath Press, Ltd. nor WIR Publications, Ltd.,' Mr James concluded. From a statement by Clare Doyle, company secretary of both firms, on 7 January 1977, he again suggests that money was coming from readers in an organization in the constituencies whose donations were not declared in *Militant*.

Let us turn to my accountant, who is perhaps more illuminating. He stated that long and careful scrutiny of the full accounts of both WIR Publications and Cambridge Heath Press revealed no accounting irregularities, and indeed, the audit certificates provided by the accountants involved must be regarded as *prima facie* evidence of correct accounting treatment and compliance with the law.

Cambridge Heath Press, he found, was entirely dependent on WIR for funds and would otherwise face bankruptcy. There was no evidence in the accounts to suggest where WIR obtained its funds. But one important feature emerged from an analysis of bank interest.

In 1973-4, for example, the net WIR cash inflow, assumed to be mainly from donations, amounted to £17,000, which had it been received uniformly over the year could at current rates have earned £850 interest. But interest received amounted to only £169, with £163 payable. Perhaps internal accounting and administration were remarkably poor, but otherwise, it suggested that the bulk of donations was received late in the year. If they were in fact so received and not uniformly over the year, it could imply only one or two generous 'benefactors'. Similar reasoning would apply to subsequent years. So, was a large lump sum given by some unknown source late in the financial year? In any case, the source remains unknown.

Mr Taaffe also informed the Labour Party that total loans from WIR to Cambridge Heath totalled £148,500 in 1975-8. This was not so. The total, as can be worked out from the accounts, was £215,466. By January 1980 they were substantially higher at £284,666, following another £69,000 loan, and will be still higher since, bringing the total to well over £300,000.

Further odd facts emerge from expert scrutiny of the accounts. Not immediately obvious in those of WIR are two further loans, of £40,077 in 1977-8 and £26,900 in 1978-9, which do not appear in Cambridge Heath accounts for those years. To whom they were granted remains a mystery. My accountant noted that £40,077 was a decidedly odd amount for a loan, rather than a round figure. Could it, he wondered, be the exchange figure for a sum of foreign currency? This loan was also not specifically declared in the 1978 accounts but was included under the total of 'Debtors and Pre-payments'. It was also not mentioned in the directors' report, although this did note that the additional long-term loan had increased by £50,000. The £40,077 loan first became apparent in the 1979 accounts by way of a revision of the previous year's comparative figures. A similar disclosure was recorded in the 1978-9 accounts for the £26,900.

In 1975-6 there was a change of accounting policy of Cambridge Heath Press on the treatment of donations. It meant that the comparative figures for 1974-5 were revised to show a loss not of £28,792, but of £8,102. The reason was that the loan of £20,690 which had been included as an adjustment to the profit-loss account was now being used to reduce the trading loss. The effect was to distort the trading figures and show a marked increase in the trading loss in 1975-6. Not only was this a variation on the previous year's treatment, it was inconsistent with the treatment of donations in the WIR accounts. There, they continued to be incorporated in the balance sheet, or 'below the line' in the profit-loss accounts.

The loans made by WIR to Cambridge Heath, totalling £284,666 in January 1980, and higher since, were made interest-free until 1 April 1986. In 1977, 1978 and 1979, commenting on the annual loan, the accountants involved added the rider to their report: 'We consider that this loan may be irrecoverable and that a provision should have been made in full for this in the profit and loss account. No provision has been made as the directors are of the opinion that the loan will be ultimately recoverable.' Subject to this reservation, they were of the opinion that the accounts gave a 'true and fair state of the affairs of the company' and complied with the Companies Act 1948.

Whether the loans could ever be recoverable seems doubtful, since Cambridge Heath, through which the Militant Tendency's staff are presumably paid, has practically no assets and makes losses. In March 1980 there was a further interesting development, when Cambridge Heath received a mortgage from WIR, a 'floating charge' on all assets and property, securing all monies due on any account whatsoever. The total indebtedness covered then was £284,666. It is noteworthy that at March 1979, total assets of WIR amounted to only £11,000. The purpose of the mortgage covering contingent liability was not clear. But a libel writ was issued against Cambridge Heath in July 1979, which it believed it could successfully defend. Even so damages and or costs could have proved a heavy burden beyond its ability to carry.

All these observations about the Militant Tendency's finances can be backed up by detailed figures for each year from the registered accounts.

What is clear is that it has a considerable income estimated at £200,000 a year. Its members and employees are expected to pay or repay a tithe on their earnings, which in the third quarter of 1978 averaged £1.17 a week, against an average of £1.22 in 1977. Contributions are sought by banker's order or debit to a holding fund. In 1980 the *Militant* fighting fund reached a total of £93,849. For 1981 the target was set of £120,000, half of it by 11 July, with specific targets set for each area – again a sign of systematic fund collection with an organization to back it. A table is published weekly in *Militant*, with eighteen named areas and more unspecified. On 26 June 1981 *Militant* announced that with only two weeks to go to its 12 July fighting-fund target of £60,000, only £39,569 had been raised. It appealed to readers to set something apart from their holiday bonus for the fund. The pressure of the Militant Tendency's fund-raising is relentless.

Militant itself is run as cheaply as possible. It has much unpaid help in despatch and sales, and pays low wages. Nevertheless, it is a considerable operation, running rallies, Marxist schools, publishing numerous Trotskyist pamphlets and selling them from its World Books shop at Mentmore Terrace, as well as an *International Review*.

Several hundred thousand pounds have flowed into the Tendency through WIR Publications then out of it through Cambridge Heath Press with almost nothing in the accounts of either company to show where it came from or how it was spent. Certainly it is not kept in their bank accounts, beyond a working minimum. Presumably it goes on the widespread agitation which has brought the Militant Tendency such power and influence in the labour movement.

As Lord Underhill, noting numerous references in the Tendency's minutes to fund-raising efforts and appeals, has observed, members also belong to the Labour Party. 'Money is raised through Militant which is drawn from Labour Party and trade union organizations, and is therefore lost to the Labour Party.' In contrast, the Labour Party in 1979, with 130 full-time workers, about double those of *Militant*, received £1,800,000 in official union affiliation fees, but only £300,000 from individual members and other sources. In 1981 it again faced a severe financial crisis, being practically broke, and facing the prospect of starting from scratch to raise the funds to fight the next general election.

With both the Militant Tendency and other larger Trotskyist organizations, the question remains: where does all the money come from, whatever the explanations? It has proved virtually impossible to establish facts by the many who have tried. But there is a wide range of theories based on evidence available.

Some money is believed to come from the United States from Trotskyist organizations there. About 1971, the British port employers found evidence that dock strikes were being financed by American Trotskyist money, and made representations through the British embassy in Washington in an attempt to stop it. Then there is the suspicion of Arab funding, so angrily denied by the Workers Revolutionary Party despite its daily espousal of Arab causes. According to Western intelligence sources, the United Arab Emirates, in particular, maintain secret bank accounts in Switzerland from which Arab activities and publications, at least, are funded. It is normal for anyone, be it only by a charitable banker's order, to contribute to a cause with which one is sympathetic. Also to answer special appeals.

Another theory is that in the past, cash has come from Sri Lanka, a strong Trotskyist centre. Yet another suspicion has been that money has come from or via South Africa, possibly through black liberation movements. Another, again, is that help has been received from West Germany, via the JUSOS, but with its origin in East Germany, and before that stage, the Soviet Union. Trotskyist organizations scorn, from ideological reasons, suggestions of 'Moscow gold'. But such reasons are unlikely to deter the Russians where disruptive activities in the West can be furthered. Indeed, John Tomlinson asserted in his book that at the end of January 1980, the KGB sent a top specialist agent from Paris to infiltrate the Militant Tendency to protect it as far as possible from damaging exposure. The Trotskyists can be taken care of when the day comes.

It seems clear, however, that one way or another, plenty of cash is available, however passing the crisis. As the *Daily Telegraph* aptly commented, 'Always in the Red, But Never Broke'.

7 Unions

The trade union movement has always been a prime field of Far Left activity. Involvement by the Trotskyists and their sympathizers, which is increasing, is a relatively new development over the last ten to fifteen years. The commitment of the Communist Party, a more disciplined and experienced organization, goes back much further.

A generation ago, when I was young, there was fierce opposition to the Communists, who were regarded by old-fashioned Labour and TUC stalwarts as the main enemy. They were barred from office in a number of unions, including the Transport and General Workers and NATSOPA. The triumvirate of Arthur Deakin, TGWU, following on in the tradition of Ernie Bevin, Will Lawther, the viking-like leader of the Mineworkers, and Tom Williamson, of the General and Municipal Workers, maintained a rigid barrier against them. The TUC general council was barred to Communist membership. There were able and likeable Communists, more devoted to their unions and members than the Party. There was, for instance, Joe Scott, of the AEU, as it then was, who died aged eighty-one in June 1981. But the ban remained. It was relaxed in the early 1960s when Will Paynter, also of the Mineworkers, and an honest man who commanded respect, was admitted to the TUC general council. He has been followed by others, Ken Gill of TASS, the Technicians' union, and George Guy, of the Sheet Metal Workers. The TGWU also ended its ban on Communists holding office, and since then the Party's influence has grown, with several members on its executive and a significant say in policy.

A ban on Communists holding office still continues in the Electricians' Union (EEPTU), which they controlled through ballot rigging and corruption twenty-five years ago. But the battle to regain influence continues. The Far Left still fights in the unions in an uneasy alliance with the 'Broad Left', which can mean different things in different unions. A prime and constant activity is the quick exploitation of disputes. Much is known about this already, but it is instructive to read what the Trotskyists particularly have had to say for themselves, though this is written largely for private consumption.

In October 1979 the central committee of the Socialist Workers Party gave a review of 'Industrial Perspectives' for members only. 'Workers' power', it declared, 'is in the workplace. That is why we are obsessed with building the SWP in the workplace. ... For us the trade unions are the most important working class organizations with which we have to struggle for influence and leadership.'

Predicting that unions' leaders would not demonstrate the 'same naked class collaboration' as they had done under Labour with the social contract and 'concordat', the central committee nevertheless predicted continuing fraternization and vacillation. However right the SWP might have been about this, the unions have not succeeded under Mrs Thatcher. Even left-wing leaders, however, the central committee thought, while wanting to see the back of the Tory government, believed that parliament and the Labour Party (hopefully led by Mr Wedgwood Benn) was the mechanism for change. 'We must support all action that Scargill, Benn, Fisher, Evans, etc. might initiate against the Tories. But at the same time we have to make clear their political inability to lead an all-out fight. . . . In fighting the Tory Government we shall be continually stressing rank and file self-reliance, and why we cannot trust the trade union leaders. . . .'

The central committee also noted that shop stewards' organization, after scoring past successes, had been seriously undermined. But strikes by public sector workers, bakers, journalists and lorry drivers had shown that 'the class' had not yet been defeated. Even so, partly due to the control of the right-wing Engineering Union executive, 'the traditional Broad Left has collapsed as a national force. . . .'

Problems to be faced included lack of systematic work on the shopfloor. During the next twelve months, 'industrial work must become the obsession of each member of the Party – students, unemployed, lecturers etc. etc. A local strike must be considered more important than a local Nazi march.' Despite some successes in various strikes, 'our strike interventions are still too slow off the mark. We still "miss" too many strikes. Every strike represents another group of workers more open to our rank and file trade union advice on "how to win" *and* to socialist politics. Ten minutes on a picket line and the conversation soon ranges from how to get wood for the brazier to what role the TUC are playing, to what bastards the Tories are, how serious the crisis, inflation and socialism. A strike missed is an opportunity gone forever – workers learn more and become more open-minded in two weeks of picketing than in twenty years of passive work routines.'

Conclusions were:

1. There is no room for a small group of experts [*sic*] to be the only ones to go near a picket line. With so many places to cover, every comrade must be involved.

2. Every member must be involved (including students, teachers, lecturers, unemployed) in working systematically round a particular workplace – selling *Socialist Worker*, producing bulletins, visiting shop stewards and militants so that even if they will never join the SWP we slowly build up a relationship of trust with some of the best workers inside. For the majority of our members this work must become a priority. In every branch we must win the argument that laying the foundations for expanding our industrial strength is more important than chasing the National Front....

3. Individual branches, *not just district committees*, must take responsibility for work around workplaces and strike interventions....

4. Individual branches, *and not just district committees*, must take responsibility for monitoring the network of contacts and sympathetic trade union bodies we can pull round to us through strike solidarity work, Code of Conduct, RTW, R&F Papers, working inside the local trades council etc....

Students must be involved in industrial work. But this doesn't mean abandoning systematic work in the colleges, or abandoning SWP branches in the colleges.... Student support for strikes, local picket lines etc. can help us in the colleges. All student members will need to sell *Socialist Worker* at a factory or workplace each week as part of general drive by the Party to establish new bases in workplaces where we have no members. More than that, students can play a more active role in the Right to Work Campaign....

Some years ago, the SWP published a lengthy pamphlet co-ordinated by Peter Robinson, 'A Guide to Workplace Bulletins'. It is an illuminating publication giving fifteen pages of how to agitate on the shopfloor. It followed a 'national school' to teach agitators how to write and distribute such bulletins. There is highly professional advice: 'How the Shop Stewards react to Bulletins'; 'How to argue back'; 'Confronting the Stewards'; 'Shop Stewards Elections – Throw Them Out'; 'Avoiding Victimization'; 'Personal Insults'; 'Self Praise'; 'Beware of the Rule Book'; 'Management–Union Collusion'; 'Rules of the Thumb'; and much other practical advice on how to produce a bulletin, including how to avoid dismissal by being humble or obstructionist; being careful of rumours; and technical advice on stencils, good typing and types of paper.

Recommending the guide-book the central committee said, 'The bulletin is our organized link with hundreds of workers in a factory.... The bulletin became the centre of the work-in and then of the lockout. . . . It became our weapon for leading the fight-back against the management.'

The Socialist Workers Party deserves mention for other intervention and activity on the labour and industrial front. It is active in Fleet Street, both through journalists and print workers. Former members of the International Socialists include John Palmer, European editor of the *Guardian*, Alix Palmer, formerly of the *Sun*, now a contributor to the *Daily Star*, and Barbara Dalziell, of the *Financial Times*, till recently lay secretary of the Central London branch of the NUJ. Other like-minded Trotskyists include Aidan White, a skilled sub-editor on the *Guardian*, and formerly a Trotskyist activist both on the executive of the NUJ and on London suburban newspapers. Paul Foot, an expellee, is a *Daily Mirror* columnist and Campaigning Journalist of the Year. There are other Trotskyist SWP members among print workers, on the *Sun* and the *Daily Mirror*. As often as not, when serious losses of production occur over some relatively trivial dispute involving highly paid print workers – many of whom earn far more than doctors or MPs, or even junior Ministers – one hears later that a leading role was played by the local Trot. Trotskyist journalists are not only prominent in the leadership of the National Union of Journalists and Fleet Street, but also in the Book and Magazine branches. Not to mention suburban and provincial branches. Another leading official of the NUJ who may be deemed among the Far Left, although he does not bear any political label, is Ron Knowles, editor of the union's paper, *The Journalist*. His editing has led to frequent controversy with allegations of political bias, omission and one-sidedness, which he has consistently denied.

But the Socialist Workers Party is also extremely active in the Civil Service, particularly through the 240,000-strong Civil and Public Services Association, the largest Civil Service union comprising lower- and middle-grade clerical staff, and for twenty-five years a battleground between the left and right wings and moderates. As the 1981 pay dispute demonstrated, militant control of the union could, at the least, severely disrupt the mechanics of government. According to Peter Sloman, its secretary, the SWP Civil Service fraction has a total of 120 members, most in the CPSA, but others in the 107,000-strong Society of Civil and Public Servants, into which CPSA members, including some noted militants, graduate through professional promotion, and in the 67,000-strong Inland Revenue Staff Federation. In the CPSA, the Socialist Workers Party backs *Redder Tape*, the Far Left alternative to the union's official *Red Tape* journal, while in the other two unions, bulletins are issued every two months.

In summer 1980 the CPSA became involved in a dispute over two of its members at Brixton unemployment benefit office, Philip Cordell, then twenty-six, and Richard Cleverley, twenty-seven, who were both also SWP members. The 'Brixton Two' were sacked for allegedly taking unauthorized time off for union activities. They were subsequently reinstated after a Civil Service Appeal Board finding that they were wrongfully dismissed – dismissal was too severe a penalty – but with a recommendation that they be posted to another office without payment for time suspended, work under strict supervision and be warned that further 'misconduct' could result in dismissal. To this they agreed. Transfer of five other staff, including three supervisors, was also sought by the Employment Department, because of objections by staff remaining to working with them.

But this affair provided the SWP with an opportunity for intervention in a dispute on a large scale. During the prolonged unofficial strike, mass picketing took place outside the Brixton office, which resulted in eighteen arrests, and a police limit on no more than six pickets. John Deason, a member of the SWP central committee and organizer of the Right to Work Campaign, admitted that many of the leading activists who helped organize the mass picketing were SWP members. 'We are not ashamed of this involvement,' he said. 'Indeed, we expect our members to behave in such a manner in any and every trade dispute. We believe that working-class interests are only advanced through mass struggle, and that the necessity to beat the Tories on the picket line is for the moment our prime objective.'

Two Labour MPs, Reg Race (Wood Green), former research chief of the National Union of Public Employees, and Stuart Holland (Vauxhall), also played a prominent part at Brixton, leading a march in protest against police curbs on pickets. Subsequently, Kenneth Thomas, CPSA general secretary, issued a circular to his 240,000 members. In it, he blamed the SWP and its 'offshoots' for being largely responsible for the angry Brixton scenes. The union's official machinery, he said, had been misused during the dispute which resulted in the 'calculated and callous exploitation of a trade union issue by a small faction'. Mr Thomas continued, 'On this occasion there was absolutely no justification for prolonged and bitter unofficial action. It split the union; it could have endangered our objectives and was subsequently exploited by some whose trade unionism is suborned by their political aims.'

Mr Thomas also accused those who took part in the action as being 'in the game of political martyrdom. Over the years I have respected and enjoyed the friendship and sometimes shared the aims of many Civil and Public Services Association people on the Left. But there is within this union the dafter end of the political spectrum whom we have tolerated, initially with amusement, but in recent years, because of our toleration, they have increasingly and totally unrepresentatively misused the machinery of this union as a result of which our name has sometimes been a joke in the trade union movement. For once therefore let us not mince words. The Socialist Workers Party and its officials, certainly in the latter weeks, have been largely responsible for the Brixton affair.' Mr Thomas also attacked the Left-backed Brixton Unemployment Benefit Office Campaign for Trade Union Rights, saying they 'bamboozled money out of our members and branches, trading cheaply on natural trade union loyalty for the underdog'. He urged the union to 'grow up and stop indulging in school-boy politics'.

Mr Thomas, who was attacked by the SWP and Mr Deason for his plain-speaking circular, also wrote to Mr Race, demanding an explanation why, as a former union official, he did not have the courtesy to inform the CPSA of his plans to join the 'unofficial and politically-inspired action'. Mr Holland, apart from being attacked by Tory Ministers, was condemned by Len Murray, TUC general secretary, for his involvement. Mr Murray said, 'Interference in industrial relations issues from Labour MPs or anyone else, without consulting the union concerned, is neither welcome nor productive.' Confirming that he was referring to Mr Holland, he added after a meeting of the TUC's employment and policy committee which had criticized the intervention, 'He appears to have been in touch with some political elements involved in the dispute, but made no effort to consult the union concerned.'

Among SWP claims of success were the use of a striker's flat as a headquarters with telephones permanently manned, production of thousands of leaflets and a tour of the country by a number of Brixton strikers to seek rank-and-file support by addressing over two hundred meetings. Several thousand pounds were collected from the CPSA and many other trade unions, Civil Service and industrial.

Despite Mr Thomas' concern, however, the SWP national committee, in an internal document of the same period, was not too happy about its lack of progress in the CPSA, where Mrs Kate Losinska, its redoubtable president, Charlie Elliott, Bradford vice-president, and other moderates had regained control and introduced postal balloting. As has been demonstrated in the Engineering Union, there is no greater setback for the Far Left than the secret postal ballot which nullifies the old tactic of entryism, packing meetings and staying until all moderates have gone, if they were there in the first place.

The SWP leadership conceded that a year earlier 'we were feeling optimistic about the growth of the rank and file group in the Civil Service. There were a number of local Redder Tape groups with their own bulletins and activities. The Redder Tape conference in June was well attended and two weeks later the Defend Our Unions Conference produced an excellent response from Civil Servants – with some 150 delegates – nearly 15 per cent of the total. But our expectations have not been borne out.' There had been a 'number of serious defeats'. The Broad Left had suffered from complacency. There had been a 'schizophrenic situation', resulting in a Cuts Campaign Conference initiated by Redder Tape being 'not a great success'. Membership 'declined markedly – the SWP branches in Hackney, South London, Manchester and Birmingham were folded up. . . . The behaviour of the Broad Left executive had been appalling. . . . The BL seemed to learn nothing. They sailed blindly on into the new year. . . .' Further criticism was expressed of the 'Socialist Caucus', comprising the International Marxist Group, International Communist League, Workers Socialist League and Revolutionary Communist Tendency.

Pulling itself together, however, the SWP national committee urged fresh action. '*We* should organize for a co-ordinated response to the pay conference. We should think about how to campaign to make certain it happens, moving resolutions throughout the union, and then trying hard for some form of agreement about what we want to see from it. . . .' Where such approaches failed, 'we go for our own initiatives. But the Phil Cordell case is the best specific example. We need to bring the greatest pressure to bear on all activists to organize meetings in solidarity with Phil – providing them with the Brixton campaign leaflets, posters, badges etc. and getting meetings sponsored by branch committees, individuals, areas, regions and so on. . . .'

In the event, and despite militant feelings resulting from the pay dispute, the Far Left made only limited headway in the Civil and Public Services Association. At its May 1981 conference, Mrs Losinska was re-elected, beating off challenges for the presidency from Kevin Roddy, a

Trotskyist from the Department of Health and Social Security in Washington, and moderates remained firmly in control of the union, with a majority of eighteen to ten on its national executive.

In the in-fighting in the CPSA, however, there are some unpleasant and odd manifestations. At the end of its May 1980 conference at Southport, Mrs Losinska was called by the local police to identify three bags which appeared to have been forgotten by three delegates leaving hurriedly for London from the car park used for the conference. I have the names of the three delegates alleged to have forgotten the baggage, one of whom, it is suggested, is a supporter of the Palestine Liberation Organization and even himself an Arab or of Arab origin. For obvious reasons, they cannot be identified.

But when the police asked Mrs Losinska to confirm the bags' contents, they were found to contain Arab documents, plastic guns and much cash. Not the kind of baggage to forget in a car park. It was retained by the police, and subsequently the episode has been discussed at the highest level in Whitehall. Despite details being published in the *Daily Telegraph* in March 1981 and being the subject of discussion at the union's last conference in May 1981, neither a rejoinder nor complaint has been made by those involved.

The department of dirty tricks goes further. At the union's special pay conference at Central Hall Westminster early in 1981, a leaflet was distributed under the name of *Daylight*, 'issued by the national moderate group in the Civil and Public Services Association'. It was in the names of the group's officials, Charlie Elliott, and Mrs Losinska, the group's chairman, giving home telephone numbers. It purported to be last-minute guidance, 'produced early this morning', on how to vote on a series of motions for 'undecided or unmandated delegates'. In fact, it was a clever forgery.

I have in my possession a curious collection of well-produced bulletins, their titles redolent of Arab or even Nazi terminology. Some carry the heading, 'Popular Front for the Liberation of the CPSA (United Command Council)' and the sub-titles: 'Communiqué, South Midlands Brigade, Beds, Bucks and Oxon' or 'Communiqué from Forward Battle Group VALKYRIE'. Another is from the 'Committee of Public Safety' of the Popular Front's 'General Command'. Yet another is the 'Communiqué from the Peter the Painter Squad of the Fortress London Brigade'. All are Far Left propaganda, attacking Mrs Losinska and her colleagues, not only on policy differences, which most would think legitimate, but on drinking, minor road accidents, support for Solidarity, the Polish trade union movement, alleged liaisons, racial origin, religious adherence and so on. While they are written in a would-be satirical style, they are purely offensive. One ends: 'The Committee of Public Safety say: DEATH TO THE FALANGE! DEATH TO THE INFIDEL! AN END TO ALL ADULTERERS! MICRO-CHIPS TO THE WALL! NO SELL OUT! NO JOB LOSS! DEATH TO THOSE WHO TRAVEL IN CONSORT WITH POLES DONKEYS ASSES LITHUANIANS AND ALL OTHER UNCLEAN SPECIES! LONG LIVE THE GLORIOUS REVOLUTION! LONG LIVE THE COMMITTEE OF PUBLIC SAFETY!'

Good clean stuff from the Far Left? But the propaganda and constant conspiratorial tactics illustrate the relentless fight for control of the machinery of government. As with other Trotskyist activity, most of the public, and the patriotic citizens of this country, are unaware of it.

Inside the CPSA, there are also myriad ideological differences between various factions which they take seriously, but to outsiders seem pedantic. For example, *Redder Tape*, organ of the Socialist Workers Party, is at odds with the Broad Left, which comprises other groupings. In January 1981 Steve Allen, the editor of *Redder Tape*, was complaining about four fruitless approaches to the Broad Left for unity. Mr Sloman, SWP fraction secretary, who works for the Medical Research Council, was similarly plaintive. For its part, the CPSA Broad Left publishes *Broadside*, which also attacks the union's moderate leadership. Kevin Roddy gets a platform, as in other Trotskyist journals.

Many groups have a vested interest in pursuing Far Left aims in Britain's largest Civil Service union. They include the Militant Tendency, which occasionally publishes a special issue of *Militant* as well as *Unity*, 'The Voice of *Militant* in the CPSA', for its adherents. Early in 1981, the moderate leadership of the CPSA discovered (such oversights are frequent in large organizations), that a large number of its sectional journals were being printed by the Cambridge Heath Press, printers and publishers of *Militant*. They included *Aviation Organizer*, *Viewpoint* for members in the Department of Health and Social Security, *New Environment* for the Department of Environment colleagues, *Voice* for the Inland Revenue members and *Union Voice* for the Land Registry. They are typical red-and-black offset-printed broadsheets. No one has ever suggested they were not well printed at competitive commercial rates. But the individual and total cost was unknown. The reason was that each CPSA section was allowed a global budget to spend as it thought best. But through what amounted to a back door, financial support was being given, quite legitimately, to a major Trotskyist organization. I deal with Militant Tendency's and other Trotskyist and Communist finances in Chapter 5. But the Cambridge Heath Press was able to tender cheaply for such work because of cheap or free labour. Committed Militant Tendency employees are expected to pay back a 'tithe' of their earnings. Others, young supporters or those on the dole, rally round on Saturday nights and Sunday mornings to despatch the paper free. If the Cambridge Heath Press were a normal commercial operation, such cheap printing rates would hardly be possible.

Just like the Socialist Workers Party and other Trotskyist organizations, the Militant Tendency devotes much thought to exploiting industrial disputes and extending its influence in unions, now a major objective after its advances in the Labour Party, through the formation of 'caucuses'. In *British Perspectives, 1979* and the previous *Summer Bulletin*, attention was given to the 700,000-strong National Union of Public Employees. NUPE was once a minor, comparatively peaceful trade union, representing road sweepers, hospital porters and similar occupations. During the past ten years, it has been transformed into a militant, mass organization of nearly 700,000 members, involved in 'dirty jobs' strikes, in which Trotskyists have been prominent, nasty hospital disputes, and so on. Its general secretary is Alan Fisher, due to retire in June 1982, and in 1981 chairman of the Trades Union Congress. Mr Fisher's strident speeches have much power but little content. But there is a widespread view that the real motor in the union is Bernard Dix, a haggard, Mexican-moustached figure, who was formerly its Press officer and now assistant general secretary. Mr Dix is the left-wing mind behind the union's transformation into a mass, left-wing movement. He is at present taking a year's sabbatical leave to write a history of the union. Other left-wing NUPE lieutenants include Reg Race, MP, its former research officer.

In the light of all this, the views of the Militant Tendency on NUPE and Mr Fisher are illuminating. 'Even a national strike of the entire membership of NUPE, carried out in a determined fashion, could paralyse the country,' *British Perspectives* stated. 'Such is the power of the working class under modern conditions.'

But Mr Fisher, perhaps to his surprise, did not come so well out of a statement from the Militant Tendency executive board in an answer to Oxford members on 'Tactics in the Public Sector Manual Wages Dispute'. Admitting tactical errors in exploiting the industrial action through NUPE, the Militant Tendency said 'NUPE had the beginning of a network of shopstewards, but in general, these stewards lacked the experience to play an immediate leading role in an all-out strike'. The organizational framework was sparse. Many full-time officials had never before been involved in national industrial action and would have found it impossible to sustain all-out strike action without active support from shop stewards. 'Our approach took these factors into account and gave the necessary flexibility for the action to be tightened up as the dispute progressed and as the confidence and organization improved. We called from the start for all-out action in strong areas and in areas where there was a strong tradition of militancy, such as water, sewage and dust collection. And we called for the organization of local strike committees across union and service boundaries in order to make the overall action as effective as possible. . . .

'With Alan Fisher, in particular, we had to be extremely careful. A personal attack on Alan Fisher could have resulted in our tendency being cut off from the Left moving activists in NUPE, the majority of which would have had serious criticisms themselves of the way Fisher had come out against his own EC, even to the point of threatening resignation if things did not go his way. We must always be constructive when we distance ourselves from the union leaders. Alan Fisher especially had – and still has – a huge fund of goodwill among NUPE members who remember the personal role he played in the growth of the union and even in the low pay campaign itself.

'Because of their respect for him, they are willing to make enormous allowances, as T&GWU members and AUEW members used to make allowances for the actions of Jones and Scanlon. Their attitude would be that Fisher had made a genuine mistake under pressure. They would rally to his defence if they thought he was coming under unjustified attack. The tone we adopted in relation to Fisher was therefore correct.'

British Perspectives also commented: 'The process of change that has begun in the Bakers Union, NUPE, in the CPSA and in other unions, will be intensified in the coming period. In the smaller unions the voice of Marxism is getting a more and more respectful hearing at the present time. In the decisive unions – the T&GWU, the AUEW, the GMWU, the EEPTU and other industrial unions – Marxism can become an increasingly important factor. But as in the case of the AUEW and the EEPTU, of course, for a whole period of time there can be a period of black reaction.' Nevertheless, the Militant Tendency believed that even these unions under moderate leadership could be pushed into industrial struggle.

Apart from NUPE, Trotskyist influence is strong in the Fire Brigades Union, Agricultural Workers, where the campaign against pesticides has proved a valuable platform, the Union of Communications Workers (Post Office), the Post Office Engineering Union, the Engineering Union, the Construction Workers where, however, Communists are also strong, as in the Transport Union and the NUT and NALGO. In the latter two important white-collar unions, which have a combined membership of one million, new Far Left targets include securing their affiliation to the Labour Party – they are traditionally politically non-aligned like Civil Service organizations – which would greatly increase opportunities for entryism and left-wing influence.

Few better examples exist of specific Trotskyist intervention in an industrial dispute than the bulletin of *Socialist Organiser*, a comparatively new Trotskyist front organization like others operating behind this weekly paper, led by John Bloxam, but with branches throughout the country. I deal with *Socialist Organiser* in more detail on Trotskyist penetration in Labour Party fringe organizations (Chapter 10), but there is strong internal evidence that it is closely linked with the International Communist League.

In late 1980 nine shop stewards at British Leyland's Longbridge plant were sacked after leading a violent rampage through the premises. One of them was Jim Denham, like three others a Transport Union shop steward and alleged to be a member of the International Communist League. Certainly, Mr Denham reported on the dispute, which following an inquiry resulted in reinstatement of some of the men, for *Socialist Organiser*.

On 8 December 1980, *SO* 'Info 10' was published, duplicated on orange paper. To give it due credit it is a classic blueprint for industrial disruption. Commenting that dismissals had included 'one of our comrades' and been followed by strike action, it added, 'Since then the CP-dominated works committee has managed to end the strike in "return" for a postponement of the appeal.... Three of the stewards (including our comrade) are known militants, two of them Labour Party members. Some of the other workers are also militants. But some of the victimized workers are not trade unionists at all – just men who have crossed the foremen or supervisors.

'Almost certainly the sacking was ordered from BL central management. The first reaction of the Longbridge management after the so-called "riot" was to play it down.' The appeal, the bulletin added accurately, was 'certain to go against the workers, though the bosses may let one or two off to make things look better. Our aim is to get immediate strike action after the appeal.'

The following course of action round Longbridge was spelled out:

a, A SO bulletin on Monday

b, Pressing for a joint shop stewards' committee meeting as soon as possible and a mass meeting before Friday

c, Pressing for section meetings to discuss the issue

d, Sales of the SO broadsheet

e, (We hope) a special bulletin containing extracts from witnesses' statements prepared in support of the victimized men

f, A bulletin on Thursday (probably) from the Leyland Action Committee (a united-front organization of militants in BL in which our comrades participate). This will be given out in other Birmingham BL factories as well as Longbridge.

g, (We hope) a public meeting with Tony Benn [*sic*] or someone like that speaking

h, Organizing a defence committee

i, Organizing the stewards and other militants who are committed to fighting for strike action

At the JSSC, we will press for:

A decision to call a mass meeting before Friday and recommend a strike if the nine are not reinstated

Election of a strike committee

Section meetings to prepare for the mass meeting and organize picket rotas.

The problems the strike will face are (a) threats from Edwardes; (b) probably, an instruction from the AUEW and the EEPTU for their members to cross the picket line.

In the week before the appeal, and in the period up to the New Year, what we can do outside Longbridge is:

a, Sell the broadsheets. Shop stewards etc. should be got to take bundles of 20 (or 40, or 60, or 100) at the bulk rate to hand out at their workplaces. All possible contacts should be chased up. (Please note that the mention of a particular worker's name in the bottom article on the front page must be blotted out with a felt tip pen before the broadsheet is sold.)

b, Get messages of support from individuals, union branches, TCs, CLPs, MPs etc.

c, Get speakers from the victimized men invited to labour movement meetings.

A real sense of urgency, and a real commitment to throw all available resources into this work, is vital. The issue is important generally: if the BL bosses get away with this now, it will mean more victimizations later. It is specially important for SO: a socialist political movement cannot possibly develop and survive without a strong commitment to active defence of its comrades and organization.

We CAN defeat BL. We can certainly give them so much of a fright that the BL bosses will hesitate before trying it on again, and SO influence in Longbridge is bigger at the end of the struggle than before it.

Further instructions include organization of *Socialist Organiser* meetings, 'jointly with the CDLM if appropriate', as well as 'broad labour movement' meetings. Should the Communist Party and bureaucrats succeed in heading off a strike, there would be recourse to an industrial tribunal and continuation of the campaign, 'and for the sake of maintaining and increasing the influence of SO, the maxim noise and agitation are vital.'

Final steps, should the strike come off, would be to argue for: 'Official support; extension of the strike through BL (On these two points comrades or contacts in relevant unions should be pressed to put resolutions); rank and file support (Comrades should organize collections, meetings, messages of support, and sales of the broadsheet); occupation if Edwardes threatens closure.'

This illuminating bulletin had some interesting sequels. The Longbridge workers did not go on strike; although 50,000 leaflets were printed, they thought survival and employment was more important. Mr Denham commented in *Socialist Organiser* on 10 January 1981: 'I don't blame the membership. ... We had no positive leadership from the T&G, no proposals for strengthening the action from the works committee. And we were faced with the AUEW's usual scabbing role.' Members lacked confidence.

Following my publication of abbreviated details of this bulletin in the *Daily Telegraph*, *Socialist Organiser* issued a special bulletin 'for immediate release' by Mr Bloxam. On the Longbridge bulletin, it said: 'We plead guilty!' Mr Jonathan Hammond, elected earlier in 1981 as vice-president of the 32,000-strong National Union of Journalists, which means he will become president in 1982, is chairman and contact man of *Socialist Organiser*. According to Mr Bloxam, he was quoted as saying: 'We are proud to plead guilty! Indeed, there is no point in Baker referring to our duplicated circulars except to support his contrived air of mystery. The same message was proclaimed as loud as we could proclaim it in our fortnightly newspaper and in a special broadsheet.

'Was that sinister? Not in our eyes, nor, we think, in those of any labour movement activist. But Blake Baker perhaps thinks that such activities are criminal....'

It is worthy of note that Mr Hammond is an NUJ official, but that most of his energies appear to be devoted to Far Left aims in totally unrelated areas, such as ailing British Leyland, and the Labour Party. He is 'proud to plead guilty'. He is also due to become, in public eyes at least, the 'spokesman' of the great majority of British journalists, when he will doubtless pursue familiar aims of greater public control of the Press, disciplining those with whom he does not agree or who can be found to have broken the rules.

Another specific example of how Trotskyists use very dirty tactics to exploit an industrial dispute was provided early in 1981 during the Ansells brewery strike in Birmingham. Ansells, a famous name in the Midlands, is a subsidiary of Allied Breweries, and because of falling beer sales, the management decided to introduce a four-day week. It would have meant wages falling by £30, to £145 a week, and when this was rejected, the Aston brewery was closed. The strike of 1,000 workers without Transport Union support failed. The *Daily Mail* reported the dispute as follows.

The Trotskyist group which latched on was Workers Power. Pamphlets were distributed urging the Ansells strikers to increase action as a 'strike against the Government'. A leaflet said: 'Steps should be taken to make sure pickets are prepared for police attack – with defence squads ready to physically defend the pickets.' During the stoppage, the brewery began supplying its public houses and clubs in the Midlands from other breweries, including Romford. Most landlords and managers, not to mention customers, were happy for new supplies. But then intimidation against both them and delivery drivers began.

Depots were raided, with wire-cutters being used to break in and air-brake lines on vehicles, radiator hoses and tyre-valves were cut. Drivers were followed to their homes and threatened. Some drivers were not only abused but beaten up. One driver was about to deliver a load of keg beer to the Newton Inn, Great Barr, Birmingham, when six men rushed into the forecourt as he opened the cellar hatch. One used a billiard cue to hit him over the head before pushing him ten feet down the cellar shute. Then a 22-gallon metal keg of beer was rolled down on top of him before the gang smashed his lorry windscreen and drove away.

On 11 March 1981, another driver's leg was broken when a cellar door was slammed on it as he was unloading beer at the Camp Inn, King's Norton. Next day, another delivery crew were trapped inside the Shareholders' Arms, Aston, while their lorry was attacked. Intimidation of landlords included smashing of pub windows with bricks and sticks, threatening telephone calls, including threats to wives and children, and verbal threats and abuse. An attempt was made to set fire to Ansells' offices with petrol. Drivers began to deliver in threes for self-defence, with one company calling in a security firm as escorts. The violence was predictably condemned by Midland officials of the Transport Union, whose 'blacking' of the Fox and Goose pub, Birmingham, had previously led to a brief suspension from the TUC congress of Britain's largest union. But the episode is revealing. Union authority is defied, as is law and order, and violence is used to achieve Far Left ends.

Meanwhile, the Far Left fight for control of the unions continues. The Engineering Union is in the throes of a crucial round of elections in which the Broad Left, led by the Communist Party, hoped to reverse the moderate tide. The Right-Left war in this union goes back over decades.

But a comparatively recent development is the bid by the Broad Left, comprising both Communists and Trotskyists, to secure control of the 132,000-strong Post Office Engineering Union, which maintains Britain's telecommunications. The union has been traditionally moderate, controlled by a group known as the Block. But as a result of organization, the Broad Left have made substantial advances. Early in 1981 they had nine supporters on the union's executive of twenty-three and were fighting to gain at least another three to give them the majority. A few years ago, the left-wing minority was only four. In 1981 they controlled fifty of the union's 300 branches, and published *Spark*, 'the Voice of the POEU Broad Left', printed by the Militant Tendency's Cambridge Heath Press. The group also organize nominations in union elections and give advice on voting at the June annual conference.

Moderates in the union were worried by an article in the International

Marxist Group's *Socialist Challenge*, which stated: 'The Post Office Engineering Union has the power to cripple the City of London, the banks, finance houses, big companies and Government departments. But the right-wing majority on the union executive refuses to take up the challenge.'

Bryan Stanley, general secretary and a former member of the Labour Party executive, warned members in the union's journal in March 1981: 'In recent weeks a number of members have approached me to ask what I am doing to fight against what they regard as the efforts of extremists to take over control of the union and to take over control of the Labour Party. My answer will always be: If you do not agree with a particular line being adopted either by individuals, branches, the union or the Labour Party, then fight within the organization to establish your point of view.

'To be frank, it is useless for members to complain to me about decisions taken at branch meetings when they themselves do not attend those meetings. There is only one way to make sure that your opinions are taken into account and influence the policy-making process. That is to attend branch meetings.'

Through the summer of 1981 the Socialist Workers Party mounted a campaign to influence both individual union conferences and the TUC's annual congress in September. All readers of *Socialist Worker* likely to be delegates were asked to contact: Conference (SW), PO Box 82, London E2 or ring 01-986 5491.

The paper also published on 13 June 1981 a 'model resolution' from the Right to Work Campaign, for which it was 'vigorously campaigning. Get it passed through your union branch now.'

This ... (TU body) calls on the 1981 TUC congress to instruct the general council to:
  1. Ensure that all TUC affiliated trade unions guarantee unemployed membership and the retention of full rights for those made redundant;
  2. Establish a TUC National Unemployed Workers Union....
  3. Give the National Unemployed Union full representation on local trades councils and within the TUC Congress;
  4. Encourage the establishment of unemployment centres staffed by democratically elected unemployed officers controlled by the unemployed themselves and funded by trade union donations.

The advertisement included a long list of union branches, trades councils and other organizations which had already passed the 'model resolution'. Thus are union and even TUC conferences influenced or fixed in advance.

But at the Post Office Engineering Union's conference in early June 1981, the left-wing bid for power was defeated. Nor did Trotskyists succeed, against executive opposition, in getting through motions expressing support for Anthony Wedgwood Benn for the Labour Party deputy leadership. The balance of power on the executive remained fourteen moderates to nine 'Broad Left'. Brian Macey, a POEU left-winger, commented in *Socialist Worker* on 13 June 1981, 'Now the Left in the POEU may have to ask themselves some serious questions.'

In the equally important Electrical Trades Union (EEPTU), its leader, Frank Chapple, once a Communist but now the most right-wing member of the TUC general council, is under constant Far Left attack. But so far, with characteristic toughness and outspokenness, he has managed to keep a tight grip on the union's affairs.

I deal with Communist Party involvement in the unions separately. But it is remarkable how often, when disputes occur, there proves to be a Far Left involvement or exploitation on the picket lines and extensive encouragement in their publications, through pamphlets, leaflets and bulletins.

8 Education and Local Government

Education is seen by the Far Left as an important long-term investment. They have had considerable success in penetrating colleges, polytechnics and schools, as well as teachers' organizations. None has been more successful than the Socialist Workers Party. A rival contender, also strong among academics and students, is the International Marxist Group. Many of its middle-class intellectual members would previously have joined the Communist Party, as they did in the 1930s. But now the Communist Party, despite its efforts to dissociate itself from Moscow with 'democratic' home 'socialism', or Euro-Communism, is tarred with the brush of identification with the Soviet Union and all its sins.

The SWP is well established in some Oxford colleges and provincial universities, notably Sussex, Lancaster, Aberystwyth and North Wales. It is also strong in polytechnics, such as Sheffield and North-East London. In the National Union of Students, whose president David Aaronovitch is a Communist, as was a predecessor, Sue Slipman, and Digby Jacks, once NUS general secretary, Trotskyists still face powerful competition from the Communist Party. From time to time, vying Far Left factions in education have collaborated, only to split again.

In 1974 the SWP, ending co-operation with the IMG and other Far Left organizations, set up the National Organization of International Student Societies (NOISS); in later years it has also been known as the Socialist Workers Student Organization (SWSO). When it first got going it led university and polytechnic occupations, sit-ins, boycotts, and protest marches, and campaigned in the National Union of Students. *International Socialism* No 75 stated: 'There are great opportunities for the development of a national student organization with direct links to a revolutionary workers' organization ... NOISS will be built through its intervention through students.'

Its founding conference at Leeds University in November 1974 was attended by delegates from twenty-eight universities, eleven polytechnics and six further education and technical colleges. By May 1975 a membership of five hundred was claimed with fifty NOISS student cells and a small number of branches. By 1978 a confidential SWP bulletin stated: 'The Socialist Workers Student Organization (NOISS) consists of 800

SWP members and an organized periphery of around 2,000. The 3,000 members of SWSO are spread over 150 colleges, some in larger societies (50 +), some in colleges of ones and twos. There are still 650 colleges where we do not have members. . . . We are still very weak in the North East and North West. . . . Over the coming year if NOISS is to grow, SWP branches should be built in the colleges where we only have a toe-hold.'

Like other SWP front organizations, NOISS had its own semi-auton-omous structure and policy. Its activities included building up groups of Women's Voice, the Anti-Nazi League, and work for the Palestinians and against South Africa. In the NUS it emerged as the principal opposi-tion to the Broad Left, and tried to mount increasing opposition to the Communists through rival seminars to the so-called 'Communist Universities'.

In 1976 the Party had founded the Socialist Worker Youth Movement with indifferent success. It is now known as Red Rebel. In August 1979 Mike Pearse, SWP youth organizer, gave a report in the internal bulletin. Rebel, he said, was started in 1978.

In that time we have produced five copies of our newspaper *Rebel* which has a paid sale of 1,400. We have interviewed around schools and in several cases initiated school student strikes. It is because of our activity around the schools that we now control the leadership of the National Union of School Students.

The original idea of Rebel was to be a school student/young workers' organization. From the beginning, and more so now, we found this was not viable, mainly because of the different oppressions young workers and school students find. At the moment there are about a dozen active Rebel groups meeting regularly and producing *Rebel* and NUSS school bulletins etc. All the groups apart from one are solely made up of school students. The other one, Brixton Rebel, is made up of all young workers. We should not be opposed to Rebel groups of young workers, but because we now control NUSS, the cuts in education will give Rebel a campaign to get stuck into. The main orientation for Rebel must be in the schools. One of the problems of Rebel has been that there has not been a campaign it can get its teeth into. NUSS is that campaign.

Mr Pearse added that many comrades would know that Rebel 'took over NUSS at the last conference' – from the Communist Party. 'Three out of four full-time positions are now in the hands of Rebel members, but there are circumstances to justify this.' At the NUSS conference,

attended by 100 delegates from all over the country, the 'political composition' was: Rebel, 37; Revolution (IMG), 20; Socialist Youth League
(Workers Socialist League), 8; Young Communist League, 15; Labour
Party, 6; Scottish National Party, 2; non-aligned, 20. 'It was clear from
the start that we had the largest number of delegates from any political
group.... NUSS has about 4,500 members of which we are probably
responsible for recruiting 1,500.' It was also very noticeable that the
Young Communist League had not managed to build NUSS as in the
previous few years, due to a 'substantial decrease in their membership
and readership of their paper *Challenge*. Normally the YCL manage to
flood conference out with delegates and observers. This year, however,
they just did not have the people to do it.' But the Communists were still
committed to penetration.

At that conference, Mr Pearse added, the Socialist Workers Party
'would get the proposals we wanted'. These included: Support for the
Right to Work Campaign, School Kids Against Nazism (SKAN), the Anti-
Nazi League, and the August 12 Troops Out Now demo; no crossing of
teachers', meal staff, or any school workers' picket lines; rank-and-file
control of the NUSS and its magazine *Blot*; boycotting of classes taught by
racist teachers; disbanding of the Special Patrol Group; working with
Rank and File Teacher; a 'more democratic' structure for the union. The
NUSS was run between conferences by a seventeen-strong national com-
mittee, all school students, in which all political groups worked. The
International Marxist Group would have preferred 50-50 control with
the SWP. 'No deal!' Composition of the national committee resulted in
six SWP members, four Young Communists, three IMG, one Socialist
Youth League, one Labour Party, one non-aligned and one Scottish
National Party.

But the nine-man executive committee of four full-time and five school
student members resulted in the election of four SWP and one IMG
members. Mr Pearse continued, 'The way to build is through militant
activity - strikes, sit-ins etc. If the NUSS is handled in the right way, the
potential is enormous.' All SWP school student members had to join and
build branches in their schools, using local bulletins to exploit specific
issues.

Blot first appeared in October 1978. The first, and particularly semi-
literate and vicious issue of the magazine, caused controversy when it was
learned that it had been financed by a grant from the Gulbenkian Trust.
Later, officials of the Trust said they had no inkling of what kind of
magazine was planned. There was widespread protest at *Blot*'s use of bad

language, articles on masturbation, contraception, truancy and sexual discrimination. A copy was sent to the Director of Public Prosecutions.

The next issue, also of 10,000 copies, appeared in early 1979 dealing with sex, abortion, the 'gay' movement, puberty and with attacks on religious education and the school system. At this time, the NUSS membership was estimated at about 10,000 with between 300 and 350 branches of members mostly aged fourteen and over paying between 20p and £1.40 a year. It had two full-time officers, the president, paid about £1,000 a year and a national organizer, usually students taking a year off between school and university. Support in cash, facilities and information was received from the National Union of Students.

Further attention was attracted by the National Union of School Students, whose president, Hardy Desai, is an SWP member, in March 1980. The organization had prepared a leaflet entitled, 'How to disrupt your school in six easy lessons', and a conference was held, attended by nearly 100 pupils aged between twelve and eighteen at Central London Polytechnic. Speakers included John Deason, secretary of the Right to Work Campaign, Simon Turner, national committee member of the SWP, Tony Cliff, its leader, and Maggie Wren, editor of *Women's Voice*, who gave a talk, 'We want more sex' on sexual politics, the right to be homosexual and women's liberation.

Hardy Desai gave lessons at the two-day 'teach-in' on the disruptive leaflet. He told one youth with a can of lager, 'It's all right. This is not like school. You can drink in here.' But lessons were cancelled after fighting broke out between left-wing and right-wing Iranian students at a separate meeting, and the building was closed.

In July 1980 the NUSS conference was attended by 150 delegates, and Mr Desai claimed that in the previous year, strikes had been organized 'from Luton to Sheffield, from London to Exeter'. At a previous conference in March 1980, Danny Ashton, an executive member, told sixty delegates there would be a 'massive wave of school strikes'. But criticism was expressed of the SWP's prominent role by both the International Marxist Group, the Communist Party, which spoke of a 'Nuremberg rally for Rebel', and the Workers Socialist League through *Red Youth*, organ of its own Socialist Youth League.

The SYL itself announced: 'From the autumn we are launching a new paper for school students – *Class War* – which, coupled to recruitment drives that SYL school students are planning will be our contribution to the fight to construct a mass, fighting school students' union.' It added: 'The first thing is to organize leafleting of the school and places frequented by youth. . . . Then arrange a secret meeting inside the school. . . . If the head finds out what is going on, he won't know who the full-time organizer is.' Campaigns should be organized, against school uniforms for example, a bulletin be produced, and an open letter sent to the NUSS branch demanding recognition. 'The NUSS needs to be permanently mobilizing for council lobbies, pickets, demonstrations and agitating.'

As a result of Far Left activities in the NUSS, all links with it were severed by the National Union of Students in December 1980 because its behaviour had become too embarrassing. At the students' conference in Margate it was disclosed that the pupil body, then claiming a membership of 8,000, had overspent its budget during its short lifespan by £7,000. In 1980 it had been given a final grant by the National Union of Students of £2,200. According to one senior NUS official the notorious *Blot* had achieved 'nothing but ill-feeling towards students in general'.

Hardy Desai, then only seventeen, denied that the NUSS was run by Trotskyists. But he conceded, 'It's true that six of our eleven executives belong to the Socialist Workers Party. I am a member myself and proud of it. But this does not mean that party is running the NUSS.'

Far Left infiltration of schools is not limited to pupils. Teachers, often members of the Socialist Workers Party, play a prominent role. Communists are also strongly represented in the National Union of Teachers, but have faced increasing competition from the Socialist Workers Party, the Militant Tendency and the International Marxist Group for the past decade. The result of the Far Left drive was formation of the Rank and File Teachers movement, a classic Trotskyist term, led by the SWP.

The leadership of the NUT was not unaware of the threat. In 1976 the union introduced Rule Eight giving its executive the right to suspend or expel members indulging in unofficial strikes, walk-outs or other unconstitutional action. In 1977 rules were again altered to ensure local officials and delegates to the union's annual conference were elected by secret ballot. The union also voted in 1978 not to affiliate with the Anti-Nazi League.

Nevertheless, the Far Left remained active. On the Communist side, the most prominent included Max Morris, former president and vice-president who has since left the Party, and Sam (S. A.) Fisher. For the Socialist Workers Party, the most prominent activist has been Chanie Rosenberg, also known as C. Dallas, wife of Tony Cliff. The Rank and File Teachers movement was formed in the 1960s and centred, as is usual with Trotskyist movements, round its publication, *Rank and File Teacher*.

This first appeared in January 1968, to be published eight times a year. Chanie Rosenberg was its first editor. Aims of the movement, as expressed in December 1978, were predictable: opposition to cuts in education expenditure; national sanctions and strikes; reduction in class sizes; large pay rises; control of the NUT by rank-and-file members, rights of school students to organize; opposition to racialism – who is not against it?; women's rights and equal pay. But a prime aim was also to indoctrinate pupils, through, for example, the SWP offspring, Teachers Against Nazis, with information kits and films available.

Several prominent SWP members of the National Union of Teachers have at times attracted public and union attention. In June 1980 Jeff Burford, an SWP member, established a 'teachers' resource centre' in London to challenge the 'all too common bias, in terms of class, sex, race and culture, in the school syllabus'. It was in memory of the late Blair Peach, and a poster was distributed by the East London branch of the National Union of Teachers, well produced in green and yellow showing a rising phoenix, the mythological bird which rose from its own ashes. Blair Peach taught at the Phoenix School in East London. The poster advertised a series of lectures by left-wing teachers on 'Workers History: the culture of working class struggles', 'English Racism', 'The French and Russian Revolutions' and 'School Children's and Students' Culture in the Classroom'. It also claimed that Mr Peach was killed 'opposing racism and fascism on the streets of Southall. ... But there was more to Blair's teaching than just anti-racialism. He clearly saw the need to put the interests of his pupils at the forefront: to value the ideas and traditions of working people.'

Mr Burford told the *Daily Telegraph* (2 June 1980) that he and his friends were trying to persuade more and more teachers to use the classroom materials they were producing. Subsequently, Dr Michael Birchenough (*sic*), chief inspector of schools for the Inner London Education Authority (ILEA), decided to investigate such material with a view to recommending whether it should be used for teaching. He said: 'The first line of responsibility lies with the head of the school to see that no material is used which is obscene or grossly biased and that a range of views is presented on a political subject. I will certainly look into this.' Dr Birchenough decided to conduct his inquiry after being reminded that in 1979 he insisted on seeing work-sheets used in Eltham Green School for teaching children about NATO. This followed complaints by Ron Hayward, general secretary of the Labour Party, and Frank Allaun, left-wing Labour MP. These teaching aids, he subsequently ruled, which were also used at Gordonstoun, Chislehurst and Sidcup Grammar School, were perfectly suitable for children.

But one of those involved in the left-wing campaign was Dick North, a prominent Trotskyist teacher belonging to the Socialist Workers Party and then a member of the NUT executive for Inner London. He said: 'In the past in education there's only been one viewpoint, and that's the orthodox viewpoint. Our aim is to replace that with a socialist or left wing interpretation. We want pupils to cultivate a critical faculty.'

The campaign coincided with increasing criticism by moderate teachers of left-wing bias in schools. Nigel de Gruchy, assistant secretary of the National Association of Schoolmasters and Union of Women Teachers, said: 'Without the permission of the governors or local authorities, these teachers are trying to establish in-service training courses which are politically biased. This is very dangerous and will lead to a further crisis of confidence in the community and among parents on the lines of the Tyndale scandal.' This North London row resulted in six left-wing teachers being banned from teaching after a parents' revolt at their methods. Blair Peach was an official 'friend' of one of them at the inquiry. A 'friend' is permitted to act as an observer for a teacher during the course of a disciplinary inquiry.

Further ructions over Trotskyist activities in the National Union of Teachers came at its annual conference in April 1981. Mr North and five other colleagues who had urged strike action in Lambeth against Conservative government spending cuts against union instructions – the NUT is not politically aligned or affiliated – lost an appeal against disciplinary action. A union appeals committee confirmed that the six members had broken rules. Mr North was banished from the union for twelve months and barred from office for two-and-a-half years. The other five were suspended for six months. The penalties were confirmed despite appeals by the three Lambeth Labour MPs.

The six disciplined NUT members were: Dick North, John Easterson, Gary Jones, Jackie North, Vanessa Wiseman and Hilary Tarr. In the SWP *Women's Voice* of April 1981, Jeannie Robinson reported Jackie North as saying: 'I think they picked on Lambeth because we have a good record of always supporting militant action against cuts. ... I would ask all readers of *Women's Voice* to raise this issue in their trade unions and stress that our "crime" was to fight cuts.' An appeal was made for motions and messages of support to be sent to NUT headquarters and for picketing of it when appeals were heard. More information was available from *Rank and File Teacher* at SWP headquarters.

Mr North is a teacher at the Dick Sheppard School, Brixton, and represented London teachers on the NUT executive for seven years. According to *Socialist Worker* of 11 April 1981, he was 'elected on the militant platform of the SWP-led Rank and File Teachers which opposed all cuts in education, backed by action, unofficial if necessary'. As stated, unofficial action is forbidden under Rule Eight of the NUT. Mr North, a long-haired, bearded, bespectacled figure, associated with the Right to Work Campaign since 1975 and a 'leading campaigner' for disbandment of the Special Patrol Group, boasted of the 'chaos' he had caused in teaching cover in other schools.

Apart from the North affair, the at times stormy NUT 1981 conference, which ended in confusion, resulted in a decision to clamp down on left-wing extremists who infiltrated and disrupted meetings of its larger branches contrary to rule. At least twenty-six union members were to face disciplinary action. Senior union officials said that the 14,000-strong Inner London Teachers Association, the union's biggest single division, had been unable to hold a proper annual general meeting for three years because of left-wing infiltration. Lambeth branch, with 1,400 teachers, had passed resolutions giving full support to Ulster hunger strikers. It had also decided to re-affiliate to the Troops Out Movement, in which Trotskyists are active. Roy Porter, of Greenwich, said the ILTA could not conduct its business properly because it was beset by 'mob rule'. There was no guarantee that some of those who had infiltrated meetings were 'even teachers at all'.

Of the Lambeth decisions and London developments, Fred Jarvis, general secretary, said, 'We cannot have union money being used for such purposes. Obviously we cannot know of everything that is going on in our local associations', which total about eight hundred. 'But we firmly reject any intrusion into this union by elements with party political allegiances. I don't say that the union never takes any action of a political nature. But we are not in any way aligned to any political party or group.'

Mr Jarvis also attacked the many extremist splinter groups outside the conference who, as at the TUC, Labour Party and other major conferences, made the 1,800 delegates and hundreds of other observers and visitors run a gauntlet of distributions of political leaflets, pamphlets and broadsheets, apart from the chanting of slogans and abuse and calls to sign petitions, which are both a daily trial and make a strong police presence necessary. 'We reject attempts by the Ultra Left to interfere with and intrude in the business of this conference,' Mr Jarvis declared. 'We will have nothing to do with the Rank and File and other fringe bodies that peddle their goods outside this hall'.

In autumn 1980 a propaganda campaign was launched in British universities from Communist Europe. Hundreds of posters arrived unsolicited calling on students to fight against planned cuts in government spending on education. Headed 'Fight the cuts – Education needs adequate financing', they came from the International Union of Students in Prague. The National Union of Students' Communist president, David Aaronovitch refuses to be a member of this organization 'because the IUS is so blatantly unrepresentative'. IUS membership is based in Russia, Czechoslovakia, Bulgaria, East Germany, Poland and Hungary.

In May 1981 Russia launched yet another propaganda campaign in British schools throughout the country. Parcels postmarked in Watford, Herts, and sent to teachers, contained books written by the head of the international department of the Soviet Communist Party, Boris Ponomarev. One volume was 202 pages long, entitled *Disarmament: Soviet Initiatives*, in the name of President Brezhnev. Others, distributed by Novosti Booklets (Novosti is the 'trendy' Russian news service) included: *Privileged Class* (for children); *Soviet Democracy at Work*; *Young People in the USSR*; *Invincibility, the Liberation Movement*; and *The Great Vital Force of Leninism*. For sports teachers, there was a book on the 1980 Olympics. Others works covered the geography of Russia. An anti-Chinese work was called *Injustices behind the Wall*.

Mrs Victoria Cherneyeni, who launched the campaign from an address in South-West London, wrote to teachers that it would be a free booklet service of about forty a year. With textbooks at a premium and in short supply, such propaganda was, if not welcome, not rejected. Other material came from Orbis, a Prague-based news agency. Books ranged from *USA and Human Rights* to *Chile: An Accusation and a Warning*.

Education, both in schools and colleges, will always be a prime target of Far Left activity and agitation, since the youth of today may become the revolutionaries of tomorrow. A blind eye is almost certain to be turned to much of this activity by the 'socialist republics' which are spreading in local government in Scotland, South Yorkshire, the West Midlands and more recently London.

Most teenagers are impervious to it. Others turn to the National Front. Many college students soon lose their left-wing sympathies. But the Far Left also has its successes. The only remedy is vigilance and firm action by those responsible for education, parents or, as with the National Union of Teachers, by unions when political indoctrination in the classroom is identified.

Further advances by the Far Left, which became more evident in 1981, were in local government. As noted above, there are the so-called 'socialist republics' of South Yorkshire, based on Sheffield with the powerful backing of Arthur Scargill, Marxist leader of the Yorkshire miners; Lothian in Scotland, and Sandwell, centred on West Bromwich, Walsall, both of which became involved in closed shop disputes and sackings of rebels.

In London, there were Camden and Lambeth, where Ted Knight, a former full-time worker for the Socialist Workers Party, ruled at Brixton, but failed to get elected for Norwood in the GLC elections. Nevertheless, a key political post was found for him soon afterwards. Most important of all, Ken Livingstone, who denies being a Marxist, but suggests Britain should become a republic, who espouses Far Left causes and appears regularly, in interviews or articles, in Trotskyist journals, become leader of the GLC.

Mr Livingstone came to power as Labour leader within eighteen hours of the GLC election result, deposing Andrew McIntosh, the moderate who had led Labour to victory. In the early hours, Mr McIntosh had confidently discounted predictions of an imminent putsch. Before the day was over, he was out, bitterly attacking Mr Livingstone and his supporters.

'The working class is in charge now, and we're going to make a lot of changes,' declared Mr Livingstone. Nevertheless, he was soon embroiled in a dispute with the National Union of Railwaymen, which had given him substantial aid in his election campaign, but complained that a pay rise for Underground workers had not been increased as expected.

Mr Livingstone, apart from threatening to cut grants for the Royal Opera House, decided that the GLC should boycott Prince Charles' wedding. Some councils wanted to fly the Red Flag on the wedding day. At least one encountered staff resistance and changed its mind.

The new Marxist councils have been engaged in a running fight with Michael Heseltine, Secretary for the Environment, over government proposals for reduced spending. Others have been deliberately obstructive over sales of council houses, which more than 250,000 tenants wanted to buy. Applicants were deliberately frustrated or even 'intimidated', being told their house could not be re-painted like others on their estate because they wished to buy it. In Sheffield, the housing department sent out letters to applicants saying that having bought their home, they might be left with a property they could not sell because neither the council nor building societies might allocate funds. In Sheffield, as elsewhere, there were delays in dealing with applications to buy because of 'internal problems'. There was also resistance in Greenwich, South-East London, and in Lambeth nearly two hundred application forms were for a time 'impounded' by NALGO members. Resistance was widespread.

Moves, which proved unsuccessful, were also made to impose the same kind of political control over Labour local government candidates and councillors as over MPs through re-selection. In *Socialist Organiser* of 4 April 1981, Nigel Williamson, a member of the Campaign for Labour Party Democracy's local government action committee, gave advice on 'How Labour can control the councillors'. Arguing for greater account-ability to the rank and file, he made detailed proposals, such as writing into standing orders commitments to follow Party policy, election of the Labour group leader by a joint meeting of the group and district Party, as at Stirling - where the PLO flag is displayed in the council chamber - and a grass-roots campaign over eighteen months to achieve such aims at the 1982 Labour Party conference.

'The rearguard action against local government democracy is going to be even more bitter than the arguments over accountability of MPs,' he wrote, 'if only because instead of one elitist group, the PLP (Parliamentary Labour Party), we have 454 Labour Groups all attempting to preserve their privileged and elitist position. Nevertheless, we must remain con-fident that we can win this crucial reform.' The Far Left battle for control of local government, which could be at least as far reaching as that for Parliament, is still on.

On 10 July 1981, after a week of rioting throughout Britain, Mr Livingstone addressed a meeting of the Anti-Nazi League attended by two hundred people at a locked and guarded Brixton townhall. Mr Livingstone blamed the police for the troubles. Of the London police and its Special Patrol Group, he said, 'They regard themselves as a Clint Eastwood, gung-ho World War Two elite. There can be no doubt that over the last twenty years, there has been a dramatic shift to the right by police. With every day that passes the force becomes less representative of the community as a whole.' He had been brought up in Brixton and had himself been harassed by police. 'This kind of police harassment has been directed not just against the black community, but against all working-class people.' He also said that the main responsibility for the riots must lie with the government.

The meeting was chaired by Dick North, who said that he would keep proceedings short. 'I am sure you all want to get out on the streets yourself,' he said. Outside, shops were being smashed and looted. The new leader of the GLC was forbidden by a police officer to walk about because rocks were lying around and people might throw them. When Mr Livingstone protested he was told, 'I do not care who you are – there is one law for everyone.'

The Claimants and Unemployed Workers Union, a somewhat amorphous organization, devoted to securing the best social security and unemployment benefits available, but not to be confused with an orthodox trade union, was founded in May 1970 by Joe Kenyon, a former Barnsley miner. He had left mining in 1961 due to pneumoconiosis, the miners' 'dust disease', and after working for the National Council of Training Colleges, became unemployed in 1967. 'I tried to get jobs. I wanted to go back to the pits, but they wouldn't have me, and they said everywhere else that I was too old. So I decided to make unemployment my proper career.'

Mr Kenyon, who had become an unofficial adviser on benefits, much in demand, borrowed £7 worth of paper and ink, ran off his own leaflets and distributed them at employment offices around Barnsley. Soon, he had 1,500 members in twenty-three branches. There were no constitution and no rules, and he denied accusations of building a 'scroungers' charter'. Membership grew to 10,000 in seventy-eight branches. Backing came from Michael Meacher, Labour MP for Oldham West, now Mr Wedgwood Benn's campaign manager.

Far Left influence increased, and a 'Handbook for Strikers' was issued in 1972, helping single miners strikers to obtain benefits. The Claimants Union, however, kept going. In July 1975 the *Daily Telegraph*, saying it had no legal, financial or official trade union backing, quoted members as saying; 'Any Tom, Dick or Harry can start a Claimants' Union in his area if he has been, or is claiming benefit and agrees to abide by our charter.'

Although non-political and non-sectarian, members agreed it included left-wingers, Communists, International Marxists and other Trotskyists. It was called by some trade unionists and social workers the 'deadbeats social club'. Its charter laid down 'minimum policy': the right to an adequate income without a means test; a socialist society in which all necessities are provided free, managed and controlled directly by the working class; non-secrecy and a right to full information; no distinction between so-called 'deserving' and 'undeserving' cases.

It had no secretariat or officers and no financial structure, with minimal subscriptions to pay expenses, but produced a paper and leaflets. Its activities led to social security staff shutting down the Southend office in 1978 and calling the police. It is, therefore, illuminating to read the latest Trotskyist advice on how to form a Claimants Union branch.

In *Socialist Worker* of 18 April 1981 an article tells readers, 'It's easy to set up a claimants union.' It is by S. McNee and C. Joseph, of Crawley, Sussex. They say the Claimants Union was started in Crawley by two unemployed SWP members.

The reasons and need for such a union became apparent after the two members started a paper sale at the dole queue. We decided that the best way that a Claimants Union could be started was to write a leaflet and hand them out on the dole queue.

It is easy to set up a Claimants Union. All you need are two unemployed members and a leaflet. For an address we used a trade union club. Next we informed the local Press. Got two reports, one on the front page. This on its own has led to four new contacts.

When it comes to going to the Department of Health and Social Security with a claimant, you don't need to know very much. Find out about the claimant's case. Do not give your name, just tell them that you are from the Claimants' Union. Don't be fobbed off by any DHSS staff saying you should not be there.

Insist on seeing a supervisor or manager. Don't be frightened off by thinking you do not know very much. First, just by being there and listening you will learn a lot quickly. Second, the DHSS officials do not know how much you know and your very presence scares them. You'll soon have built up a pool of knowledge, you'll need a boat to get across it. Write off for literature from any helpful source you come across.

We have been told, although we have not done it yet, that the Child Poverty Action Group is one of the best sources. Use your local library reference section. You'd be surprised at the lie-cracking tools to be found there wrapped up in cardboard.

We now have eight hard-core committee members. Twenty willing contacts. And dozens of positive conversions (ex-Battle of

Britain pilot included). If we can do it in Crawley, a concrete obstacle they had to divert the M3 round, any two unemployed members can do it anywhere.

Thus is an active Trotskyist cell formed. And small wonder if resentment increases against 'scroungers', both among the public and among social security benefits staff.

Unemployment provides a fruitful field for Far Left agitation. A classic example was the 'People's March for Jobs' from Liverpool to London with ancillary efforts in May 1981. Sponsored ostensibly by the TUC, which kitted-out marchers, ranging from brave pensioners to punk rockers and skinheads, all provided with weather-proof clothing, a new pair of boots and sleeping bags, it provided a major propaganda occasion for every Far Left organization.

Although Louis Heren, deputy editor of *The Times*, Russell Lewis, formerly of the Tory Central Office, now of the *Daily Mail*, and other well-known Fleet Street journalists joined it for one or several stints, the national Press was accused, with some justification, of ignoring it. Not, I would guess, deliberately, but because such a thirty-one-day effort is not news every day. Not so the Far Left Press. Every day of the march received full-colour treatment in *News Line*, which also produced a commemorative magazine. Vanessa Redgrave was present to autograph T-shirts when the marchers finally arrived in London. *Militant*, *Socialist Worker* and *Socialist Challenge* made it their principal news item. The Socialist Workers Party distributed 50,000 leaflets on behalf of its Right to Work Campaign.

The *Morning Star*, on behalf of the Communist Party, also joined in the competition for increased influence. Mick Costello said the Communists would use the opportunity to advance their case for building a mass movement to defeat Thatcher government policies. In the end, one could only be sorry for the unemployed, deserving of pity and sympathy, but in the end, just a target for exploitation.

9 The Anti-Nuclear Movement

The Far Left flourishes on front organizations, ostensibly for a worthy moral purpose, attracting many do-gooders and ordinary people of good-will. Many of these have compromised, or even made fools of themselves. Others have earned the sobriquet of being 'fellow-travellers', sometimes well deserved – 'If the cap fits, wear it'....

The Communist Party and its Moscow backers have been adept at creating and exploiting front organizations. There have been, and are still, various 'friendship societies'. There is the World Peace Council an ancillary 'peace' movement, still going strong. The aim is not peace, but the weakening of the West and the spreading of Russian influence while the Soviet Union continues to arm on a scale unprecedented in the history of the world.

Recent years have seen the re-birth of the Campaign for Nuclear Disarmament, fuelled by genuine concern over the dangers of atomic radiation and the stationing of nuclear weapons in Britain. CND, a some-what amorphous body, which nevertheless has attracted a large member-ship, is supported by more than seventy organizations including such well-meaning groups as broad centre environmentalists, Friends of the Earth, Ecologists, the Liberal Party and so on. There are anarchists, the so-called 'brown bread and sandals brigade', Church representatives, including Mgr Bruce Kent, Roman Catholic CND general secretary, and Canon Paul Oestreicher, Anglican, local residents groups – in fact, a complete hotch-potch.

There is also the Far Left in considerable strength, the wolf in the fold. Sally Davison, CND national organizer, is a Communist Party member. So, too, are an appreciable number of other officials and national council members. But the Communists were not the only party on the Far Left to see the opportunities for entryism and front organization influence offered by CND. The Trotskyists, mainly through the Socialist Workers Party and the International Marxist Group, also moved into it in force. For much of the past year, although it has been little publicized except in Far Left publications, CND has been a battleground between the Communists and Trotskyists, between rival Trotskyist groups, and between them and the do-gooders who have found themselves in the middle of in-fighting at which the Far Left is adept, but in which they have little experience or expertise.

The Communist Party, as ever disciplined and well organized, ensured it was well represented on CND's national and local organization from the start. But not until early 1981 did CND appear to wake up to the fact that it was being heavily penetrated and diverted into unrelated causes by the SWP and IMG. Members of both parties are highly professional in organizing endorsement for pre-planned resolutions, exploitation of conference procedure and other tactics. They went to work with a vengeance, ostensibly to mobilize still greater support for CND, but in fact to swing it behind other objectives, such as exploitation of unemployment through the Right to Work Campaign and political opposition to the Thatcher government.

On 28 March 1981 there was a CND 'Labour Movement Against the Missiles' conference, attended by more than 700 delegates, in Manchester. This was intended to be little more than a public mass rally, expressing general support for CND. In fact, the organization, procedure and agenda were overturned by determined Trotskyist intervention. Another major development was the founding of Youth CND late in 1980, only to find it was being taken over by Revolution Youth, the newly-formed youth section of the International Marxist Group. Surprisingly, neither of these rows was reported in the national Press. The evidence is not fabricated. It comes in print in Trotskyist publications, albeit with a notable silence by the Communist *Morning Star*, and in such publications as *Peace News*. It led the national council of CND early in 1981 to issue statements dissociating themselves from the SWP and IMG. Whether these attempts to prise off the Trotskyist octopus have proved successful remains to be seen. The SWP, certainly, has declared its intention of holding CND to the non-nuclear policies which it forced through in Manchester. Scarcely a Trotskyist publication appears without a page devoted to nuclear disarmament.

Let us take the internal evidence. Late in 1980 the Socialist Workers Party began to organize local protest groups in East Anglia, where most Cruise missiles will be stationed. One was at Norwich, called the Norwich Anti-Nuclear Campaign, led by Dr Ian Gibson, biology lecturer and SWP member. They aimed to mobilize union action against Cruise missiles. Feelers were sent out to other towns. In Halesworth, Suffolk, the Suffolk Anti-Nuclear Campaign was started, mostly with Friends of the Earth supporters. *Socialist Worker* began to publish a 'No Nukes' section of small ads, giving details of demonstrations, marches, day-schools and so on throughout the country. *Socialist Challenge*, organ of the IMG, printed 'Jobs not Bombs' next to its front-page title.

There followed the Manchester conference, attended by more than 150 supporters of *Socialist Challenge*, who, according to it, had been 'delegated', a revealing phrase. SWP members also came as 'delegates', armed with resolutions from union branches and elsewhere. The organizing committee had decided not to accept resolutions, but its decision was overturned by Trotskyist in-fighting. Subsequently, an SWP motion was approved, committing CND to its aims, such as support for the Right to Work Campaign and political opposition to the Tories. Ironically, there was also internecine warfare at the conference, not only between the SWP and IMG, but with lesser Far Left organizations, such as the Revolutionary Communist Tendency and the Spartacists, who wanted support for the IRA.

Socialist Worker, on 2 May 1981, published a revealing article on the Manchester conference by Phil Marfleet, under the heading 'Whose Side are we on?', in reply to a reader, Terry Doughty, of Birmingham. He had written saying he had been told by his local CND members that the SWP did not have the best interests of CND at heart, that some members had been 'disrupting' the movement and trying to 'discredit' its leadership. 'Please tell me what is going on,' said Mr Doughty, since he had assumed the SWP supported CND. Mr Marfleet said SWP was fully committed to CND, but Mr Doughty's comments were not isolated ones. *Peace News* had reported the Manchester conference as having been disrupted by a determined attempt to take over the proceedings. The official CND Press statement afterwards, he said, spoke of the 'sour note' struck by the SWP and 'disruptive tactics'. In South Wales, a CND national council delegate had reported: 'It was noted that the SWP and International Marxist Group are attempting to discredit CND and that there will be no future collaboration with those organizations, whose commitment to the disarmament struggle is negligible.' Mr Marfleet commented: 'This is strong stuff. Nothing could be clearer – the SWP is out to disrupt CND, and CND should have nothing to do with this divisive organization.' The CND had not replied to a request for comment. 'This is unfortunate, for all over the country, SWP members are doing their best to build the movement.'

Mr Marfleet became more specific. Many new CND groups had been established over past weeks. 'Many will have been established by SWP members – and particularly in the unions – Engineers Against the Bomb, Teachers Against the Missiles, Council Workers Against Missiles, Journalists Against Nuclear Extermination – the initial effort has involved many of our members. The accusation that the contribution is negligible is simply foolish....' At Manchester, Mr Marfleet continued, 'many delegates were *Socialist Worker* supporters who had taken the trouble to raise the issue of missiles in their workplace and union branches in order to attend conference, report back, and so commit their fellow union members to *more* determined CND activity. No such delegate "disrupts" a union conference.

'A number of SWP members who had been delegated and sent to the conference with branch resolutions asked conference to hear what their branches were proposing. Some 80 per cent of the delegates wanted to hear the resolutions moved. When delegates explained the key resolutions, they again received the overwhelming support of the conference. As *Peace News* admitted, "they (the SWP) managed to take the majority of delegates with them".'

Mr Marfleet went on to show how the SWP was trying to deflect CND from being purely an anti-nuclear movement into other ends of its own. 'The successful resolutions called for CND to get behind all those who are fighting unemployment and the cuts; that "Jobs not Bombs" be amongst our principal demands and that we work to build CND where we, the workers' movement, have the greatest strength – in our workplaces and unions.

'Here, perhaps, we do disagree with the CND leadership. Their emphasis on the "broad church" of CND seems to mean that they do not want to build a movement with real teeth.' It would be blindness to ignore what civil servants at Faslane nuclear submarine base had shown, 'that the organized strength of the workers gives muscle power to the movement and that is the key to shifting any government's missile strategy. And who can say that the fight against missiles is not directly connected to that against the dole queues? ... It is no surprise that conference delegates again agreed, and that on the recent Easter marches, the main slogans have been "Jobs not Bombs" and "Maggie Out".'

Mr Marfleet ended with a discussion of future tactics. 'We can look forward to receiving reports of the conference, copies of the resolutions passed and a commitment by CND to see these agreed policies are followed up. We can start by seeing CND fully behind the forthcoming "People's March" for jobs, as agreed by conference.' The SWP was committed to 'making the all-important connection between the *working class* movement and that against missiles. The CND leaders may not agree – and of course they have every right to contest our point of view.'

The SWP was not the only Far Left organization to publicize its active intervention in CND affairs. Let us, again, take the International Marxist Group at its own words. In *Socialist Challenge* of 7 May 1981 Brian Heron, of London, replied to criticisms by Alasdair Beal, a member of the CND national council. Mr Beal had wondered what the IMG had achieved when it overturned the decision of CND labour conference organizing committee not to take resolutions, and had taken them to task for their attitude to 'multi-lateralism'. Mr Heron denied the first charge, saying that more than 150 *Socialist Challenge* supporters who had been 'delegated' to the conference abided by the no-resolution decision, with Martin Collins, a supporter and member of the organizing committee, speaking in favour. But, said Mr Heron, 'The last national council of CND was treated to a series of accusations about *Socialist Challenge* disruption from CND officers.' No attempt had been made to present or discuss such complaints. '*Socialist Challenge* supporters initiated and led the fight – and it *was* a fight – to get CND to support the labour movement conference. In the course of this fight we had to defeat some silly ideas being put forward by the Socialist Workers Party. Faced with the hostility of CND officers to the idea of the conference, the SWP wanted us to "go it alone". They wanted a *Socialist Challenge*/SWP/Manchester against the Missiles conference. But we said "No": we wanted a genuine CND conference which would involve important forces in the labour movement.'

Mr Heron went on to describe further in-fighting in which the IMG and SWP joined to argue for a statement of policy from the conference, but were defeated by seven votes to six on the organizing committee – this shows the strength of Trotskyist organizations on the committee. In the event, the conference voted for resolutions to be put, but was also 'treated to less than inspiring speeches from the RCT [Revolutionary Communist Tendency, another small Trotskyist group] that we should be discussing Ireland, and from the Spartacists, denouncing us all for supporting imperialism!' The conference became increasingly fed up with this wrangling. 'The final "Appeal", moved by myself, was the only resolution that no-one voted against,' said Mr Heron, who then complained that this was not mentioned either by the CND Press statement nor by two accounts published by the Socialist Workers Party.

Back to the Socialist Workers Party in its journal *Socialist Review* of April–May 1981. Pete Goodwin wrote that the Manchester conference was a 'quite unprecedented event' attended by more than 700 delegates, half from unions and half from local Labour organizations, showing 'how great is the immediate potential for rooting the anti-bomb movement in the labour movement', but complained that it 'missed a real opportunity to fulfil that potential. And responsibility for that must be squarely put on the shoulders of strangers, a strange combination of the International Marxist Group and the CND leadership. It was the IMG that initiated the conference last autumn from Manchester Against the Missiles. But there the credit stops. For, having initiated the conference, they then decided to accept an ultimatum from the CND leadership that the CND leadership itself appoint the overwhelming majority of the conference organizing committee. Most of the key CND leaders involved here are either members of or politically close to the Euro-Communist wing of the Communist Party. For them the labour movement is only one front among many of a "broad" campaign. . . . Not surprisingly the format of the conference they decided reflected these concerns: a platform composed of the likes of Ron Todd and Frank Allaun, no workshops, no resolutions and no declaration . . . despite the influence of CP members in the CND leadership, the CP scarcely even mentioned the conference in the *Morning Star* and CND itself gave it a miserable four paragraphs in its paper, *Sanity*. About the only real mobilizer obtained from officialdom was circulation of all Labour Party branches for the conference, which must undoubtedly have increased the number of delegates from Labour Parties present.'

Nevertheless, Mr Goodwin continued, 'the turnout on the day, coming very heavily from the Far Left and the newer CND activists was even more impressive'. But at the conference, the chairperson, Olive Gibbs, a former CND vice-president, 'resigned from the chair when her incredibly insensitive efforts to stop the Lee Jeans speaker were overturned. Of the resolutions passed two, moved by myself and another SWP member, constituted just the sort of declaration the conference should have had in the first place. It emphasized withdrawal from NATO (but it was opposed by the IMG because it also included opposition to the Warsaw Pact), a "Jobs not Bombs" orientation (calling for CND support for the People's March and the CND demonstration in October to be on that theme) and the pressing need to establish nuclear disarmament groups in every union and industry. . . . If this conference was a very faltering step, then the second step must be directed to developing exactly that discussion and providing us with some of the tools to wage the campaign among the rank and file.'

According to *Sanity*, the CND bi-monthly journal for June–July 1981, which announced the run-up for the movement's annual conference in

London on 13–15 November 1981, CND had achieved more than 22,000 national members, 1,000 local groups and hundreds of affiliated organizations. Its organizer was Duncan Rees, vice-chairman and a Communist. It was previously planned to hold a Christian CND conference in Coventry Cathedral on 12 September, which would be addressed by a member of the Dutch Inter-Church Peace Council.

In *Socialist Review*, Colin Sparks and Marta Wöhrle of the SWP reported: 'The most striking thing about the anti-bomb movement to date is its sheer size. It is much larger than the Vietnam Solidarity Campaign was at its height in the late 1960s. It is probably larger than CND was in the early sixties. It is a *mass* movement. Although there are numerous peace groups and anti-nuclear groups, which have grown up in the last few months or have been churning on for years, the main pole of attraction is CND.'

New members were 'flooding in' and showings of *The War Game*, the anti-nuclear film, were attracting large audiences. SWP advice on how to form an active CND group included:

1. Advertise a founding meeting in the local press.
2. Book *The War Game* and hire a big hall.
3. Advertise the showing as widely as possible.
4. Print lots of local memberhip cards and think of lots of local activities.
5. Show the film, and you are away [*sic*].

The article continues, 'Of course, the number of activists who are prepared to attend regular business meetings and work consistently for the campaign is very much smaller than the hundreds who will come to a big public meeting or film show.' But 'people are very, very keen.... By every standard that you can think of, CND is going very well indeed.' But it faced real problems, since like every other mass campaign, it could very quickly decline, and had barely touched the manual working class and other large sectors of the population. 'People in the local groups are racking their brains for fresh activities which can keep up the momentum.... It will take more protest marches, even enormous protest marches.... But the current shape of CND makes this rather difficult. The bulk of the activists in every local group are "middle-class": they are men and women in their twenties and thirties from the middle grade of white-collar work. Many of them are completely new to political activity of any sort whatsoever. Some, perhaps the majority, are members of trade unions, but they do not automatically make the connection between the union card in their pocket and the struggle against the bomb, for they are rarely experienced trade unionists. . . . A lot of the things which are almost second nature to regular readers of *Socialist Review* are new to many people in CND.' These included such things as 'targeting special leafleting at council estates, special showings of *The War Game*, leafleting factories and factory gate meetings'. An illuminating example of Trotskyist tactics follows. 'The fact that it is possible to walk into a well-organized factory, ask to see the convenor, and get him or her to raise CND on the shop stewards' committee is not widely appreciated.'

But some successes were cited at Gloucester and Bristol, where the 'few articulate middle-class people' were soon outnumbered by industrial workers and unemployed. Comrades Sparks and Wöhrle continued: 'Finally, there is a problem with the national organization. It has done very little to build local groups. . . . All the co-ordination is being done by ourselves. There just does not seem to be any national leadership. We never see their publications – although we seem to survive without them. No-one knows what the national organization is arguing for and frankly no-one cares.'

They added: 'There are no hard and fast political lines in CND. The old-style CP-Quaker leaderships at local level have been swamped by a flood of new people. Where they have hung on, as in King's Cross in London, they have been a major obstacle, prepared to sacrifice activity and growth to the goal of retaining control. In most places, the people involved have little previous experience; many are passive supporters of the moderate Left in the Labour Party.

'There is sometimes hostility to revolutionary ideas, but anyone who has proved that they are prepared to work hard for CND can usually rely on other people supporting them in fighting off attempted witch-hunts.' Some on the extreme Left had been reluctant to get heavily involved in CND despite supporting its aims. There were an 'enormous number of things to do and it can mean that CND gets pushed a long way down the priority list. Against that, it should be obvious that CND ties in with so many other things that it is folly to turn your back on it.' One prominent London militant had said, 'It is full of vicars and faith-healers and I am not going again.' The two comrades commented: 'It should be obvious that there is more to the movement than that, but unless the work is done soon, it is the vicars and faith-healers, or even worse the people who see the election of Michael Foot as the answer to all problems [*sic*], who will lead the campaign. And they will lead it into a blind alley.'

Clearly, CND has its problems with the Far Left at adult, national level, with 'vicars and faith-healers' and other do-gooders, including middle-class people, merely worried about radiation and their children, hardly able to cope with professional militant in-fighting by experienced agitators. But that is not the whole extent of CND's problems with the Far Left. Youth CND has been the object of a take-over by Revolution Youth, the youth section of the International Marxist Group.

The Campaign for Nuclear Disarmament founded Youth CND in autumn 1980. They had not reckoned with the entryism of Revolution Youth which soon caused problems and resentment. The evidence is provided in *Socialist Challenge* of 9 April 1981, when Richard Rozanski, of the IMG Revolution Youth national committee, responded angrily, under the headline 'Revolution Youth Refutes Witch-Hunt', to it 'becoming the victim of a red-baiting witch-hunt, orchestrated by national officials of the Campaign for Nuclear Disarmament'. He continued: 'At the December 1980 conference of the YCND, seven members of Revolution Youth were elected to the 18-person national *ad hoc* committee of the YCND. This reflected the role which we had played in re-building YCND as a mass campaigning body.' The 'first whiff' of an orchestrated campaign against them by 'independent' and Communist Party 'activists' emerged at a meeting of the London YCND on 4 March 1981.

'Accusations were made that YCND was being "dominated" by a non-existent body, the "International Marxist League".' This was followed by a national *ad hoc* committee meeting on 21 March 1981 that the Revolution movement was dominating the campaign. At the same meeting, Sally Davison, CND national organizer and a member of the Communist Party, produced a copy of a document alleged to be a perspectives resolution passed by the Birmingham branch of Revolution Youth. The document referred to building YCND and winning supporters of YCND to the ideas of Revolution Youth. Sally Davison had alleged that this meant 'we were trying to "take-over" YCND'.

National CND officers had expressed the view that membership should be limited to those under twenty-one, making it a school student organization with relatively little say in the campaign. Their view was that CND should be a people's movement, not 'one which prioritizes the labour movement and youth – as Revolution have argued'. Both some non-affiliated members of CND and the Communists were worried about the influence of Revolution Youth, Mr Rozanski wrote. But 'Revolution Youth has never made any secret of the fact that while it strives to build the campaign as a united front body, it also attempts to win young people in YCND to socialist ideas. . . . We pledge ourselves to loyally build YCND, but not at the price of keeping quiet about our politics.'

In *Peace News* of 1 May 1981, Harry Brighouse reported: 'The weekend conference of Youth CND held April 11-12 was to take the form of one day's discussion on the constitution, resolutions and elections to the National Committee, followed by a day in workshops. The "discussion" on the constitution was more like a pitched battle, with the well-disciplined Trotskyist group, Revolution Youth, pushing through a clause which should eventually raise the age limit to 25, and another clause divorcing YCND regions from CND regions, both of which will enable RY to increase their dominance.

'Of the 200 who attended on the Saturday, less than 50 remained on the Sunday. Discussion was brief and not very productive. . . . As yet YCND is not in sectarian hands, but it could well be soon. It is up to young "independents" to try and ensure that YCND, a vital part of the growing movement, does not come under the control of an unrepresentative authoritarian minority.'

Both the Socialist Workers Party and the International Marxist Group remain clearly determined to maintain the ground gained and to continue to push through their objectives. The Communist Party remains deeply entrenched in the CND leadership. It makes CND suspect, whatever its members, with the active backing of Michael Foot, profess. The truth is that with the fading of the Anti-Nazi League, the Campaign for Nuclear Disarmament is the latest mass left-wing front organization supported by, and exploiting, the anxieties of many young parents and other well-meaning people. There can also be little doubt that, probably unwittingly, it actively serves the political, strategic and military aims of the Soviet Union, which last year is said, by Dr Joseph Luns, NATO general secretary, to have provided £6 million for funding of the international nuclear disarmament movement, principally in Western Europe. There is no CND in Russia, certainly no Trotskyists, and such mass popular movements would be ruthlessly suppressed.

10 The Labour Fringe

One field of political activity that is a great target for Trotskyist penetration is the fringe organizations of the Labour movement through which the Far Left can formulate policy at grass-roots level and, with luck, steer it through annual and special conferences. A prime example is the work of the Militant Tendency. The Tendency declared its support for Anthony Wedgwood Benn, the 'enamel mug proletarian', in his campaign against Denis Healey, the former Chancellor, for the deputy leadership of the Labour Party early in 1981.

But the Party itself apart, there are a number of other organizations in which Trotskyists have been active. One is the umbrella organization, the Rank and File Mobilizing Committee for Labour Democracy, formed in 1980 and based at 10, Park Drive, NW11, home of Vladimir Derer. It comprises ten organizations, including the Militant Tendency, following similar aims. They include the Campaign for Labour Democracy, run by Mr Derer. This was set up in June 1973 by a group of rank-and-file Labour Party members following Harold Wilson's rejection of the proposal in the Party's 1973 programme to extend nationalization to twenty-five of Britain's hundred largest companies. In that year the Campaign also decided to concentrate on the right of constituency parties to re-select their MPs. Although mandatory re-selection was defeated at the 1974 conference, the proposal received two million votes. The battle was finally won at the 1979 conference. Undermining the Labour Party was underway.

A founder member of the Campaign for Labour Democracy was Mrs Frances Morrell, former political adviser to Mr Benn and now deputy chairman of the Inner London Education Authority. Other prominent members are the MPs Reg Race, Michael Meacher and Joan Maynard. Among the vice-presidents is Bernard Dix, assistant general secretary of NUPE.

Then there is the Labour Co-ordinating Committee, run by Nigel Stanley from 9, Poland Street, WC1, the headquarters of the Rowntree Trust, as well as other left-wing organizations. The LCC is openly for Mr Benn, and Mrs Morrell also works closely with it. Other Far Left groups include Clause 4, Independent Labour Publications, based in Leeds, the Institute for Workers' Control, of Nottingham, the National Organization of Labour Students, and the Socialist Campaign for Labour Victory, run by John Bloxam, from 5, Stamford Hill, N16.

An illuminating account of Trotskyist penetration is found in a set of internal bulletins from the International Communist League, an entryist organization. In the bulletin of 13 August 1980 reminders to members included a 'model resolution on gay-baiting at the Young Socialists summer camp' (where there had been a fracas over homosexuals); 'try to get Young Socialists to sponsor B. [Bloxam?] and report to the centre'; 'CLPD membership (£3 to V. Derer, 10, Park Drive, NW11); 'LCC renewals'; 'visitors' cards for Blackpool' (TUC or Labour Party conference?). A 'checklist' included: Socialist Committee for Labour Victory special conference; an anti-National Front conference in Birmingham; the League's own conference in Birmingham; a 'fightback lobby' of the TUC conference; a 'barricade lobby' of the Labour Party conference; and various other fringe organization and Lambeth conferences.

By 18 August further instructions had been issued. On the Labour Co-ordinating Committee elections, members were told: 'Comrades should be asked to vote *tactically* so as to give John Bloxam the best chance of getting on. This means voting for: Tony Banks, John Bloxam, Bob Cryer, Dave Gardner, Peter Hain, Stuart Holland, Michael Meacher, Frances Morrell, Chris Mullin, Stuart Weir, Audrey Wise.'

On 17 October 1980 the tone was harsher. Dealing with the Labour Co-ordinating Committee, Campaign for Labour Party Democracy and Labour Committee on Ireland elections, this bulletin stated: 'From the replies to the questionnaire about the LCC elections, it seems that many comrades are still not LCC members. *This sort of looseness in discipline could ruin us if we do not cure it.* All our members must be LCC, CLPD and LCI members. This is not a request, it is an instruction. Comrades who are hard-up financially should be helped by better-off members in their branches. If the whole branch is desperately hard-up, appeal to the centre for help. Financial problems are in no case a valid excuse for failing to join up.

'Branch organizers must take personal responsibility for seeing comrades join up. Take envelopes, stamps, paper etc. with you to the next S* group meeting and join up everyone there and then.' (S* occurs regularly, and appears to stand for *Socialist Organiser*. 'We should also encourage as many S* supporters as possible to join LCC, CLPD and LCI. But it is the responsibility of our own comrades to give a lead, to set an example, and to do what needs to be done whether the other S* supporters do it or not.'

On 25 November 1980 there was a further warning: 'CLPD, LCC, LCI; Comrades are remined that it is compulsory for all comrades to be members of all these campaigns.' After further details of subscriptions and addresses and of financial help, this bulletin added: 'To be able to act promptly and effectively in relation to these important campaigns, we must be able to mobilize what forces we need without any delay. It is important that we get all our comrades into these campaigns *now*, while there are no problems of getting in. To repeat: this is a matter of discipline.' There followed instructions on attendance. About thirty comrades were needed for the annual general meeting of the Campaign for Labour Party Democracy, thirty for that of the Labour Committee on Ireland and ten for the Labour Co-ordinating Committee meeting. On Ireland, 'it is vital we *win* certain issues (hunger strikers, troops out now, political status ... and a role for us in running the LCI). At the CLPD and LCC meetings we want enough comrades to make sure our policies get a good hearing.' Further instructions were given on how to vote on various resolutions, both for and against.

The most explicit bulletin of all is dated 9 December 1980. It bears no identification. I was told it is from the International Communist League, but it also bears a handwritten note about an 'SO discussion meeting'. The following comrades, duly qualified by membership, were ordered to attend the conference of the Campaign for Labour Party Democracy at the Conway Hall, Red Lion Square on 13 December: 'Lejeune, Butler, Paul, Matthews, Glover, Hamilton, Swing, Deedes, Landis, Macaulay, Armstrong, Fraser, Short, Rossing, Lamarre, Kelly, O'Keefe, Ramsey, Roger W., Hellmann, Oliver, McKelvie, Joe B., Ross C., Avebury (if poss.).'

These, I was informed, were code names. For the simultaneous Labour Committee on Ireland meeting at Caxton House, St John's Way, N19, the following comrades were given attendance orders: 'Foster, Callaghan, Mellor and all the other NW London cdes., Les H., Van Helsing, Appleyard, Lewis, Cambell, Ritchie, Evington, Mike F., Steve (Leics.), Curtis, Amanda B., Ali, Zero, McInnes, Alan.'

Those ordered to attend the Labour Co-ordinating Committee meeting at the NUFTO Hall, Jockeys Fields, WC1 on 14 December, were: 'Keith, Foster, Lejeune, Fraser, Short, Weightman, Butler, O'Keefe, Macaulay, Walsh, Ramsey, Ritchie.' All, again, may be code or cover names. The bulletin said: 'In the CLPD our aim is not to take the campaign over or to use it simply to make propaganda. There are a whole number of people in and around the CLPD who have come across us for the first time through the democracy campaign, but who may be doubtful of us for one reason or another. We need to work with them in CLPD and gain a hearing.... We are therefore standing several comrades for positions in the CLPD. We are also proposing a resolution that the CLPD take the fight for Labour Party democracy more strongly into the unions with a rank and file orientation.'

For the Labour Committee on Ireland, 'there will be a caucus at 12 noon.... We will be aiming to get a number of our cdes. onto the London regional cttee.... If cdes. have written off for membership of the LCI and have not received any reply, *they should still turn up to the conference.* Apparently the LCI mail has not been collected from the forwarding address for some time, so it will be difficult for them to refuse people admission.' At the Labour Co-ordinating Committee, 'we will not be making a major intervention at the LCC conference as on past experience, there are usually not very many people there. Our aim is to involve the LCC in a debate around our differences with them on strategy....'

A circular calling a branch meeing at the Metropolitan, Farringdon Road for Sunday, 14 December 1980 is merely signed 'Ramsey'. According to some International Communist League members, code names are also used for Mr Bloxam and Jim Denham, the sacked Longbridge shop steward.

An interesting new development has been the emergence and development of *Socialist Organiser* on lines reminiscent of the Militant Tendency and *Militant*. *Socialist Organiser*, a fortnightly journal, is 'sponsored' by the Socialist Campaign for Labour Victory of which John Bloxam is secretary, Jonathan Hammond, vice-president of the National Union of Journalists, chairman, and John O'Mahony, treasurer. John Bloxam also runs *Socialist Organiser*.

But as with *Militant*, what has happened is that under the cover of the paper, *Socialist Organiser* (which also has 'supporters' rather than 'members'), there has been developed a political organization throughout the country, with Jonathan Hammond, again, as its chairman, or 'chairperson' as Mr Bloxam puts it. Following my articles on the Far Left in the *Daily Telegraph* in spring 1981 which mentioned this development and other Trotskyist activity, Mr Bloxam circulated a memo to supporters on 28 March 1981 in an attempt at rebuttal which in fact, apart from odd interpretations reflecting the Far Left's inherent conspiratorial thinking – they assume everyone is as conspiratorial as themselves – contained much tacit confirmation.

Denying any sinister activity, the circular said:

The running of Socialist Organiser is in fact perfectly open and democratic. Socialist Organiser was launched by the Socialist Campaign for Labour Victory, a left-wing grouping in the Labour Party and trade unions.

SCLV is run day to day by a steering committee and a secretariat elected by democratic, publicly-advertised conferences. Since last August Socialist Organiser has broadened out. Socialist Organiser groups have been established in most major towns. They are not conspiracies or cabals but active campaigning groups, advertised in our paper each fortnight, open to anyone who supports our Marxist policies and is willing to make their support practical by selling a quota of the paper and by making a financial contribution to keep the paper going.

These groups send delegates to regular national meetings to decide our policy. The delegate meetings elect and supervise a secretariat and editorial team for the paper. There is no secret about the Socialist Organiser information circulars either; they are sent out by the secretariat to the local groups to keep them up to date with activities, meetings, fund-raising efforts etc.

This organizational work has continued. After six-and-a-half months of *Socialist Organiser* and the new groups, the organization held its first national rally at the Islington central library on 21-22 March 1981. At this conference-cum-'day school', a women's caucus was set up to meet at least four times annually with a commission based in London to deal with its day-to-day running. Some problems had arisen. In 1980 the organization had launched *Women's Fightback*, a front paper and organization for women, secretary Rachel Lever. But, Gerry Byrne reported (*Socialist Organiser*, 4 April 1981), some SO women had become more identified with the new organization than with the original movement which was tending be seen as the 'men's paper'. More co-ordination was needed.

Martin Thomas also reported that the 'day school' had 'discussed the need for a higher profile for SO. The SO Secretariat proposed that we should adopt the name "Socialist Organiser Alliance" as preferable to the vague description "Socialist Organiser groups". The basic idea of a new name was widely accepted, but the specific proposal "Alliance" was narrowly voted down. So we're looking for new ideas.'

Other issues discussed included factory bulletins, support work for industrial disputes, the role of Marxist councillors, the Liverpool to London jobs march and local government in special detail. A 'workshop' on youth discussed plans for *Barricade*, the 'youth paper linked with *Socialist Organiser*'. This, it was also felt, should be more popular in character.

As these details and activities indicate, there is every sign that while masquerading as a Labour Party fringe organization, the Socialist Campaign for Labour Victory-cum Socialist Organiser is really a fast-developing political organization in its own right. While it has some co-operation with other Trotskyist groups, such as Alan Thornett's Workers Socialist League, there is also considerable internal evidence of close links with the International Communist League.

I have a number of *SO* bulletins as well as others from the ICL, which in places refer to 'S*', suggesting a veiled abbreviation for SO. While the two sets of bulletins are not typed on the same typewriter, they have a remarkable similarity in format. This similarity apart, a number of names have been published in both *Socialist Organiser* and publications of the ICL, such as *International Communist*, of which Martin Thomas, is executive editor, and *Workers Action*. They include: Andrew Hornung, John O'Mahony, Sam Richardson, John Bloxam, Jim Denham, Bruce Robinson, Alasdair Jamieson, Rachel Lever, Colin Foster, Jo Thwaites, Bas Hardy, Dave Spencer, Alexis Carras and Sean Matgamna, national secretary of the International Communist League.

In January 1981 Sean Matgamna published an article in *Socialist Organiser* concerning the activities of the WRP which has since become the subject of a libel action by Vanessa Redgrave. *Socialist Organiser* set up a petition in protest against the legal action, which was signed by more than one hundred left-wing politicians and others, including Mr Benn, and three other Labour MPs, Dennis Skinner, Ernie Roberts and Reg Race. Mr Bloxam commented, 'What is at stake here is people's freedom to criticize political parties. In law, no political party can sue for libel. Vanessa Redgrave claims that criticism of WRP defames her. Virtually all political parties contain some well-known members. If this principle became generally accepted, it could severely inhibit political comment and inquiry.'

On 13 June 1981 *Socialist Organiser* reported moves for formation of a 'new revolutionary youth movement'. It said that on 6 and 7 June 160 young people 'from as far away as Glasgow in the North and Weymouth in the South' had met in Coventry. The conference was called by Barricade and Red Youth and laid the groundwork for a 'National Left-Wing Youth Movement'. They elected an editorial board-cum-steering committee, 'which will produce a new revolutionary youth paper and plan for a bigger conference in the autumn'.

The purpose of the conference was to follow up the involvement of young people in the so-called People's March for Jobs in May 1981. *Socialist Organiser* commented: 'There is no socialist youth movement able to lead the fight. Labour's official youth movement, the Labour Party Young Socialists, is kept in a half-dead condition by the preachers' socialism of the dominant Militant Tendency.... Over the summer, the new movement will be campaigning hard.... It will be present in force, arguing its point of view, at the LPYS summer camp in August.... Transforming the YS into a real fighting force is a major aim of the NLWYM as part of the work of revolutionizing the whole labour movement.' There was a detailed report on the various 'workshops', a Trotskyist euphemism for discussion groups, on treatment of apprentices, youth unemployment, 'organizing the dole queues, including the Unemployed Workers and Claimants Union, the IRA H-block hunger strikers, women's and 'gay' rights. 'The gay workshop tackled the knotty [sic] problem of raising gay liberation at work. Attitudes are generally very bad, the usual response being: "Are you a poof?" if you even discuss the question.'

The proposed paper, said Ms Jo Thwaites, should relate to youth, and 'have coverage on music and sexuality as well as youth at work and Youth Campaign for Nuclear Disarmament'. There were disagreements on names for the new paper. 'This summer looks like being a long and hot one, and we have no time to lose. Youth are already fighting back.... We want to organize and give political direction to that fight, and aim to transform the LPYS into a force to do that.'

The Militant Tendency clearly faced a new challenge. The new organization, based at *Socialist Organiser*'s new headquarters at 214, Sickert Court, London N1, elected as its executive board: Caroline Lees, Weymouth; Carole Hollier, Welwyn and Hatfield; Jo Thwaites, *Barricade* editorial board; (?) Constantin, *Barricade* e.b.; Judith Bonner, Coventry North East; Alex Owalade, National Union of School Students; Mick Liggins, National Council of Young Workers; Dale Ackroyd, *Red Youth* editorial board; Andrew McDonald, Aylesbury; Bas (?), Coventry Anti-Racist Defence; and Ruth Davies, Wallasey. All, where not stated, Labour Party Young Socialists.

Few better examples of the success of persistent grass-roots agitation for pre-determined objectives exist than the Labour Party's special conference at Wembley on 24 January 1981 which resulted in approval of a new electoral college for choosing the Party leader on the basis of 40 per cent for the unions, 30 per cent for the Parliamentary Party and 30 per cent for the constituency parties.

Attempts have been planned since to reverse it at the October 1981 conference. But at the time, despite the strength of Mr Benn's support, approval of the final formula came for many not immersed in the internal in-fighting of the Labour movement as a surprise. Michael Foot, new Party leader, came badly out of it. There were also suggestions, which were strongly denied, that there had been eve of conference wheeler-dealing on voting, as happens at TUC conferences, between Clive Jenkins, of the Association of Scientific, Technical and Managerial Staffs, Moss Evans, of the Transport Union, and other union leaders.

That the result was anything but an 'accident', however, is shown by items in Trotskyist publications. In its special conference report of 30 January 1981, credit for the result was claimed by *Militant*. Eileen Short, a delegate from Bethnal Green and Bow Labour Party, writing in a personal capacity, said:

> This 30-30-40 college is the formula put forward by *Militant* after last year's annual conference, when the broad principle of a wider election franchise for the leadership was adopted.
>
> Over recent years, supporters of *Militant* have played a prominent part in the fight for Party democracy, both on the issue of re-selection of MPs and the election of the leader. It was *Militant* supporters who played a key role within USDAW (Union of Shop, Distributive and Allied Workers), ensuring that this union submitted the 30-30-40 proposal, which was eventually adopted by the special conference.

At the time, there was some surprise that USDAW, a traditionally moderate, politically quiet union, had come up with the left-wing formula which was finally adopted. But as *Militant* made clear, it had been made a target for change, which, as those familiar with the trade union movement will know, depends on concerted action in union branches getting through motions for its own annual conference, adopting left-wing delegates and the right mandate long before the conference takes place. Just as parallel efforts in constituency Labour parties has brought the Militant Tendency considerable influence on the political front. Militant supporters, including Patrick Wall of Shipley, and Tony Banks of Tooting, played a leading part in the Wembley debate. *Militant*, claiming a 'great victory', called for further political action in constituencies, union branches and in local government elections.

But *Militant* could not claim all the credit. Before the Wembley special conference took place, at least two detailed instructions on how to vote, and on the likely course of the conference were given by John Lansman, secretary of the Rank and File Mobilizing Committee. In *Socialist Organiser* of 10 January 1981 he told, 'How to mandate delegates for Jan. 24th.' Mr Lansman gave an extremely detailed analysis of the six proposals likely to come up at the conference, and the various possible compositions of the electoral college. He concludes, 'It is certain that the result will be very close. In fact, it is likely to hang on the 430,000 votes of USDAW. . . . The aim must therefore to be to hold USDAW votes. . . . The best chance may well be in allowing USDAW to move its own proposal with the support of the Left. . . . If USDAW holds the balance, the compromise should not involve splitting the difference on proportions, but rallying support for USDAW!'

Two weeks later, on 24 January 1981, in the eve-of-conference issue of *Socialist Organiser*, and next to a long interview with Mr Benn, Mr Lansman gave final, more explicit instructions on left-wing tactics at the conference. He warned, 'There are two ways in which the Left could be defeated at the special conference. There could be no decision at all, or an electoral college could be agreed which gave 50 per cent of votes to MPs.'

After further analysis of likely or possible right-wing, national executive and trade union leaders' moves, he continued: 'A Left victory will almost certainly depend on retaining support from the Right Wing union USDAW. It will be essential, both at the group meetings on Friday and at the conference itself, to maximize the chances of retaining USDAW support.' After further examination of pre-conference moves, he concluded, 'In the conference itself, maximum support from the very first ballot must be given to USDAW's resolution, or failing that to some formula giving 40 per cent of the votes to the trade unions.'

Mr Lansman's guidance was repeated by *Socialist Organiser* in its editorial. Despite their doubts whether the Far Left would really pull it off, the result of Labour's special Wembley conference turned out exactly in accordance with their previous analysis and tactical and voting instructions.

The battle of the Far Left for still greater influence both within the Labour Party, the unions and the fringe organizations continues. The aim is eventual power with Mr Benn as the figurehead leader. For those outside, as with other Trotskyist and Ultra-Left activity, it is a subterranean world. Yet the struggle is obsessive and should never be forgotten. For its successes are becoming increasing apparent, both within the divided Labour Party and equally important, local government. Complacency in combating it can only lead to a Marxist-ruled Britain.

11 The International Connection

Trotskyism is in some ways more of an international movement than Communism which has for sixty years been largely subservient to the aims of the Soviet Union. Trotsky himself advocated international revolution through the proletariat to overthrow Western society. For that reason, he was expelled from Russia in 1929 when the Stalinist line of first building Communism at home prevailed. For that reason, too, he was assassinated by a Stalinist agent by an ice-pick through the head in Mexico in 1940.

But Trotskyism remains full of international links with its long history of international secretariats, splitting, re-forming and splitting again over ideological differences. Most of it is public history. What is interesting is how those links persist today and become involved in new causes, notably the Palestine Liberation Organization, and new revolutionary movements. British Far Left groups, too, maintain widespread connections with similar groups in many other countries.

The Militant Tendency took part in the founding conference in London in April 1974 of a new international, the CWI, the Committee of the Workers International. The gathering was attended by forty-six comrades from countries including Britain, Ireland, Sweden, Germany, Spain, India, Ceylon, Pakistan, Jamaica and Iraq. The first bulletin produced by the CWI commented, 'This represented a great step forward for our tendency. Nevertheless, there were only four established national sections, in Britain, Ireland, Sweden and Germany.' The resolution adopted said: 'We regard this committee as the germ of the mighty workers' international which will within the first decade become the decisive force on the planet.... An international executive committee shall be established.... Each national section must pay to the IEC the equivalent of £5 per member per year.' Publication of main documents of the tendency must be undertaken in six languages, with a printed international bulletin as soon as possible in other languages. The first meeting of the international executive was held in Britain in August 1974. British members visited Spain and Portugal.

By January 1975 the CWI was able to report: 'We have fully established national sections in Britain, Ireland, Germany, Sweden and Belgium, and sections in the process of formation in Greece and Spain.... By far the strongest section is the British, with a membership of over 600, an eight-

The Far Left

page weekly paper and 22 full-time workers (including one full-time for the CWI).'

Charles James in his study of the Militant Tendency observed wide-ranging international links from the May Day 1978 issue of *Militant* through fraternal greetings and advertisements for parallel foreign Marxist papers. He also noted similar items and contributions in foreign publications. These included: '*Voran – Marxistische Zeitung für* SPD, *Juso and Gewerkschaft*', not an official publication of the West German Social Democratic Party, but aimed at militant young Marxists, the JUSOS, trade unionists and others; *Nuevo Claridad*, Spain; *Offensiv*, Sweden; *Voorwarts*, Netherlands; *Vonk*, Belgium; *Xekinema*, Greece. These publications also carried articles about the movement's activities in other countries. For example, François Bliki, editor of the Flemish edition of *Vonk*, also wrote in *Voorwarts*, while the latter's editor, Frans Hoffman, also wrote for both *Vonk* and *Militant*. The Militant Tendency also sells foreign publications, while some of its own pamphlets, including some by Ted Grant, are advertised in Holland. Some posters bore a strong resemblance to each other despite being printed in different languages.

This evidence of close international links continues. In 1979 *British Perspectives*, reporting on the 'prospects for the development of Marxist tendencies in other countries', described the 'recent visit to India, where the objective situation is very turbulent and exceptionally favourable'. It referred to proposals to translate material into all Indian languages and to 'set up bookshops stocked with the tendency's material'. It added, 'On the basis of contacts already established, it is entirely possible that there could be Marxist tendencies in every country of Western Europe, and in several countries in other continents. The problem on an international scale is a shortage of available experienced personnel. Fleeting visits or occasional correspondence are not enough to develop viable tendencies. On the other hand, it would be fatal to dissipate resources by making pilgrimages everywhere.'

In May 1981 *Militant* again carried greetings from *Vonk*. It reproduced an article, 'Workers of the World Unite', by Elma Louw from *Inqaba ya Basebenzi* (Workers' Fortress), the South African Marxist journal. Further greetings came from the Nava Sama Samaja, Trotskyist party of Sri Lanka. Leo McDaid, a member of the Paderborn SPD reported on unemployment and JUSO activity in West Germany. Demand for *Militant International Review* had outstripped supplies. Clearly the international links and co-operation continue.

In June 1981 an International Socialist Youth rally was held in Vienna, attended by delegations from Irish Labour Youth, German, Swedish, Dutch and fifty members of the Labour Party Young Socialists, Militant Tendency supporters. Reporting on the rally under the heading 'Red Vienna', *Militant* recorded on 19 June 1981 that they had sold 600 copies, as well as 340 copies of *Socialist Youth* and several hundred badges. During the camp, more than £400 was raised for the *Militant* fighting-fund.

But Kevin Ramage, LPYS chairman, was critical. 'While the congress marked a consolidation of the Left leadership, gained over the Right Wing in 1979, at the same time it showed the failure of the bureaucratic methods of the Left leadership to develop IUSY [International Union of Socialist Youth]. Political debate was minimal. Most of the two and a half days were spent on endless reports and bureaucratic wrangles.' Delegates were 20 per cent down in number from 1979. Only the Militant Tendency had called for mass action on unemployment, a march on Common Market headquarters. He quoted an amusing anecdote on the selling of *Militant* to drivers in Vienna: ' "Oh my God," came the cry from one well-heeled driver of a Volvo, "you're not in Vienna as well!" Yes we were.'

Similar links are maintained by other Trotskyist organizations. A full account of the activities of the Workers Socialist League, the Oxford-based group led by Alan Thornett, was given by Robert Porter, industrial correspondent, and Harry Longmuir, investigative reporter, in the *Daily Mail* in summer 1980 after a deep inquiry. At its annual conference in April 1981, Mr Thornett told the 112 delegates that some comrades would soon be sent back into Turkey to form a Trotskyist group. A total of £500 to finance this group had been raised and more money promised. They also described further international contacts. At a WSL summer school the Socialist League of the United States had shown film of members in gun battles with extreme right-wingers in Detroit. Others were: the Egyptian Revolutionary Communist League, operating illegally against President Sadat; the Bolshevik Workers' League, a Chilean organization based in Paris, fighting the Pinochet regime; a Trotskyist cell at Tokyo University, Japan; the Danish Trotskyist Workers League; and activists in Greece. Still more were: Spanish revolutionaries, of whom a representative, 'Marcos', addressed the conference; Austrian Trotskyists, who had visited Britain and taken part in a Young Liberals Ireland demo as well as Cowley and other picket lines; and the Italian Bolshevik Leninist

Group, whose leading member, Fernando Viscintin, visited Oxford in April. His group and the Marxist Revolutionary Front had members in Austria, France and West Germany, and claimed to have engineered a major dispute at Fiat in Turin.

Further developments included a report by Keith White, a member of the WSL's American Commission, who reported on contacts with Steve Sultzer, leader of the Socialist League of America, also due to visit Oxford. Mr White said American Trotskyists relied heavily on WSL literature, and had learned how to infiltrate industrial disputes from Mr Thornett, who visited them at Christmas 1978. Mr Sultzer, he added, had asked for a WSL activist to be sent to live and work with them in the United States. Danish Trotskyists had also asked for political guidance, and the Austrians for a lecture tour there by a WSL activist. Leaders of the WSL also decided to use a £550 gift to send an activist to work with a revolutionary group in Greece.

To further these international links, the Workers Socialist League itself founded an International Tendency aimed at promoting world revolution. Approaches and contacts were both ways. Mr Thornett visited Paris and Italy as well as America to seek affiliations with foreign Trotskyist groups. Robert Sutcliffe, another leading member and lecturer in politics and economics at Kingston Polytechnic, told the April conference he had travelled 63,000 miles by air in two years and attended seven international conferences and three national Trotskyist group meetings. He had visited revolutionary groups in Spain to further formation of a Spanish Trotskyist alliance of 4,500 members from three groups, the Workers Revolutionary Front, the Communist League and the Revolutionary Communist League.

Neither Mr Thornett nor Mr Sutcliffe were prepared to talk to the *Daily Mail* investigators about either their international or domestic activities. Oxford may seem a strange centre for a network of international revolutionary activity, but where else could be more appropriate? It is an intellectual centre – and Mr Thornett's group includes academics – with a constant flow of visiting luminaries and others.

Facts about international Trotskyist links in view of the obsessive secretiveness of the movement are hard to come by. But as Peter Shipley, an expert on Trotskyism, has observed, the movement has 'probably been more prolific in Britain than any other Western country'. Only in France, with six separate Trotskyist groups, could a membership of 10,000 or more be claimed. At that time, he estimated that in West Germany, where Communism, thanks to the proximity of East Germany, is a much greater threat, there were only 1,200 Trotskyists in ten rival groups. In Portugal, the *Liga Communista Internacionale* claimed 6,000 members.

According to the annual report of the *Bundesverfassungsschutz*, the German Special Branch and security service, for 1979, the largest German group with about 500 members was the 'Group of International Marxists – German Section of the Fourth International', subordinated to the 'United Secretariat' in Brussels. The 'League of Socialist Workers' with a youth organization, 'Socialist Youth Federation', had altogether only 250 members. Other small factions included Spartacists and Posadists.

Spartacists in Britain are linked with those in America and distribute their literature. The Socialist Workers Party has its own international organizer, Peter Goodwin, who reported in 1979: 'In the past we have had relations with many groups on the Western European revolutionary Left, but on the whole they didn't get very far – partly that was our own fault.' But 'systematic and promising relations' had been developed with vs (Left Socialists), Denmark and su (Socialist Youth), Norway. International conferences had been organized or attended. 'In this sort of international work you get very used to pinching yourself every so often to make sure you are not living in a dream world. Well, with regard to Western Europe we've pinched ourself so much that we're blue with bruises.' But he felt 'cautious optimism'.

The May Day 1981 edition of *Socialist Worker* carried greetings from a number of fraternal foreign organizations and publications. They included: *Workers' Action*, of the International Socialists of Canada; *The Worker*, for Workers Power and International Socialism, of the Socialist Workers Movement of Ireland; *The Battler*, of the International Socialists of Australia; the *Sozialistische Arbeiterzeitung*, of the Sozialistische Arbeitergruppe of West Germany; *Socialist Worker*, paper of the International Socialist Organization of the United States; and the *Mouvement Militant Mauricien*, of Quatre Bornes, Mauritius, Indian Ocean. Other greetings came from the British anti-Zionist Organization, Palestine Solidarity, printed also in Arabic, saying: 'Victory to the Palestine Liberation Organization! For a democratic and secular state in all of Palestine!' Yet more messages called for support for the Turkey Solidarity Campaign and the Support Committee for the Chilean Metal Workers.

Another new development has been the formation of the Communist Workers Organization, based in Glasgow and London. In its quarterly *Workers Voice* of winter 1980–1, it reported that the first congress of the cwo was held in London on 15–16 November 1980, and 'was attended by comrades from France and Partito Communista Internazionalista (Italy)'.

Apart from these often fragmented contacts, however, there is one notable characteristic about some Trotskyist international liaison activity. That is the Arab connection. The most outstanding example is the Workers Revolutionary Party, with its figurehead Vanessa Redgrave. Not a week passes without *News Line* publishing favourable articles about Colonel Gaddafi, the Libyan revolutionary leader, the Palestine Liberation Organization and other Arab causes. Similar favourable coverage is given in other Trotskyist publications.

But the WRP stands out, with Vanessa Redgrave having visited Colonel Gaddafi in Tripoli, Beirut, Abu Dhabi and other centres. Whatever the truth about allegations of 'Arab gold', which the WRP have angrily refuted, the relationship between Arab and Clapham-based revolutionaries is striking. When Gerry Healy addressed a rally, said to be 1,000 strong, in London on 17 August 1980, among those present as a fraternal delegate was the official representative of the Arab Ba'ath Socialist Party, Abdul-Zahra al-Hashimi. Other delegates came from West Germany, France, Spain, Greece, Australia and the United States as representatives of the international committee of the Fourth International. The rally was to commemorate the fortieth anniversary of the assassination of Trotsky, himself, ironically, a Jew.

There is another darker side to international revolutionary links and activity. That is terrorism. I am not by one whit suggesting that links exist between the WRP or any other British Trotskyist group and foreign terrorist organizations. They all condemn violence and terrorism. But some of those whose policies they espouse, including the PLO, the Libyans and the Iraqis, practise assassination and other forms of terror in London and elsewhere. Probably only the world's secret services know the truth, and they do not talk. But according to Western intelligence agencies, contacts exist between Baader-Meinhof extremists in West Germany, the Red Brigades in Italy, the Red Army in Japan, the IRA and various Arab organizations. Some Trotskyists, in Britain, as distinct from their parties and leaders, are not averse to practising physical violence on picket lines, demos and elsewhere. It is a dangerous world.

Postscript

As stated at the outset, the purpose of this book was to inform, not moralize. I do not make recommendations, since my opinions are unimportant, and intelligent men and women can draw their own conclusions. Doubtlessly, eagle-eyed critics on the Far Left may find this or that detail wrong. More could be said about fringe or other dubious organizations. Anyone who read the range of Far Left literature notes the recurrence of certain addresses, of the same printing firms, the parallel international links.

But some observations are valid. Today, to be 'Leftish' is fashionable. To be against the Far Left or the permissive society is to appear 'reactionary'. To be chaste is to be ridiculous. Violence is more or less tolerated. Many of the sins of Western society are not tolerated in the Soviet Union; there, they still shoot people.

What the Far Left condones, encourages and furthers with its propaganda or through its adherents in television and elsewhere are causes and acts which it would ruthlessly suppress were it itself in power: street violence, civil insurrection, homosexuality, the IRA. It does so because of the ultimate aim of undermining established society until a take-over is possible. It professes democracy, but is itself undemocratic. It claims to abhor violence, but practises it.

The Far Left has made impressive advances, not least in local government with the Red Flag flying over town halls. Sir Harold Wilson was shocked at the clenched fists raised at the end of the Labour Party conference. The only moral which I would draw is the need for vigilance by those who still believe in freedom. If this book helps to inform, it will have been worth the effort.

Index